ADVANCES IN MERGERS AND ACQUISITIONS

ADVANCES IN MERGERS AND ACQUISITIONS

Series Editors: Cary Cooper and Alan Gregory

ADVANCES IN MERGERS AND ACQUISITIONS

EDITED BY

CARY COOPER
UMIST, Manchester, UK

ALAN GREGORY
University of Exeter, Exeter, UK

2000

JAI
An Imprint of Elsevier Science

Amsterdam – London – New York – Oxford – Paris – Shannon – Tokyo

ELSEVIER SCIENCE Inc.
655 Avenue of the Americas
New York, NY 10010, USA

First edition 2000

Library of Congress Cataloging in Publication Data
A catalog record from the Library of Congress has been applied for.

ISBN:0-7623-0683-1

The paper used in this publication meets the requirements of ANSI/NISO Z39.48-1992 (Permanence of Paper).
Printed in The Netherlands.

CONTENTS

LIST OF CONTRIBUTORS

Anup Agrawal

William A. Powell Jr. Chair of Finance and Accounting, Culverhouse College of Business, University of Alabama, Tuscaloosa, AL 35487–0224, USA
E-mail: aagrawal@cba.ua.edu
http://www.cba.ua.edu/xeaa.html

John Doukas

Professor of Finance, Department of Finance, School of Business and Public Administration, Old Dominion University, Norfolk, VA 23529–0218, USA
E-mail: jdoukas@odu.edu

Laura Empson

Fellow of St. Anne's College, University of Oxford, Said Business School, Oxford OX2 6HS, U.K.
Fax: +44 (0) 1865 274899
E-mail: laura.empson@sbs.ox.ac.uk

Martine Cardel Gertsen

Associate Professor, Department of Intercultural Communication and Management, Copenhagen Business School, Dalgas Have 15, DK-2000 Frederiksberg, Denmark
Fax: +45 38 15 38 40
E-mail: mg.ikl@cbs.dk

Philip K. Goulet

The Darla Moore School of Business, University of South Carolina, Columbia, SC 29208, USA
E-mail: Goulphp3@spanky.badm.sc.edu

Jeffrey S. Harrison   Professor, Management Department,
                                   College of Business Administration,
                                   University of Central Florida, Orlando,
                                   FL 3286, USA
                                   Fax: (407) 823–3725
                                   E-mail: jeffharrison@bus.ucf.edu

Martin Holmèn   Assistant Professor of Finance, Stockholm
                                   University, Stockholm, Sweden
                                   E-mail: mah@fek.su.se

Robert E. Hoskisson   Rath in Strategic Management and
                                   Professor of Management, College of
                                   Business Administration, University of
                                   Oklahoma, Norman, OK 73019–0450, USA
                                   E-mail: rhoskiss@ou.edu

Jeffrey F. Jaffe   Department of Finance, The Wharton
                                   School, University of Pennsylvania,
                                   Philadelphia, PA 19104, USA
                                   E-mail: jaffe@wharton.upenn.edu

R. J. Limmack   Professor of Accountancy and Finance,
                                   Department of Accounting, Finance and
                                   Law, University of Stirling, Stirling
                                   FK9 4LA, U.K.
                                   Fax: 01786 467308
                                   E-mail: R.J.Limmack@stirling.ac.uk

Hugh M. O'Neill   Associate Professor and Chair, Management
           •   Kenan-Flagler School of Business,
                                   University of North Carolina, Chapel Hill,
                                   NC 27599–3490, USA
                                   E-mail: hugh_oneill@unc.edu

Richard Schoenberg   University of London, Imperial College
                                   Management School, 53 Prince's Gate,
                                   Exhibition Road, London SW7 2PG, U.K.
                                   E-mail: r.schoenberg@ic.ac.uk

David M. Schweiger

The Buck Nickles/Sluor Daniel Chair
Professor of International Business
The Darla Moore School of Business,
University of South Carolina, Columbia,
SC 29208, USA
E-mail: Schweiger@darla.badm.sc.edu

Anne-Marie Søderberg

Associate Professor, Department of
Intercultural Communication and
Management, Copenhagen Business
School, Dalgas Have 15, DK-2000
Frederiksberg, Denmark
Fax: +45 38 15 38 40
E-mail: ams.ikl@cbs.dk

Sudi Sudarsanam

Professor of Finance & Corporate Control,
Department of Finance & Accounting,
Cranfield University School of
Management, Cranfield MK43 0AL, U.K.
Fax: 44 1234 75 2554
E-mail: p.s.sudarsanam@cranfield.ac.uk

INTRODUCTION

Cary Cooper and Alan Gregory

One of the enduring puzzles in the finance and management literature has been the propensity of companies to engage in acquisitions and mergers despite evidence that on average these are not successfully carried out. The finance literature suggests that acquisitions and mergers at best do not add value to the acquiring firm, and that more probably they are seriously detrimental to shareholder wealth in the longer term. In this literature, the comparative metric is some model of 'normal' returns. In essence, these models attempt to compare the returns earned on a portfolio of acquiring firms compared to some risk-adjusted benchmark portfolio return. By contrast, the management literature has addressed the question of acquiring firm performance using a more diverse range of tools, including questionnaires and case study investigations of acquiring firm management. A considerable number of human resource and organisational behaviour specialists have focused upon both pre merger and post merger issues involving employees. Many questions have been asked pre merger about the 'culture fit' or otherwise of two organisations in merger talks, or in deciding who would be an appropriate suitor. In addition, the relationship that develops pre merger or the process engaged in can have an impact on post merger behaviour and any problems that might materialise. Another issue is how to manage the communication process with employees post merger, or indeed the whole process of structural change – usually poorly managed, accounting for many merger or acquisition failures.

The first thing that strikes us from the many papers on acquiring firm performance from the very different traditions and methods of the finance and management literatures is that the weight of the evidence in both disciplines leads to the conclusion that the post acquisition performance of acquiring firms

Advances in Mergers and Acquisitions, Volume 1, pages 1–5.
2000 by Elsevier Science Inc.
ISBN: 0-7623-0683-1

is disappointing. This does not, of course, appear to dampen the appetite of firms to embark upon the acquisitions trail. At the time of writing, one of the most common clichés used to describe the recent spate of take-overs is that of a 'tidal wave' of merger and acquisition (M&A) activity. One characteristic of this latest merger wave has been an increase in cross-border activity. In part, this upsurge in activity has been a motivation in starting this current series. However, the second thing that concerned us as editors coming from the different disciplines of management and finance is how little inter-action there is between the management literature and the finance literature[1]. Our discussions on this led us to think about ways of increasing awareness of researchers, students and practitioners of the inter-disciplinary possibilities for research into M&A.

Those discussions give rise to this JAI series on recent advances in the area. In this first volume of the series, we include some review papers from both finance and management perspectives. We start with a major and wide-ranging review article from Anup Agrawal and Jeffrey Jaffe, *The Post Merger Performance Puzzle*, that examines the international literature on long-run performance of acquiring firms. They conclude that a diversity of different research in the U.K. and the U.S. largely supports the hypothesis that mergers (in U.K. terms, agreed or friendly take-overs) give negative long-run wealth effects. However, returns are non negative following tender offers (roughly equivalent to a hostile bid in the U.K.). In terms of explaining this negative performance, the authors find wide-ranging support in both the U.K. and U.S. for the 'methods of payment' hypothesis – equity offers perform far worse than cash offers. It is interesting to note that in the U.S., most tender offers use cash as the form of consideration because the use of equity requires compliance with the U.S. 1933 Securities Act, which can lead to a substantial delay (Martin, 1996). This is not the case with the U.K., where there appears to be no strong relationship between hostility and financing (Gregory, 2000). The second explanation the authors find support for is the performance extrapolation hypothesis. Recent evidence from the U.S. suggests that the market wrongly assumes that 'glamour' firms will continue to perform well post-merger. This explanation is compatible with the evidence on 'glamour' versus 'value' stock performance in general (Lakonishok, Schleifer & Vishny, 1994).

Our second review paper comes from the management literature on the influence of national cultures on post takeover performance. *The Influence of Cultural Compatibility Within Cross-Border Acquisitions: A Review*, by Richard Schoenberg. This paper assesses the issue of cultural compatability in cross border acquisitions, drawing on the literature within the corporate culture field and organisational behaviour research. The role of culture fit and compatibility on subsequent acquisition performance seems to depend on the post acquisition integration process as well as the attractiveness of the acquirer's culture by the acquired. The management style in terms of participation, formal versus informal climate and the like play an important role here.

The third paper in this section is *Integrating Mergers and Acquisitions: An International Research Review*, by David Schweiger. This chapter goes further down the line of factors influencing mergers and acquisitions, exploring not only national and organisational cultures and the implementation process but also the integration decision making process and the management of the integration. This is a thorough review of the international literature, drawing together all the relevant research, culminating with research opportunities in the future.

The fourth review paper *Takeovers As A Disciplinary Mechanism?* by Robin Limmack concludes that research to date has been unable to provide a definitive answer on whether the takeover market acts as a effective disciplinary tool. He highlights the potential problems of possibly conflicting takeover motives together with methodological difficulties. Limmack also points out the problem of changes in the corporate control market through time, a particularly timely reminder given the recent Vodafone-Mannesmann deal, which shows that both size and country of domicile are no longer effective defence mechanisms. He goes on to conclude that issues of over-optimism and managerial self-interest still remain (although later in this volume Doukas and Holmèn provide some interesting evidence from Sweden on the latter). Last, Limmack notes that governance arrangements may have an important role to play in influencing acquiring firms' behaviour. This is a theme developed later by Sudarsanam.

The last of our review papers, *Corporate Governance, Corporate Control and Takeovers*, by Sudi Sudarsanam, looks specifically at the role of corporate governance in acquisitions and mergers. He looks at alternative governance mechanisms and the possible inter-actions between them. One of the main themes from this paper is that no clear and conclusive results can be reached on the superiority of one governance mechanism over another. The author calls for the development of more theories on combinations of governance mechanisms and for empirical tests of those theories.

The second section of this volume looks at more specific studies that span the finance, strategy and organisational processes of mergers and acquisitions. Jeffrey Harrison, Hugh O'Neill and Robert Hoskisson's paper, *Acquisition Strategy And Target Resistance: A Theory Of Countervailing Effects Of Pre-Merger Bidding and Post-Merger Integration*, is particularly important for the success of any business combination, post merger. The authors examine what goes on pre merger in terms of the acquisition strategy, the resistance of the target organisation, and what impact these approaches have on subsequent post merger relationships and integration. The more there is 'relatedness' and open co-operation pre merger, the greater the likelihood of 'operating synergy' post merger. The more the top executives resist in terms of premium-increasing tactics the more problems subsequent to a merger. This is an important piece of research in terms of minimising the likelihood of a 'two plus two equals three' scenario that emerges in many mergers and acquisition.

The second paper in this section, *Managerial Ownership and Risk-Reducing Acquisitions*, by John Doukas and Martin Holmèn focuses upon Swedish mergers and acquisitions and investigates the particular issue of risk reducing (diversifying) takeovers between 1980 and 1995. The authors investigate announcement period returns and find that, consistent with managers diversifying the risk of their human capital, such takeovers are shareholder wealth reducing when acquiring firm managers have no equity stakes in their company. However, when managers have an equity stake in their firms, risk-reducing takeovers increase firm value. The authors go on to present simultaneous equation estimates that suggest managerial ownership affects the acquirer's shareholder returns, while there is no evidence of reverse causality. This paper is a particularly interesting complement to the earlier papers by Limmack and Sudarsanam.

Laura Empson's paper, *Mergers Between Professional Services Firms: Exploring An Undirected Process Of Integration*, explores a range of approaches used by professional service organisations to engage in merger activity, which is very different from the corporate sector. She identifies an undirected model of organisational integration, where the pace and approach of integration is slower and more constrained, and led by the professional staff themselves. This contrasts sharply with the traditional CEO-led approach in most organisations.

Martine Cardel Gertsen and Anne-Marie Søderberg's paper, *Tales Of Trial And Triumph: A Narratological Perspective On International Acquisition*, on the other hand, examines the reality of the experience of a merger or acquisition as perceived by the people involved. A narrative is defined by the authors as 'an account of events over time' and this qualitative account of people involved in several mergers highlights the dilemmas, aspirations, fears and impact of these major structural events on the lives, hopes and behaviours of those at the receiving end of mergers and acquisitions.

NOTES

1 An exception is the strategic management literature where a certain, if rather limited, cross-fertilisation takes place.

REFERENCES

Gregory, A. (2000).The Long-Run Performance of UK Acquirers: Motives Underlying the Method of Payment. *Accounting and Business Research*, Summer, 2000.

Lakonishok, J., Shleifer, A., & Vishny, R.W. (1994). Contrarian Investment, Extrapolation and Risk. *Journal of Finance*, December, 1541-1578.

Martin, K. J. (1996). The Method of Payment in Corporate Acquisitions, Investment Opportunities, and Management Ownership. *Journal of Finance*, September, 1227-1246.

THE POST-MERGER PERFORMANCE PUZZLE

Anup Agrawal and Jeffrey F. Jaffe

ABSTRACT

While the bulk of the research on the financial performance of mergers and acquisitions has focused on stock returns around the merger announcement, a surprisingly large set of papers has also examined long-run stock returns following acquisitions. We review this literature, concluding that long-run performance is negative following mergers, though performance is non-negative (and perhaps even positive) following tender offers. However, the effects of both methodology (see Lyon, Barber & Tsai, 1999) and chance (see Fama, 1998) may modify this conclusion. Two explanations of under-performance (speed of price-adjustment and EPS myopia) are not supported by the data, while two other explanations (method of payment and performance extrapolation) receive greater support.

1. INTRODUCTION

Most research on the financial performance of mergers and acquisitions has focused on stock returns surrounding announcement dates. Virtually all researchers have reported large positive average abnormal returns to targets, a result that is not surprising given the significant premiums typically involved

Advances in Mergers and Acquisitions, Volume 1, pages 7-41.
Copyright © 2000 by Elsevier Science Inc.
All rights of reproduction in any form reserved.
ISBN: 0-7623-0683-1

in takeovers. Conversely, these same researchers have found surprisingly small abnormal returns to bidders over the announcement period. In fact, while some papers have reported significantly positive performance here, quite a few others have found either zero performance or even negative performance to acquirers. In a well-known review article, Roll (1986) concludes that the null hypothesis, of zero abnormal performance to acquirers, should not be rejected; and, while there have been many subsequent articles, the results appear to be mixed enough that Rolls' conclusion appears to hold.

Parallel to the research on announcement period returns, a smaller body of work has investigated long-run post acquisition returns. The earlier research here was, typically, a small section in a paper primarily devoted to announcement period returns. The profession often paid little attention to the results on long-run returns, perhaps because the strong belief in market efficiency indicated what the results should be. However, enough of the earlier papers reported negative long-run returns following mergers that the topic could not be completely ignored. In fact, the results caused Jensen & Ruback (1983, p. 20) to comment: "These post-outcome negative abnormal returns are unsettling because they are inconsistent with market efficiency and suggest that changes in stock prices overestimate the future efficiency gains from mergers."

Over the years, the initial trickle of studies has widened to a steady stream. We count 22 different papers examining long-run post-acquisition returns, with 10 having seen print in the 1990s. As the literature has grown, we have witnessed three concomitant developments. A number of the more recent papers have been fully devoted to long-run returns and perhaps an equal number have searched for explanations of the phenomenon, both signs of increased academic interest. In addition, recent papers have adopted the more sophisticated empirical methodologies now available.

Because of the substantial body of work in the area, we believe that a review of the literature is called for. Our chapter seeks to answer two questions. First, does the accumulated evidence suggest that post-acquisition performance is, indeed, negative? The evidence on this question is presented in Section 2 of our chapter; the answer to this question seems quite important. In addition to the obvious implication for market efficiency, an answer clearly informs the debate on gains from mergers. Studies focusing on announcement period performance conclude that mergers produce wealth gains to stockholders of the target and acquiring firms combined. A finding of negative performance after mergers can overturn this conclusion. Second, what are possible explanations for the literature's findings on long-run performance? Of course, if long-run performance is, generally, insignificantly different from zero, no explanation is needed. However, if past research suggests under-performance (or out-performance), a convincing explanation enhances the plausibility of that finding. The evidence on this question is presented in Section 3. Section 4 provides a summary and conclusion.

2. LONG-RUN PERFORMANCE FOLLOWING ACQUISITIONS

We start by providing a summary of the literature, in Section 2.1. Section 2.2 provides a detailed review of the individual studies that have examined this issue in various contexts.

2.1 Summary of the Evidence

Section 2.2 reviews 22 articles that have examined the stock price performance of acquiring firms following acquisitions. All of these articles are listed in Table 1. We now attempt to summarize this body of research, a task made easier by separating mergers from tender offers. In addition, since Franks, Harris & Titman (FHT) (1991) altered this literature, both by devoting their entire paper to post-acquisition performance and by using more sophisticated measurement techniques, we separate pre-FHT from post-FHT findings.

2.1.1 Pre-FHT Findings on Performance Following Mergers
The first thirteen articles listed in Table 1 all occurred prior to FHT.[1] Of the 13, we exclude Dodd & Ruback (1977), because it deals with tender offers,[2] Firth (1980), Barnes (1984), Dodds & Quek (1985), Franks, Harris & Mayer (1988) and Franks & Harris (1989), because they do not separate mergers from tender offers.[3] Of the remaining seven, Mandelker (1974) provides the least support for negative post-acquisition performance. The CAARs, though negative, are not economically significant. In addition, while no t-statistics are provided for his entire 40-month post-acquisition period, t-statistics for both a 10-month and a 20-month period are insignificant. On the other extreme, Asquith reports CAARs of –0.072 in the 240 days following merger outcome. This return is both economically and statistically significant, providing perhaps the strongest evidence against the null hypothesis of zero abnormal returns.

All of the other five papers are ambiguous to some extent. Using the same data but different methodologies, Magenheim & Mueller (MM) and Bradley & Jarrell (BJ) reach opposite conclusions. MM find what are most likely significant CAARs over three years, while BJ find insignificant results over the same time period. We are inclined to put more weight on BJ's results, since their approach specifically avoids MM's methodological problem. However, BJ do

Table 1. Summary of the Studies on Post-Acquisition Performance

The table summarizes the data, methodology and results of 22 studies on the long-run stock price performance of acquiring firms after acquisition via merger or tender offer.

Study	Acquisition Type[a]	Sample Period	Sample Size	Method[b]	Event Date[c]	# Months[d]	Results	Stat Sig[e]
Mandelker (1974)	M	1941-62	241	Fama-MacBeth 2 factor model	C	40 40	-0.014 Constant β -0.026 Moving β	nr nr
Dodd & Ruback (1977)	T	1958-76	124	Market model	A	60 60 13	-0.059 Successful -0.0262 Failed +0.0844 Clean-up mergers	I[f] I[f] I
Langetieg (1978)	M	1929-69	149	4 Methods Control firm	C	70 70	-0.223 to -0.2615	S I
Firth (1980)	Both	1969-75	434 129	Market model	A	36	+0.001 Successful -0.035 Failed	I nr
Asquith (1983)	M	1962-76	196 87	β-control portfolio	C	11.4	-0.072 Successful -0096 Failed	S- S
Malatesta (1983)	M	1969-74	256	Market model	A A*	12	-0.076 -0.029	S I[f]
Barnes (1984)	M	1974-76	39	Market & industry model	A	60	-0.063	nr
Dodds & Quek (1985)	M	1974-76	70	Market model	A	60	-0.068	nr
Bradley & Jarrell (1988)	Both	1976-81	78	β-control portfolio	A	36	-0.16	I
Magenheim & Muller (1988)	M T	1976-81	51 26	Market model	A	36	-0.2437 +0.0632	nr nr
Franks, Harris & Mayer (1988)	Both	1955-84	392 127 207 221	4 methods 4 methods 2 methods 2 methods	C	24	-0.018 to -0.18 US, Equity -0036 to +0.094 US, Cash -0.094 to +0.042 UK, Equity +0.0175 to +0.175 UK, Cash	

Study	Type[a]	Period	N	Method[b]	Date[c]	Months[d]	Return	Sig.[e]
Franks & Harris (1989)	Both (UK)	1955-85	1058	3 methods	C	24	-0.126 to 0.048	S
Limmack (1991)	Both (UK)	1977-86	448	Size decile adj.	A	24	-0.128	
			81	3 methods			-0.1496 to -0.0467 Successful	I
							-2.2625 to -0.0738 Failed	I
Franks, Harris & Titman (1991)	Both	1975-84	399	8-factor model	A	36	-0.0396 Event time	S
							+0.018 Calendar time	I
Agrawal, Jaffe & Mandelker (1992)	M	1955-87	937	Size and β adj.	C	60	-0.1026	I
	T		227				+0.022	I
Loderer & Martin (1992)	M	1965-86	304	Size and β adj.	C	60	-0.0075	I
	T		155				-0.01	I
	O		746				+0.0075	S
	A		93				+0.0125	S
Anderson & Mandelker (1993)	M	1966-87	670	Size & b/m adj.	C	60	-0.0931	nr
Kennedy & Limmack (1996)	Both (UK)	1980-89	247	Size adj Size adj	A	23	-0.0956 -0.0508	S S
Gregory (1997)	Both (UK)	1984-92	452	6 methods	C	24	-0.1182 to -0.18	S
Loughran & Vijh 1997	M	1970-89	788	BHAR (Size & b/m adj.)	C	60	-0.159	S
	T		135				+0.43	I
Rau & Vermaelen (1998)	M	1980-91	2,823	Size & b/m adj.	C	36	-0.0404	S
	T		316				+0.0856	S
Mitchell & Stafford (1998)	Both	1961-93	2,767	BHAR (Size & b/m adj.)	C	36	-0.02 EW	S
				Fama-French regression			-0.079 EW	S
				CAARs using: Size & b/m adj.			-0.018 EW	I
				Fama-French regression			-0.054 EW	S

[a] M = Merger, T = Tender offer, O = Other acquisitions, A = Acquisition of assets

[b] BHAR = Buy and hold abnormal return, CAAR = Cumulative average abnormal return, b/m = book/market, adj = adjusted

[c] A = Announcement date (first public announcement), A* = Announcement of board or management approval, C = Completion date, O = Outcome date

[d] Number of post-event months

[e] Statistical significance: I = Insignificant, S = Significant, nr = Not reported

[f] Probably

not separate mergers from tender offers as MM do. Langetieg (1978) reports CAARs between –0.223 and –0.2615 over 70 months using four different statistical methods. While these abnormal returns are both economically and statistically significant, his control firm approach yields insignificant returns. Langetieg places more weight on the control firm approach, though readers may not. Malatesta (1983) finds statistically significant abnormal returns for the year after the first public announcement of merger but insignificant results for the year after board/management approval. Limmack (1991) assesses post-acquisition performance over two years, finding significantly negative CAARs for two of his three methodologies. However, Limmack does not separate mergers from tender offers, leaving interpretation somewhat ambiguous. We include this article in the present section of our paper on the (perhaps dubious) premise that abnormal returns would likely have been even more negative if tender offers had been removed from his sample.

Thus, taken together, the literature at this point only suggests the possibility of an anomaly. The lack of corroboration across papers, as well as the use of empirical methodologies now considered inadequate for measuring long-run abnormal stock performance, prevents one from drawing a strong conclusion at this point.

2.1.2 Pre-FHT Findings on Performance Following Tender Offers

Prior to FHT, only two papers examined performance following tender offers. Our calculations, based on Dodd & Ruback's (1977) Table 3, yield a CAAR of –0.0591 for the 60 months following tender offers. By contrast, our calculations, based on Magenheim & Mueller's Table 11.3, yield a CAAR of 0.0632 for the three years following tender offers. Statistical significance can not be assessed for either of these calculations. However, since the CAARs are of opposite signs and of similar magnitudes (though for different post-event time periods), we conclude that the null hypothesis, of zero abnormal returns following acquisition, should not be rejected.

2.1.3 Post-FHT Performance Following Mergers

As shown in Table 1, FHT is followed by eight papers. Of these nine, we exclude FHT, Kennedy & Limmack (1996) and Mitchell & Stafford (1988) because they do not separate mergers from tender offers. Of the remaining six articles, Loderer & Martin (LM) (1992) provide the least support for negative post-merger performance. LM find that five-year performance, while negative, is not statistically different from zero. However, this is not to say that the authors provide no support for negative post-merger performance, since three-year abnormal returns are significantly below zero.

By contrast, a number of articles provide stronger evidence of negative post-merger performance. Agrawal, Jaffe and Mandelker (AJM) (1992) find a statistically significant five-year CAAR of –0.1026, under a size and beta adjustment. Anderson & Mandelker (AM) (1993) report five-year CAARs of –0.0956 and –0.0931, under a size and a size & book-to-market (b/m) adjustment, respectively. Both of AM's CAARs are statistically significant. However, one should not view these two studies as independent. The two datasets greatly overlap since AM use the 1966 to 1987 portion of AJM's data. Loughran & Vijh (1997) find a statistically significant five-year buy-and-hold return relative to a size and b/m control of –0.159. However, when overlapping cases are eliminated, the buy-and-hold return relative to a control becomes –0.142, which is only marginally significant (t= –1.69). Rau & Vermaelen (1998) find a statistically significant three-year CAAR of –0.0404. However, one is likely to view this CAAR as economically insignificant. Finally, Gregory (1997) finds two-year CAARs between –0.1182 to –0.1801 under six different models, all of which are statistically significant. Gregory uses U.K. data, providing an out-of-sample test of the anomaly. While Gregory does not separate mergers from tender offers, our discussion below suggests that post-acquisition performance would have been even worse if tender offers had been removed from the sample.

Taken together, we believe that the post-FHT articles suggest strong evidence of an anomaly following mergers. One can find some evidence of statistically significant negative abnormal returns in each of the six articles above and strong evidence of both economically important and statistically significant negative performance in a few of the articles. As a group, the studies cover a long time period and two countries (United States and United Kingdom). A wide variety of statistical techniques are used, all of which go beyond the old-style CAPM/market model approaches. While there has been a fair amount of criticism of long-run return studies in general (see e.g. Kothari & Warner (1997), Barber & Lyon (1997) and Lyon, Barber & Tsai (1999)), the differing results on tender offers (see below), as well as the differing methodologies in the six papers, suggest that something more than a statistical bias is at work here. Furthermore, in our opinion, the results discussed in Section 3 below, on explanations, strengthen one's belief in the anomaly.

2.1.4 Post-FHT Performance Following Tender Offers

Of the nine papers beginning with FHT, four examine tender offers. AJM state that five-year CAARs following tender offers are (p. 1611) "small and insignificantly different from zero. Thus, we find no evidence of unusual performance for tender offers." Loderer & Martin (LM) find that five-year abnormal performance is positive but insignificantly different from zero. Loughran & Vijh (LV) find a five-year buy and hold abnormal return (BHAR) following tender offers of 0.43. While this number is economically significant, it is only marginally statistically significant (t = 1.67). When overlapping cases are eliminated, the five-year BHAR is even greater at 0.613, though the t-statistic is still marginally significant (t = 1.86). Rau & Vermaelen (RV) find a lower, but statistically significant three-year CAAR of 0.0856.

Two related conclusions seem warranted. First, while there is strong evidence, in our opinion, of negative abnormal returns following mergers, there is no similar evidence following tender offers. Abnormal returns are predominantly positive, not negative. Secondly, one could perhaps even make the case that abnormal returns are significantly positive here, as suggested by the evidence of LV and RV. However, this might be stretching the case, because LV report only marginal statistical significance and both AJM & LM report insignificance.

2.1.5 Performance Following Failed Bids

While the profession has always been more interested in long-run returns following successful acquisitions, the literature has occasionally examined bidder returns following unsuccessful bids as well. Our Table 1 notes four such papers. Dodd & Ruback (1977) find a 60-month CAAR of –0.0262 following the announcement of tender offers that later turn out to be unsuccessful. While this appears to be economically insignificant, the absence of t-tests prevents an assessment of statistical significance. Similarly, Firth (1980) reports a CAAR of –0.035 over 36 months following the announcement of acquisition attempts that turn out to be unsuccessful. No t-test is reported over this interval. Asquith (1983) finds a statistically significant CAAR of –0.096 over the 240 days following unsuccessful merger bids. Finally, Limmack (1991) finds 24-month post-bid CAARs of –0.2420, –0.2625, and –0.0738 under three models. The first two are significantly negative, while the third is statistically insignificant.

The results above are merely suggestive at best. The finding of Asquith for unsuccessful merger bids is similar to his finding for successful bids. And, the abnormal returns are generally even more negative for Limmack. However, the results raise more questions than they answer. For example, the methodologies of these papers are not the most current. Will the results change under newer methodologies? Also, Limmack does not separate mergers from tender offers; are his negative returns driven by mergers? These questions can only be answered by new research.

2.2 Review of the Individual Studies

Mandelker (1974) is generally considered the first modern treatment of the financial consequences of mergers, with merger completion dates being precisely determined and abnormal returns (or residuals, as they were then called) being calculated relative to a benchmark. The paper analyses 241 mergers that took place during 1941–1962. Both the acquiring and the acquired firms were listed on the New York Stock Exchange (NYSE). The abnormal return for stock j in calendar month t, ε_{jt}, is calculated as:

$$\varepsilon_{jt} = R_{jt} - \hat{\gamma}_{ot} - \hat{\gamma}_{1t}\beta_{jt},$$

where R_{jt} is the return on stock j in month t
$\gamma_{ot}, \hat{\gamma}_{1t}$ are the ex-post coefficients between return and risk for calendar month t, as estimated by Fama & MacBeth (1973)
β_{jt} is the beta for security j in month t.

Mandelker's major focus is on returns around the time of the merger, with perhaps his most important finding being (p. 303): "stockholders of acquiring firms seem to earn normal returns from mergers as from other investment-production activities with commensurate risk levels. Stockholders of acquired firms earn abnormal returns of approximately 14%, on the average, in the seven months preceding the merger."

In addition, his rather exhaustive work also presents returns for the combined entity subsequent to the merger. His Table 1 shows cumulative average abnormal returns (CAARs) of –0.014 over the 40 months following merger completion, clearly an economically insignificant drop. While no t-statistics over the 40-month period are provided, Mandelker's Table 4 shows statistically insignificant abnormal returns over the first 10 months and the first 20 months following merger completion.

In his Table 1, a firm's beta for month t is measured using data over the previous 60 months. In his Table 8, the beta for month t is measured using data from months $(t - 30, t - 1)$ and $(t + 1, t + 30)$. Here, the CAAR over the 40 months following merger completion is –0.026. This CAAR, though somewhat bigger in magnitude than that in Table 1, still seems economically insignifcant.

Results on post-merger returns were given little weight in Mandelker's paper, perhaps for two reasons. Research on other market anomalies, which has questioned the efficient market paradigm to some extent, had not yet arisen. In addition, other work showing negative abnormal returns following mergers was to come later as well.

Dodd & Ruback (DR) (1977) examine stock return performance both before and after tender offers. They compile a sample of 124 NYSE firms making successful tender offers and 48 NYSE firms making unsuccessful tender offers, over the period from 1958 to 1976. Abnormal returns are calculated from the market model.

The study measures the post-acquisition performance of acquirers over two periods, months (+1, +12) and (+13, +60), relative to the first public announcement of the bid. From their Table 3, we calculate that the CAAR, for the successful acquirers, over this entire 60-month period is –0.0591. While this performance may be economically important, the t-statistics reported for the two periods are both insignificant. In addition, we calculate that abnormal returns are –0.0262 for unsuccessful acquirers for the same 60-month period. Again, t-statistics are insignificant for each of the two periods.

The paper also calculates post-acquisition performance following 19 cleanup mergers, i.e. offers where the acquirer owned over one-half of the target firm's shares prior to the merger. DR's Table 4 indicates that the CAAR for acquirers over months (+1, +13) is 0.0844, with a marginally significant t-value of 1.60. No results are reported for months (+13, +60).

Langetieg (1978) examines 149 mergers between NYSE firms over the period from 1929 to 1969. He begins by adjusting returns for both market and industry factors. He abstracts from market returns by using either the Capital Asset Pricing Model (CAPM) or the Black (1972) two-factor model, and employs two industry indices, yielding four measures of abnormal performance. Regardless of the measure, the results in his Table 1 show large negative returns over three intervals (months (+1, +12), (+13, +24), and (+25, +70)) after the merger. Our summations over the three periods yield cumulative abnormal performance over months (+1, +70) between –0.223 and –0.2615.

However, in his Table 2, Langetieg uses a control firm approach as well. His control firm "represents the firm in the merging firm's two-digit industry having the highest residual (i.e. returns net of market influence) correlation to the merging firm" (p. 371). He calculates abnormal performance as the difference between the acquiring firm's performance, using one of the four measures above, and the performance of the control firm using the same measure. We calculate his cumulative abnormal performance over months (+1, +72) to be –0.055, which is much smaller in magnitude than his first set of results. He summarizes his results as follows (p. 376): "If we were to draw preliminary conclusions based only on the results for merging firms, we would be forced to conclude that the post-merger excess return experience is inconsistent with the efficient markets hypothesis. However, it would be wrong to draw conclusions based only on merging firm results, since the control firm results and the 'paired-difference' results must also be considered. The control firm also shows a generally negative average excess return in most post-merger time intervals. Examination of the 'paired-difference' results shows average excess returns that are still predominantly negative, but never significantly different from zero. Hence, we conclude that the post-merger excess return experience is consistent with the efficient markets hypothesis."

This quote indicates that Langetieg puts more weight on the control firm results. However, it is not clear whether this second approach is preferable. After all, the first approach abstracts from industry effects. A control firm may be superfluous in this set-up, since this firm is meant to abstract from industry effects as well. Subsequent academic studies have not used a control firm this way.

Firth (1980) examines bidders in 434 successful bids and 129 unsuccessful bids, in the United Kingdom, over the period from 1969 to 1975. Takeover bids where the bidder holds at least 30% of the target stock, six months prior to the bid announcement, are excluded from the sample. Both bidders and targets are exchange-listed firms. Abnormal performance is measured via the market model, with a moving average method used for beta estimation. Specifically, the parameters of the model for a given month t are estimated over months (t–48, t–1), excluding months (–12, +12) around the takeover bid month. His Table III shows CAARs for successful bidders of only 0.001 over the 36 months following the bid announcement. This is clearly an economically insignificant return and his Table V indicates that this is statistically insignificant as well. Table IV shows CAARs for unsuccessful bidders of 0.035 over the 36 months following bid announcement. Table V indicates statistical significance over the first year, but not over the next two years, following the bid announcement. However, the table does not allow a statistical inference over the full three-year period.

Asquith (1983) provides a comprehensive study of mergers, with particular attention given to announcement dates. As opposed to the monthly returns in the Mandelker and Langetieg studies, Asquith uses daily data, allowing him to measure returns relative to both the 'press day' and 'outcome day.' The press day is the day that *The Wall Street Journal (WSJ)* reports news of the merger bid and the outcome day is the day that the *WSJ* publishes the outcome.

The study examines 196 NYSE or American Stock Exchange (AMEX) acquir-ers in successful mergers involving NYSE targets over the 1962–1976 period. Daily abnormal returns are calculated as the difference between the return on the merging firm and the return on a control portfolio with a similar beta. To form this control, all securities on the NYSE and AMEX are ranked once a year, according to their betas, and placed into one of 10 decile portfolios.

Asquith's Table 1 shows abnormal returns from 480 days before the announcement date to 240 days after the outcome day. Bidding firms experience positive abnormal returns of 0.134 over days (–480, –40) prior to the press day, perhaps indicating that firms are more likely to make acquisitions after performing well. However, cumulative excess returns are –0.072 over the 240 days following the outcome, with almost all of this decline occurring after day

+60. In addition, cumulative excess returns are –0.096 over the 240 day period following the outcome day for a sample of 87 unsuccessful bidders.

While Mandelker makes little mention of the slight post-merger decline in his sample and Langetieg concludes that post-merger performance is not significantly negative, Asquith states (p. 74): "These results are surprising, especially since the post-outcome decline in equity value is delayed by sixty days or more . . . The stock price behavior of merged firms during the post-outcome period thus remains a puzzle. There is no immediate stock price reaction after a merger, but within a year there are large negative excess returns."

Malatesta (1983) examines 256 firms that acquired targets with asset size greater than $10 million over the period 1969–1974. Abnormal returns are calculated from the market model in risk premium form. For months (+1, +12) after the merger announcement, the market model parameters, α_{jt} and β_{jt}, are estimated from the 36 observations closest to a given month t, drawn from months (+13, t + 60).

Malatesta's Table 4 presents cumulative average abnormal returns for acquiring firms over months (+1, +6) and (+7, +12), relative to the first public announcement date of the merger. Abnormal returns are significantly negative over both periods, with a total CAAR (our calculation) of –0.076 over months (+1, +12). While this cumulative return is similar in magnitude to that in Asquith (1983), Asquith measures returns from the outcome date. Since the first public announcement of a merger is often made after its completion, Malatesta also looks at the subset of roughly one-half of his sample where an announcement of board or management approval of the merger appears in the WSJ. For this subset, his Table 5 reports statistically insignificant negative CAARs in both periods (+1, +6) and (+7, +12) relative to this more precise announcement date.

While Malatesta takes the significantly negative returns following the first public announcement quite seriously, he argues (p. 179): "Market inefficiency is an unlikely explanation for negative abnormal post-merger returns to acquiring firms. Information concerning mergers is widely disseminated. The general characteristics of mergers are well known. It is implausible that investors systematically misinterpret the implications of these common phenomena." Instead, he suggests the possibility that post-merger losses are mere statistical artifacts due to changes in risk parameters around the merger event.

Barnes (1984) examines all mergers between companies listed on the London Stock Exchange, over the period from June 1974 to February 1976. Post-merger performance of the resulting 39 acquiring firms was assessed using the market model with an added industry factor. The author's Figure 1 indicates that the CAAR over the 60 months following the month of announcement is –0.063. No statistical tests are reported.

Dodds & Quek (1985) examine 70 mergers, during 1974–1976, where the acquirer is listed on the Industrial Sector of the London Stock Exchange. Post-merger performance is computed using the market model. The Industrial Group Index of the Financial Times Actuarial Share Index is used as a proxy for the market. Their Table 1 shows a CAAR of –0.068 over the 60 months following the month of merger announcement. No statistical tests are reported for this interval.

Magenheim & Mueller (1988) examine 78 NYSE/AMEX acquiring firms that completed takeovers worth at least $15 million, over the period 1976–1981. The authors classify 51 of the acquisitions as mergers and 26 as tender offers. They calculate abnormal returns from the market model, estimating the parameters α and β over one of three periods: months (–60, –4), (–36, –4) or (+13, +36), relative to the initial announcement month. For the first two estimation periods, the authors' Table 11.5 presents CAARs for each of the first three years subsequent to the announcement. Our calculations show that the CAARs over the entire three-year post-announcement period are –0.1436 and –0.3896 using the first and second estimation periods, respectively. Only the CAAR over the first year (–0.0321) is presented using the third estimation period, which runs over the second and third post-announcement years. While the two three-year estimates differ substantially, they both appear to be economically significant. The authors do not report statistical significance over the three-year period. However, they present z-values (standard normal) of –1.2464 and –4.9307 for performance over months (–3, +36) relative to the month of initial announcement, using the first and second estimation periods, respectively.

The authors present post-announcement returns for mergers and tender offers separately, in Table 11.3, using only the (–60, –4) estimation period. Our calculations show CAARs over the first three years after the announcement to be –0.2437 and +0.0632, respectively, for the two sub-samples. Once again, z-values are reported for the period (–3, +36). They are –2.60 for mergers and 0.56 for tender offers. Magenheim and Mueller appear to be the first to calculate post-acquisition returns, separately for the two types of acquisitions; and, like Magenheim and Mueller, subsequent researchers generally find that returns are higher after tender offers than after mergers.

Bradley & Jarrell (BJ) (1988) criticize Magenheim & Mueller's methodology, stating (p. 255): "It is well known that market model parameter estimates based on monthly data are inefficient and non-stationary." And, indeed, financial economists have long pointed out that, if the true abnormal performance is non-zero during the estimation period, measurement of abnormal performance in the forecast period will be biased. BJ estimate abnormal returns using a method similar, if not, identical to that of Asquith (1983). Here, a daily abnormal return is the difference between the return on the acquirer's stock and the return on a portfolio of securities of similar beta. The authors find a statistically insignificant CAAR of –0.16 over the first three post-acquisition years.

Franks, Harris & Mayer (1988) examine post-acquisition returns for both the United Kingdom and the United States, as a small part of their detailed study on takeovers. The authors use a sample of takeovers over the period 1955–1985, as recorded in the London Share Price Database (LSPD). The dataset covers all U.K. companies listed on the London Stock Exchange (LSE) after 1975 and about two-thirds of the companies (generally larger firms) on the LSE before 1975. The U.S. sample includes all companies that disappeared by acquisition from the University of Chicago Center for Research in Security Prices (CRSP) files over the period 1955–1984. The CRSP database covers all NYSE-listed firms since 1926 and all AMEX-listed firms since 1962. The authors calculate post-acquisition abnormal returns in four ways:

(1) The market model approach, using α and β estimated over the 60-month period beginning 71 months before the announcement month.
(2) The market model approach, using months (+25, +60) relative to merger completion as the estimation period.
(3) The return on the acquiring firm minus the return on the market.
(4) The capital asset pricing model.

Post-merger returns are computed relative to the month of the final bid for mergers in the U.S. and the month when the merger was unconditionally accepted in the U.K. The U.S. sample includes 127 all-cash acquisitions and 392 equity acquisitions. The U.K. sample includes 221 cash and 207 equity takeovers.

For the United States, the authors' Table 8.9 shows cumulative average abnormal returns to acquirers, over the first two years following all-equity takeovers, to be around –0.18 under methods (1), (3), and (4). All three estimates are statistically significant. However, the CAAR is a statistically insignificant –0.018 under the second method. Since Method 2 may lead to a bias if abnormal performance is still negative over months (+25, +60), one might feel less confident with this method than with any of the other three. Taking this view, one would conclude that post-takeover performance in the United States is strongly negative for all-equity acquisitions. Results are quite different for all-cash deals in the U.S., with post-acquisition performance being insignificantly different from zero under each of the four methods.

Only methods (1) and (4) are used for acquisitions in the United Kingdom. Here, abnormal returns, following all-equity acquisitions, are significantly negative (–0.094) under the first method, but insignificant under the fourth. By contrast, abnormal returns following all-cash acquisitions are insignificant under the first method but significantly positive (0.175) under the fourth. One can draw two conclusions from the U.K. results. First, the benchmark is important in studies of long-run returns, as previously shown by Dimson & Marsh (1986) and others. Second, returns following cash acquisitions are higher than those following equity acquisitions, a result that the authors found for the U.S. as well. And, since tender offers are likely financed with cash, while mergers are likely financed with equity, the results of Franks, Harris & Mayer are consistent with those of Magenheim & Mueller.

Franks & Harris (1989) examine wealth effects of corporate acquisitions in the United Kingdom. While the bulk of their work concerns the time immediately prior to the takeover event, they consider post-acquisition performance as well. They use a sample of 1,058 acquiring firms, in acquisitions recorded on the LSPD during 1955–1985. Post-acquisition returns are measured over the 24 months following what they term the 'unconditional date', which occurs when a sufficient percentage of shares has been pledged to the acquirer to result in legal control. The authors begin by calculating post-takeover abnormal returns in three ways:

(1) Returns relative to the market index.
(2) Returns relative to the market model, where α and β are estimated over the 60-month period beginning 71 months before the announcement month.
(3) The capital asset pricing model.

In their Table 10, the CAAR over the 24 months following the unconditional date is approximately 0.05 and statistically significant, under methods 1 and 3. However, the CAAR is a statistically significant –0.126 under the market model. The authors state (p. 245): "The differences in model results are directly attributable, in this case, to the cumulative effects of subtracting the α values from the realized returns of bidding companies, when the market model is used. The average bidder α is 0.0095 per month (average $\beta = 0.92$), which indicates that bidding firms (premerger) were outperforming the market by almost 1% per month. A failure to repeat this performance after the merger would show abnormal losses of over 20% over a 24-month period."

In their Table 11, the authors measure each return relative to the return on the appropriate size decile portfolio. For each decile, the acquiring firms underperform their control portfolio. We calculate an average abnormal return of –0.128 across all acquirers over the two-year period. To our knowledge, this is the first paper in the post-acquisition performance literature that abstracts from a priced factor other than beta. While Franks & Harris do not express a preference between this size adjustment and their other approaches, later research generally gives primary emphasis to methodologies that adjust for size (and other empirically-based factors).

Limmack (1991) examines the post-acquisition performance of acquirers in 448 successful and 81 unsuccessful bids, announced during 1977–1986, where both target and bidder were quoted on the International Stock Exchange in London. The author measures abnormal returns in three ways. First, the market model is employed with α and β estimated from return data over months (−67, −7) relative to the announcement month. Second, adjusted betas supplied by the London Business School Risk Measurement Service (RMS) are used in the market model. The author states (p. 242): "RMS betas are estimated on the basis of regressing trade-to-trade security returns on the market returns observed over identical periods of time. The betas so calculated are then Bayesian-adjusted following Vasicek (1973)." The alpha for any company is estimated as:

$$\alpha_j = \bar{R}_j - \beta_j \cdot \bar{R}_M,$$

where $\bar{R}_j$ and R_M are the average returns on firm j and the market, respectively, over the market model estimation period. Third, abnormal performance is measured relative to the market index.

For the period from the bid month (month 0) to 24 months following the outcome month, Limmack's Table 5 reports CAARs for the acquirers of −0.1496, −0.0467 and −0.0743 for the market model, the adjusted beta model and the market index adjustment, respectively. The first and third abnormal returns are significantly different from zero, at the 1% level, while the second CAAR is significant at the 10% level. The author presents value-weighted abnormal returns as well. The numbers here are smaller in magnitude, with only the market model adjustment yielding statistical significance and only at the 10% level.

Limmack also calculates abnormal returns for unsuccessful acquirers over the same interval. CAARs are −0.2420, −0.2625, and −0.0738 for the market model, the adjusted-beta model and the index adjustment, respectively. Here, the first two CAARs are significant at the 1% level and the third is significant at the 10% level. Value-weighted abnormal performance is similar in magnitude, with two of the three abnormal returns being significant at the 5% level.

Franks, Harris & Titman (FHT) (1991) must be viewed as an important paper, in the literature on long-run returns following takeovers, for two reasons. First, FHT devote their entire paper to this topic, while previous papers consider long-run returns as a small part of their analyses. Second, the authors use a more sophisticated set of benchmarks than those in prior research.

The paper investigates 399 acquisitions, both mergers and tender offers, over the period 1975–1984. Both the acquirer and the target were on NYSE/AMEX. The authors measure abnormal returns relative to four benchmarks:

(1) The CRSP equally-weighted index.
(2) The CRSP value-weighted index.
(3) A ten-factor model provided by Lehmann & Modest (1987).
(4) An eight-portfolio model from Grinblatt & Titman (1988, 1989).

The last benchmark consists of four portfolios based on firm size, three based on dividend yield and one based on past returns. The authors prefer this benchmark, stating (p. 86): "In developing this benchmark, Grinblatt & Titman (1988) formed 72 portfolios using rankings of firms based on market capitalization, dividend yield, past returns, interest rate sensitivity, co-skewness with the equally-weighted index and beta measured with the equally-weighted index. Since these are passive portfolios (i.e., their composition does not change over time), they should not exhibit abnormal performance when performance is measured relative to an efficient benchmark. However, Grinblatt & Titman found that the single-factor model, the ten-factor model, and another benchmark, consisting of portfolios formed solely on the basis of market capitalization, all generated significant nonzero performance. This significant performance was eliminated with the eight-portfolio benchmark, which was efficient relative to various subsets of the sample, over different sample periods, and robust with respect to minor changes in the composition of the benchmark. In addition, a sample of 37 industry portfolios did not exhibit significant abnormal performance when measured against this benchmark."

The authors calculate average abnormal performance in two ways. First, for each acquiring company, excess returns (above the one-month Treasury bill rate) are regressed against the relevant set of benchmark portfolios over the 36 months since the final bid date. The intercept in this regression is then averaged across all acquirers. Second, for each calendar month in their sample, the authors form an equally-weighted portfolio of all companies that have acquired a firm in the last 36 months. The excess return on this portfolio is then regressed against the relevant set of benchmark portfolios. The authors motivate the second approach by arguing that the first approach ignores cross-correlation between the abnormal returns of different acquirers.

The basic results of FHT, as presented in their Table 2, show significantly negative post-acquisition abnormal returns using the equally-weighted benchmark, significantly positive abnormal returns using the value-weighted benchmark and insignificant abnormal returns using either the ten-factor or the eight-portfolio benchmark. Since the authors emphasize the eight-portfolio approach, they argue that post-acquisition abnormal returns are not significantly different from zero. They "conclude that previous findings of poor performance after takeover are likely due to benchmark errors, rather than mispricing at the time of the takeover" (p. 81).

The authors separate their sample by (1) size of bidder, (2) medium of exchange, (3) number of bidders, (4) opposition of target management and (5) relative size of target to bidder. While the abnormal returns on a number of sub-samples are significantly different under either an equally-weighted index or a value-weighted index and the abnormal returns on a few sub-samples are significant under the ten-factor benchmark, no abnormal returns are significant under the eight-portfolio benchmark. Because of these results under the last benchmark, the sub-samples do not cause FHT to change their conclusion of zero abnormal performance.

Agrawal, Jaffe & Mandelker (AJM) (1992) completed their paper on the heel of the Franks, Harris & Titman work. While AJM employ similar methodology to that of FHT, and even use a sample supplied by Robert Harris, AJM reach different conclusions. AJM's sample of 937 mergers and 227 tender offers (p. 1607) "represents nearly the entire population of acquisitions of NYSE and AMEX firms by NYSE firms over the period 1955 to 1987." An acquisition is classified as a tender offer if the bidder purchased at least 60% of the target's outstanding shares via tender offer.

The authors use two methods to measure long-run abnormal returns, with an adjustment for both size and beta. In the first approach, the abnormal performance of stock i in month t, ϵ_{it}, is calculated as:

$$\epsilon_{it} = R_{it} - R_{st} - (\beta_i - \beta_s)(R_{mt} - R_{ft}),$$

where R_{it} is the return on security i in month t

R_{st} is the equally-weighted return across all firms in the same size decile as firm i

β_i and β_s are the betas of stock i and the size control portfolio, respectively, measured over months (+1, +60) relative to the month of merger completion

R_{mt} is the return on the NYSE value-weighted index in month t

R_{ft} is the yield in month t on a one-month Treasury bill.

With this approach, abnormal returns are cumulated over a five-year period beginning with the month of merger completion.

The second approach combines the Returns Across Time and Securities (RATS) methodology of Ibbotson (1975) with an adjustment for firm size. The following cross-sectional regression is estimated for each month t relative to the month of merger completion:

$$R_{it} - R_{st} = \alpha_t \beta_t (R_{mt} - R_{ft}) + \eta_{it},$$

where $R_{it,}$ $R_{st},$ R_{mt} and R_{ft} are defined above.

AJM's Table I shows steadily negative average abnormal returns following merger completion under the first method, with CAARs reaching a statistically significant –0.1026 by month +60. Results for the RATS methodology are quite similar. By contrast, FHT report insignificance with a similar procedure, adjusting for size as well as past performance and dividend yield. AJM also examine long-run abnormal performance following tender offers, finding insignificance under both methods.

In addition, the authors also examine the behavior over different sub-periods in their sample. Five-year cumulative average abnormal returns are significantly negative for mergers that took place in the 1950s, the 1960s and the 1980s. However, CAARs are insignificantly positive over the 1970–79 period. Since this period overlaps with FHT, AJM also examine FHT's sample period. AJM write (p. 1614): "The last two columns of Table II show the post-merger performance over the 1975–1984 time period of the recent paper by Franks, Harris, & Titman (1991). We find no abnormal performance during this time period, a result consistent with that of Franks, Harris, & Titman. A break-down (not reported) of our 33-year sample period into five-year sub-periods (1955 to 1959, 1960 to 1964, etc.) shows that 1975 to 1979 is the only five-year period when the post-merger performance is significantly positive. This period constitutes one half of Franks, Harris, & Titman's sample. Over the remainder of their sample period, 1980 to 1984, the post-merger performance is significantly negative. Thus, the performance over the combined period, 1975 to 1984, is insignificant. We conclude that Franks, Harris & Titman's results are specific to their sample period."

Loderer & Martin (LM) (1992) examine a sample of 1,298 acquisitions over the period from 1965 to 1986. The sample includes mergers, acquisitions of privately-held corporations, tender offers and comprehensive acquisitions of the assets of individual firms. Long-run performance is measured relative to the completion date, as reported in *Mergers and Acquisitions*.

The authors use the following regression, which is a variant of the Ibbotson RATS approach:

$$R_i - R_{si} = \gamma_{oi}D_o + \gamma_{1i}D_1 + \gamma_{2i}D_2 + \gamma_{3i}D_3 + \gamma_{4i}D_4 + \gamma_{5i}(R_m - R_f),$$

where R_i is the return on firm i
R_{st} is the return on a size decile portfolio corresponding to firm i
R_m is the return on the value-weighted CRSP index
R_f is the yield on a three-month Treasury bill
D_j is set equal to 1 if the return is measured over year j+1 following the completion date.

For their entire sample, LM's Exhibit 1 reports significantly negative abnormal returns over the three-year period following completion. However, the abnormal return is insignificantly different from zero over the full five-year post-acquisition period. In their Exhibit 3, the authors also report returns for three different time periods: 1966–69, 1970–79 and 1980–86. They find that the abnormal return, over the entire five-year post-acquisition period, is significantly negative during the 1966–69 sub-period, but is insignificantly different from zero in later periods.

Loderer & Martin separate acquisitions into four categories, in their Exhibit 4: mergers, tender offers, other acquisitions, and acquisitions of assets. Abnormal performance is significantly negative for the three-year period following both mergers and other acquisitions, but is insignificant for both tender offers and acquisitions of assets. Abnormal performance is insignificant, for the five-year post-acquisition period, for all four types of acquisitions. The authors conclude (p. 77): "We find that, on average, acquiring firms do not under-perform a control portfolio during the first five years following the acquisition. They simply earn their required rate of return, no more or no less. There is some negative performance for the first three years, especially during the second and the third years after the acquisition, but it is most prominent in the 1960s, it diminishes in the 1970s, and disappears completely in the 1980s. Thus, in the later years, the post-acquisition years do not provide strong enough evidence that corporate acquisitions are wasteful, nor do they provide evidence contradicting market efficiency."

The Loderer & Martin paper makes an important contribution to the literature, both for its detailed analysis and for its strong conclusion indicated above. However, a few points should be made to put the work in proper context. First, going back to Jensen & Ruback (1983), the anomaly has always been framed in terms of abnormal performance following mergers. While LM find strong evidence that, as a group, tender offers, other acquisitions and acquisition of assets do not precede poor stock performance, their evidence on mergers is more ambiguous. They find marginally significant under-performance in the first two years following mergers and outright significant under-performance in the first three years. Insignificance occurs only over the first four and the first five years following mergers. While Agrawal, Jaffe & Mandelker (1992) find significance over the full five-year period, earlier researchers generally go out only two or three years. Second, Loderer & Martin (1992) cumulate daily returns over a long time period, which can lead to a bias (see Blume & Stambaugh, 1983). Third, AJM's results for mergers in various decades differ from those of LM. AJM find significant five-year under-performance following mergers for the 1950s, the 1960s and the 1980s. Only in the 1970s is post-acquisition performance insignificant. Further research is needed to sort out these temporal differences.

Abnormal returns in both Agrawal, Jaffe & Mandelker (1992) and Loderer & Martin (1992) are adjusted for size. Those in Franks, Harris & Titman (1991) are adjusted for size, dividend yield and past performance. However, Fama & French (1992, 1993), Lakonishok, Shleifer & Vishny (1994) and others document that, in addition to firm size, the book-to-market ratio explains stock returns. Anderson & Mandelker (AM) (1993) use both of these factors to measure post-merger performance, saying (p. 1): "One application suggested by Fama & French (1993) is that long run performance studies explicitly control for both size and book-to-market effects. Our study is one such application."

AJM's sample of mergers runs from 1955 to 1987. AM use this sample but start in 1966, since they do not have access to the COMPUSTAT dataset, from which the book-to-market ratio (b/m) can be calculated, in earlier years. Their resulting sample has 670 firms.

Control portfolios are calculated in the manner described by Fama & French (1993). Here, decile portfolios are formed based on size, with the smallest decile being further subdivided into three portfolios. Next, 10 b/m portfolios are formed within each of the 12 size portfolios. Abnormal returns are calculated in two ways. First, the return on the appropriate size control portfolio is subtracted from the return on the acquiring firm. Second, the return on the appropriate size and b/m control portfolio is subtracted from the acquirer's return.

AM's Table II shows significantly negative abnormal returns, over five years, of –0.0956 under the size adjustment. In addition, their table shows virtually identical abnormal returns, –0.0931, under the size and b/m adjustment. Thus, the authors conclude (p. 2): "In sum, the Agrawal, Jaffe & Mandelker finding of long run post-merger under-performance persists, even after controlling for the book-to-market effect."

As a small part of their study, Kennedy & Limmack (1996) examine the post-acquisition performance of 247 U.K. companies making successful takeover bids during the period 1980–1989. The study measures abnormal performance relative to two separate benchmarks, the Financial Times All Share Index and size-matched portfolios. Since abnormal returns are similar for both benchmarks, results are reported only for the second. For this second control, all companies on the London Share Price Database are ranked each year by market capitalization and placed into one of ten decile portfolios. Abnormal performance is the difference between the return on the acquiring company and the equal-weighted return on the appropriate size decile.

The CAAR is a statistically insignificant –0.0016 over months (0, +11) relative to the bid month. However, the abnormal return is –0.0492 over months (+12, +23), a result that is significantly below zero at the 0.01 level.

Next, the authors classify acquisitions as disciplinary, when a change in the CEO of the target firm occurs within two years after the bid, and non-disciplinary, when no change occurs within two years. Abnormal returns to the acquirer over the two years following the bid month are quite similar for disciplinary and non-disciplinary acquisitions.

Gregory (1997) presents a rather exhaustive work on long-run returns for the U.K. The author states (p. 976): "The data set used in this study is a comprehensive list of all successful U.K. domestic takeovers of listed companies by U.K. plcs, with a bid value greater than 10 million pounds, for the period 1984–1992." The author calculates abnormal returns for company i in month t, ϵ_{it}, according to six models:

(1) CAPM:

$$\epsilon_{it} = R_{it} - [R_{ft} + \beta_i(R_{mt} - R_{ft})],$$

where R_{it} and R_{mt} are the returns on stock i and the market respectively in month t R_{ft} is the risk-free Treasury bill rate in month t, and
β_i is the beta of firm i, measured with data for up to 36 months following the takeover completion month.

(2) Dimson & Marsh risk and size adjustment (DM):

$$\epsilon_{it} = R_{it} - [R_{st} + (\beta_i - \beta_s)(R_{mt} - R_{ft})],$$

where R_{st} is the return on a size control portfolio in month t.

(3) Simple size control portfolio (SS):

$$\epsilon_{it} = R_{it} - R_{st}$$

(4) Multi-index model (SML):

$$\epsilon_{it} = R_{it} - [R_{ft} + \beta_i(R_{mt} - R_{ft}) + \gamma_i (R_{610t} - R_{1t})],$$

where R_{610t} is the return in month t on an equally-weighted portfolio of size deciles 6 to 10, where decile 10 is the smallest
R_{1t} is the month t return on the equally-weighted portfolio of size decile 1.

(5) Value-weighted multi-index model:

$$\epsilon_{it} = R_{it} - [R_{ft} + \beta_i(R_{mt} - R_{ft}) + \gamma_i (R_{ht} - R_{mt})],$$

where R_{ht} is the return in month t on the Hoare-Govett Smaller Companies value-weighted index.

(6) Fama & French three-factor model:

$$\epsilon_{it} = R_{it} - [R_{ft} + \beta_i(R_{mt} - R_{ft}) + \gamma_i (SMB) + \delta_i (HML)],$$

where SMB is the value-weighted return on small firms less the value-weighted return on large firms and HML is the value-weighted return on high book-to-market firms minus the value-weighted return on low book-to-market firms.

Results presented in Gregory's Table 2 show abnormal performance over the two years following the month of merger completion. Two-year CAARs vary from –0.1182 to –0.18 over the six models, with all models showing statistical significance. Model 3 (simple size control portfolio) shows the least under-performance, while Model 6 (Fama & French three-factor model) shows the greatest under-performance. The under-performance here seems even greater than that in the United States. For example, Agrawal, Jaffe & Mandelker (AJM) (1992) report a two-year CAAR of only –0.0494, though their 5-year CAAR is –0.1026. Gregory reports a two-year CAAR of –0.1252 under Model 2 (Dimson-Marsh), the same approach as that used by AJM. Of course, the time periods of the two studies vary greatly, so performance differences between the two countries may be sample-specific.

Loughran & Vijh (1997) measure the post-acquisition performance of 947 firms that made acquisitions over the period 1970–1989 where both the target and the acquirer were traded on NYSE, AMEX or NASDAQ. The authors calculate a five-year abnormal return as the difference between the buy-and-hold return of the acquirer and the buy-and-hold return of a control firm, based on size and the book-to-market ratio. Abnormal returns are measured from the acquisition date.

Their Table II shows that five-year abnormal returns are insignificantly different from zero for their entire sample of acquirers. The authors also separate mergers from tender offers, finding that post-acquisition abnormal returns are significantly negative following mergers but marginally significantly positive following tender offers. These results are consistent with much of the previous literature, though Loughran & Vijh's buy-and-hold methodology is new to this area of empirical work. In addition, the five-year buy-and-hold abnormal return, of –0.159, is of the same order of magnitude as AJM's five-year CAAR, of –0.1026. Of course, the time periods of the two studies do not coincide and buy-and-hold returns differ from CAARs. Because post-acquisition periods may overlap for acquisitions of the same acquirer, the authors next remove overlapping cases. Table III shows a 5-year buy-and-hold abnormal return of –0.142, with a marginally significant t-value (t = –1.69).

Rau & Vermaelen (RV) (1998) examine 3,169 mergers and 348 tender offers completed during 1980–1991, where the acquirer is traded on the NYSE, AMEX or NASDAQ and the target is either privately or publicly owned. The authors create a control group by first forming deciles based on market capitalization. Next, securities within each size decile are placed into five quintiles, based on the book-to-market ratio. Cumulative abnormal returns on acquirers are computed relative to the appropriate benchmark. In addition, these abnormal returns are further adjusted for bias by subtracting the mean of the empirical distribution generated using the bootstrap approach from the abnormal return of the sample. The authors call these returns 'bias adjusted CARs' or BCARs. BCARs are estimated for periods up to 36 months after acquisition completion.

RV's Table 2 reports significantly negative abnormal returns over 36 months following mergers. However, the BCAR across all mergers, of –0.0404, is small in magnitude. The BCAR for acquirers where the targets are publicly-traded is only –0.0258. By contrast, AJM find a three-year CAAR of –0.0738. The BCAR is 0.0885 in the 36 months following all tender offers and is 0.0856 following takeovers of public targets. Both values are statistically significant.

Mitchell & Stafford (MS) (1998) examine performance following three corporate events: takeovers, equity issues and equity repurchases. Their sample of takeovers consists of 2,767 acquisitions (including both mergers and tender offers) of CRSP-listed firms, over the period 1961–1993.

MS measure abnormal performance in three ways. First, a three-year buy-and-hold abnormal return (BHAR) is calculated for each acquirer as the difference between the buy-and-hold return of the acquirer and the buy-and-hold return of the appropriate size and b/m portfolio. Both value-weighted and equal-weighted averages of the BHARs are computed across acquirers. Second, equal-weighted and value-weighted portfolios are formed each calendar month using the sample of all acquirers with an acquisition within the last three years. Monthly excess returns on these 'event' portfolios are then regressed on the three Fama & French factors. Third, equal-weighted and value-weighted portfolios of acquiring firms are again formed, as in the previous approach. However, an abnormal return each calendar month is calculated as the difference between the realized return on the event portfolio and an estimate of its expected return. The latter is estimated from either the Fama-French three-factor model or the appropriate size and b/m portfolio.

MS's Table 2a shows equal-weighted BHARs for acquirers of –0.02 and value-weighted BHARs of –0.05 over the first three post-acquisition years. While both returns are significantly below zero, the authors state (p. 9): "The first notable result to emerge is the strong statistical significance associated with economically inconsequential numbers for acquirers."

Table 3a shows intercepts from the Fama-French regressions (the second approach) of –0.22% and –0.08% per month, when portfolios are equal-weighted and value-weighted, respectively. The three-year cumulations implied by these intercepts are –0.079 and –0.029, respectively. The first number is statistically significant, while the second is not.

The third approach yields significantly negative average abnormal monthly returns with Fama-French benchmarks of –0.15% and –0.13% for equal-weighted and value-weighted portfolios, respectively. These numbers are similar in magnitude to those reported under the previous approach. However, the average abnormal monthly returns are smaller in magnitude and statistically insignificant with size and b/m benchmarks.

In conclusion, one should note that five of the eight abnormal returns mentioned above are statistically significant. However, the small magnitude of the buy-and-hold returns versus the larger returns under the other approaches makes it difficult to draw inferences on return magnitudes.

3. EXPLANATIONS

The previous section summarized studies examining long-run post-acquisition stock returns on acquirers. Because of the unusual findings of the literature, recent studies have searched for explanations. Below, we review this search.

3.1 Speed of Adjustment

Agrawal, Jaffe & Mandelker (AJM) (1992) argue that the negative post-acquisition abnormal returns they observe following mergers are consistent with two hypotheses. First, the market may fully react to the merger at the announcement date, with the subsequent price decline being due to unrelated causes. Alternatively, the market may adjust slowly to news of the merger. Here, the long-run decline reflects that part of the value of the acquisition not captured in the announcement period return.

AJM examine these two hypotheses with the following regression:

$$CAR_{ci} = b_0 + b_1 CAR_{ai} + e_i$$

where CAR_{ci} is the post-merger cumulative average abnormal return for firm i. The cumulation period always begins with the month following merger completion and, depending on the regression, ends one to five years after completion. CAR_{ai} is the cumulative average abnormal return for firm i over the announcement period. The study defines the announcement period as either the three-month period ending with the month of announcement or the period beginning two months before the announcement and ending with the month of merger completion. Under the hypothesis that the market reacts slowly to merger news, b_1 should be positive. That is, a high (low) return around a merger announcement should be coupled with a high (low) return following its completion. A variant of the hypothesis is that the market overreacts to the merger event, implying a negative value for b_1. By contrast, the coefficient should be zero, if the under-performance following the merger is due to factors unrelated to the merger.

AJM's Table IV shows significantly negative values for b_1 under both definitions of CAR_{ai} when the period used to measure CAR_{ci} ends five years after completion. In addition, b_1 is marginally significant in a number of cases where CAR_{ci} is measured over shorter periods. Thus, the authors state (p. 167): "The evidence seems to indicate a negative relation between the market reaction to the announcement and the subsequent performance of the firm." Nevertheless, the authors temper their conclusion after observing sub-period results. They say (p. 167): "However, when we examine these regressions by sub-period, we find that the coefficient b_1 is negative for the decades of the 1960s, 1970s, and 1980s but is statistically significant only for the 1960s. Thus, we cannot conclude that the negative relationship is pervasive over our entire sample period."

AJM also argue that if post-merger performance reflects slow adjustment, this performance should be related to the size of the acquisition relative to the size of the acquirer. They rank all mergers by relative size in order to form five quintile portfolios. They state (p. 1618): "Portfolios 4 and 5 [the largest relative size] exhibit large under-performance, particularly over four to five years after the acquisition. However, the relationship is not monotonic, since large under-performance occurs for portfolio 2 as well. Furthermore, very few of the post-merger time periods, in any of the five portfolios, exhibit significant returns. Thus, the evidence here does not suggest that the acquirer's post-merger return is a function of the relative size of the acquisition."

In addition, Franks, Harris, & Titman (1991), Loderer & Martin (1992) and Loughran & Vijh (1997) also find no relationship between post-acquisition performance and the relative size of the acquisition.

Given their evidence from the regression above, as well as the evidence from the relative size quintiles, AJM conclude that the hypothesis that negative post-merger abnormal returns are due to slow adjustment to the merger announcement is not supported by the evidence. Since they do not identify the cause of the negative performance, they merely conclude (p. 1620): "The resolution of this anomaly remains a challenge to the profession."

3.2 Method of Payment

3.2.1 Results from Individual Studies

Loughran & Vijh (LV) provide an interesting explanation, based on the work of Myers & Majluf (MM) (1984). MM argue that a firm tends to issue stock when its shares are overvalued and to issue debt, or to finance out of retained earnings, when its shares are undervalued. Consequently, a firm's share price should drop upon the news of an equity issuance. LV suggest that acquirers who issue stock are overvalued, with a stock price decline following issuance. Though MM predict an immediate drop in the price of the stock, LV look for long-run post-acquisition under-performance. Negative abnormal returns in the long-run, here, would be consistent with the finding of under-performance following seasoned equity offerings (SEOs), as reported by Loughran & Ritter (1995) and others. While a long-term price drop following equity issuance is inconsistent with market efficiency, it must still be viewed as a possible explanation, given the results reviewed earlier in this paper.

Though LV present the most detailed discussion of the differences between equity and cash financing of acquisitions, they are by no means the first to look for long-run performance for the two types of acquisitions. We identify seven studies examining performance following cash and stock takeovers, many of them published prior to LV.

Barnes (1984) appears to be the first to split acquirers into those that finance with cash and those that finance with equity. Our interpolation of his Figures 3 and 4 indicates that abnormal performance to the acquirer is approximately –0.056 and –0.054, in the 60 months following the announcement of cash and equity acquisitions, respectively. While these numbers are inconsistent with LV's hypothesis, no t-statistics are reported. In addition, Barnes' total sample contains only 39 firms, making it difficult to draw strong conclusions.

Dodds & Quek (1985) examine a sample of 34 acquisitions financed with equity and 36 acquisitions financed with cash. Their Table 4 indicates a CAAR of –0.072, in the 60 months following equity-financed acquisitions, while their Table 5 indicates a CAAR of –0.044, following cash-financed acquisitions over the same time period. Unlike Barnes, the difference in performance is in the direction predicted by LV, although the magnitude appears to be rather small. No test statistics over the five-year period are provided.

Because Franks, Harris & Mayer (FHM) (1988) always separate the post-acquisition performance following cash-mergers from that following equity-mergers, we presented their results for both types of mergers in Section 2.2. Rather than repeat this material, we quote FHM (p. 253): "In summary, acquirers that made all-cash bids on average did not suffer postmerger losses and did better than the bidders that made all-equity offers. Whether all-equity bidders have postmerger losses depends on the benchmark employed. Compared with premerger performance, postmerger returns are negative. But using a benchmark based on postmerger parameters, we find all-equity acquirers did not experience abnormal losses in the two years after an acquisition, but they did have negative α values three to five years after the acquisitions."

Table 4 of Franks, Harris & Titman (1991) reports average post-merger abnormal performance, over 36 months, of 0.26% per month, under their eight-portfolio benchmark, for 156 all-cash bids. The table also shows abnormal performance for acquirers of –0.17% per month, for 128 all-equity bids over the same time period. Though the difference is again in the direction predicted by LV, the t-value of 1.37 for the difference between the two returns is insignificantly different from zero. In addition, while the abnormal performance is positive following all-cash bids and negative following all-equity bids, both numbers are insignificantly different from zero.

Gregory (1997) examines abnormal performance, over 24 post-acquisition months, using six models. For each of the six models, average abnormal performance is lower for his sample of about 300 equity bids, than for his sample of about 80 cash bids, a result consistent with LV's hypothesis. However, acquirers with mixed offers have the highest API under each of the six models. It is difficult to square this result with Myers & Majluf, since equity financing is part of any mixed offer.

Loughran & Vijh (1997) create a two-way classification scheme, whereby all takeovers are classified by both mode of acquisition and form of payment. Their Table II shows that the cumulative average abnormal post-acquisition return over five years is –0.25 for a group of 385 equity-financed mergers and 0.617 for a group of 111 cash-financed tender offers. Both returns are significantly different from zero. By contrast, the post-acquisition returns are insignificantly different from zero for both a group of 196 cash-financed mergers and a group of 8 equity-financed tender offers. The authors state (p. 1789): "This evidence is consistent with two hypotheses. First, the post-acquisition wealth gains are greater for tender offers, which are usually hostile to incumbent managers, as compared to mergers. The wealth gains could occur because of the appointment of more efficient managers, as proposed by Martin & McConnell (1991). Second, the acquirer's managers are likely to choose stock payment when their stock is overvalued and cash payment when it is undervalued. Apparently, the market does not react efficiently to the likely wealth gains from the business combination or to the news conveyed by the form of payment."

In addition, the paper's Table V measures abnormal performance relative to a matching firm of similar size and b/m ratio that did an IPO or an SEO in the previous five years. (By contrast, the matching firms in earlier tables were selected on just their size and b/m ratio.) Now, the post-acquisition abnormal returns on both stock-financed mergers and stock-financed tender offers are insignificantly different from zero. This result provides further evidence that the under-performance of stock-financed acquisitions can be explained by the form of payment.

As discussed in section 2.2 above, Mitchell & Stafford (1998) calculate three-year post-acquisition abnormal performance in three ways: buy-and-hold abnormal returns (BHARs), monthly intercepts from Fama & French regressions and the difference between the return on the acquirer's portfolio in a calendar month and the return on the event portfolio, where the event portfolio is taken from the Fama and French three-factor model or the appropriate size and b/m portfolio.

The authors' Table 2a shows three-year BHARs of –0.09 and –0.07, for a sample of 1374 stock-financed acquisitions, where the portfolio of acquirers is equal-weighted and value-weighted, respectively. Both the returns are significantly negative. By contrast, a sample of 1393 acquisitions without stock financing has BHARs of 0.04 and –0.02 when portfolios are equal-weighted and value-weighted, respectively. The first number here is marginally significant while the second number is insignificant.

Table 3a shows significantly negative intercepts in Fama-French regressions for stock-financed acquisitions, whether equal-weighted or value-weighted portfolios are employed. The intercepts for acquisitions financed without stock are marginally significantly negative and marginally significantly positive for equal-weighted and value-weighted portfolios, respectively. The results in Table 4a are similar.[4]

Taken together, the results in the Mitchell & Stafford paper show that abnormal performance is worse for acquirers using stock-financing than for acquirers avoiding stock.

3.2.2 Summary

As with our summary in section 2.1, we separate results prior to Franks, Harris & Titman (FHT) (1992) from those after it. Three articles before FHT contrast cash with equity offers. Barnes (1984) finds lower abnormal returns following cash-financed acquisitions, than those following equity-financed acquisitions, while Dodds & Quek (1985) find the reverse. However, differences in abnormal returns between the two types of acquisitions are small in both studies. In addition, neither article presents test statistics for the entire post-acquisition time period. Franks, Harris & Mayer (1988) generally find significantly positive post-acquisition abnormal performance following all-cash takeovers and significantly negative performance following all-equity takeovers. Taken together, the above studies are not particularly supportive of the method of financing hypothesis.

The evidence beginning with FHT is generally more supportive of this hypothesis. MS report higher performance following acquisitions that are financed with cash rather than equity. Loughran & Vijh find significantly positive abnormal returns following cash-financed tender offers and significantly negative returns following stock-financed mergers. LV conclude that both the acquisition form and the mode of payment are important. Gregory (1997) finds worse performance following all-equity takeovers than following all-cash ones, for each of six models, although he does not provide statistical tests of the differences. However, FHT find that performance following cash-financed takeovers is not significantly different from that following stock-financed takeovers.

We see the evidence, taken together, as generally supportive of the method of payment hypothesis. In our view Barnes (1984) and Dodds & Quek (1985) should be accorded the least weight, because of both their small sample sizes and their less sophisticated methodologies. Of the remaining five papers, four present evidence consistent with the hypothesis.

3.3 Performance Extrapolation

Rau & Vermaelen (RV) (1998) posit the performance extrapolation hypothesis, which states that both the market and the board of directors or top management of a bidder extrapolate its past performance when assessing the value of a new acquisition. The hypothesis has at least three implications, two of which RV test. First, because of good (bad) past performance, the market assumes that glamour (value) firms make good (bad) acquisitions. Thus, glamour bidders should realize greater abnormal returns at the takeover announcement date than should value bidders. Second, the market slowly reassesses the acquirer's quality as information from the acquisition is received. Since glamour (value) firms are initially overvalued (undervalued), long-run post-acquisition abnormal performance should be negative (positive). Third, since both the board and top management are influenced by a bidder's past performance, value bidders will exercise greater prudence toward takeovers than will glamour bidders. Thus, glamour acquirers will pay greater acquisition premiums.

RV do not test the first implication, but, instead, merely state that it is consistent with the empirical observation of Lang, Stulz & Walkling (1989) and Servaes (1991), that a bidder's announcement period return is positively related to the bidder's Q-ratio. Second, RV's Table 4 shows that glamour acquirers in mergers significantly under-perform other glamour firms, in the 36 months following acquisition. Glamour acquirers in tender offers outperform other glamour firms, following acquisition, but the differences are not significant. By contrast, value acquirers significantly outperform other value firms following both mergers and tender offers. Thus, the results of RV's Table 4 support the performance extrapolation hypothesis.

The authors' Table 6 relates long-run returns to three attributes: nature of the acquirer (glamour vs. value), means of payment and type of acquisition.

Three-year post-acquisition abnormal returns are higher for value firms than for growth firms for both means of payment (cash and equity) and for both types of acquisitions (mergers and tender offers). By contrast, while three-year abnormal performance for value acquirers is higher following cash-financed mergers than following stock-financed mergers, the reverse is true for glamour acquirers.[5] Thus, the authors conclude that while these results are consistent with the performance extrapolation hypothesis, they are not always consistent with the method of payment hypothesis.

RV's Table 7 examines the third implication of the performance extrapolation hypothesis. The table shows that glamour acquirers pay significantly higher takeover premiums than do value acquirers, in both stock-financed mergers and cash-financed tender offers, results consistent with the performance extrapolation hypothesis. However, premiums are nearly equal for glamour and value acquirers in cash-financed mergers.

3.4 EPS Myopia Hypothesis

RV also posit that managers might be more willing to overpay for an acquisition if it results in an increase in earnings per share (EPS). In addition, the market might initially overvalue these acquirers, leading to poor long-run post-acquisition performance. For each merger, the authors calculate the difference between the actual growth in the bidder's EPS following the merger and the estimated growth had the merger not taken place. Table 8 does not show a significant relationship between the impact of the merger on EPS and the acquirer's subsequent long-run abnormal performance. Thus, the authors conclude that their results do not support the EPS myopia hypothesis.

4. SUMMARY

This article examines the literature on long-run abnormal returns following mergers. We focus on two issues: the magnitude of the abnormal returns and, to the extent that the abnormal returns have deviated from zero, possible explanations. We place more emphasis on the studies beginning with Franks, Harris & Titman (FHT) (1991), because of both their more sophisticated methodologies and their greater thoroughness.

In our opinion, the work starting with FHT shows strong evidence of abnormal under-performance, following mergers. Except for FHT itself, each paper shows at least some evidence of under-performance. Perhaps the greatest counter-evidence comes from research on broader topics, rather than from the studies we have reviewed. A number of recent papers, e.g. Kothari & Warner (KW)

(1997), Barber & Lyon (BL) (1997) and Lyon, Barber & Tsai (LBT) (1999), have criticized the methodologies of long-run return studies in general. In addition, Fama (1998) surveys the entire long-run performance literature, concluding (p. 304): "Consistent with the market efficiency hypothesis that the anomalies are chance results, apparent overreaction of stock prices to information is about as common as underreaction. And post-event continuation of pre-event abnormal returns is about as frequent as post-event reversal." According to this view, the papers summarized here might be nothing more than chance results.

These criticisms are quite important and cannot be dismissed easily. None of the papers that we have reviewed were specifically designed to conform to LBT, perhaps the paper with the most specific prescriptions for avoiding bias. And, it would be surprising if KW, BL, and LBT represent the last word on long-run methodologies anyway. Certainly, future research will suggest other prescriptions as well. In addition, since our survey focuses on acquisitions, we are not in a position to dispute Fama's conclusions on a much broader topic.

Perhaps the strongest rebuttal is the diversity of the research reviewed here. Many papers, using different methodologies and different sample periods, in both the U.S. and the U.K., report similar results; and, these same researchers find uniformly non-negative long-run performance following tender offers. Viewed in this context, the criticisms of KW, BL, LBT, and Fama might be somewhat mitigated.

Our paper also examines explanations for any findings of under-performance following mergers. We conclude that the evidence does not support the conjecture that under-performance is specifically due to a slow adjustment to merger news. Similarly, Rau & Vermaelen convincingly reject the EPS myopia hypothesis, i.e. the hypothesis that the market initially overvalues acquirers if the acquisition increases EPS, ultimately leading to long-run under-performance.

The evidence in favor of both the method of payment hypothesis and the performance extrapolation hypothesis is stronger. Recent papers generally report greater under-performance following stock-financed acquisitions than cash-financed acquisitions, a result consistent with the work of Myers & Majluf (1984). Similarly, Rau & Vermaelen (1998) present a number of pieces of evidence that glamour bidders under-perform value bidders, after abstracting from the effects of method of payment and form of acquisition.

NOTES

1. It is not clear whether Limmack came before FHT, since both were published in 1991. However, we treat the Limmack article as the earlier one, since it does not use the sophisticated techniques of FHT and it devotes little attention to post-acquisition performance.

2. Actually, as shown in our Table 1, Dodd & Ruback also examine performance following clean-up mergers, finding one-year CAARs of 0.0844. However, the small sample of 19 and the special nature of this type of merger reduce the informativeness of their result to our discussion.

3. Franks, Harris & Mayer (1988) do separate cash offers from equity offers. While tender offers are predominantly made with cash and mergers are predominantly made with equity, the correlation is not perfect. We leave a discussion of cash vs. equity to a later section of the paper.

4. Mark Mitchell informs us that the last two row labels in MS's Table 4a were switched. See the discussion on page 22 of their paper.

5. Since there were only seven stock-financed tender offers in RV's sample, this type of comparison is not made for tender offers.

REFERENCES

Agrawal, A., Jaffe, J. F., & Mandelker, G. N. (1992). The Post-Merger Performance of Acquiring Firms: A Re-examination of an Anomaly. *Journal of Finance, 47*, 1605–1621.

Anderson, C., & Mandelker, G. N. (1993). Long Run Return Anomalies and the Book-to-Market Effect: Evidence on Mergers and IPOs. Unpublished paper, J. M. Katz Graduate School of Business, University of Pittsburgh.

Asquith, P. (1983). Merger Bids, Uncertainty and Stockholder Returns. *Journal of Financial Economics, 11*, 51–83.

Barber, B. M., & Lyon J. D. (1997). Detecting Long-Run Abnormal Stock Returns: The Empirical Power and Specification of Test Statistics. *Journal of Financial Economics, 43*, 341–372.

Barnes, P. (1984). The Effect of a Merger on the Share Price of the Attacker, Revisited. *Accounting and Business Research, 15*, 45–49.

Blume, M. E., & Stambaugh R. F. (1983). Biases in Computed Returns: An Application to the Size Effect. *Journal of Financial Economics, 12*, 387–404.

Bradley, M., & Jarrell G. A. (1988). Comment. In: J. C. Coffee, L. Lowenstein, Jr. & S. Rose-Ackerman, (Eds.), *Knights, Raiders & Targets: The Impact of the Hostile Takeover*, New York: Oxford University Press.

Dimson, E., & Marsh, P. (1986). Event Study Methodologies and the Size Effect: The Case of UK Press Recommendations. *Journal of Financial Economics, 17*, 113–142.

Dodd, P., & Ruback, R. (19770. Tender Offers and Shareholder Returns: An Empirical Analysis. *Journal of Financial Economics, 5*, 351–373.

Dodds, J.C., & Quek, J.P. 1985. Effect of Mergers on the Share Price Movement of the Acquiring Firms: A UK Study. *Journal of Business Finance and Accounting, 12*, 285–296.

Fama, E. F., (1998). Market Efficiency, Long-Term Returns, and Behavioral Finance. *Journal of Financial Economics, 49*, 283–306.

Fama, E. F., & French, K. R. (1992). The Cross-Section of Expected Stock Returns. *Journal of Finance, 47*, 427–465.

Fama, E. F., & French, K. R. (1993). Common Risk Factors in the Returns on Stock and Bonds. *Journal of Financial Economics, 33*, 3–56.

Fama, E. F., & MacBeth, J. D. (1973). Risk, Return, and Equilibrium: Empirical Tests. *Journal of Political Economy, 81*, 607–636.

Firth, M. (1980). Takeovers, Shareholder Returns, and the Theory of the Firm. *Quarterly Journal of Economics, 94*, 235–260.

Franks, J. R., & Harris, R. S. (1989). Shareholder Wealth Effects of Corporate Takeovers: The U.K. Experience 1955–1985. *Journal of Financial Economics, 23,* 225–249.

Franks, J. R., Harris R. S., & Mayer, C. (1988). Means of Payment in Takeovers: Results for the United Kingdom and the United States. In: A. J. Auerbach, (Ed.), *Corporate Takeovers: Causes and Consequences.* Chicago: University of Chicago Press.

Franks, J., Harris, R S., & Titman, S. (1991). The Postmerger Share-Price Performance of Acquiring Firms. *Journal of Financial Economics, 29,* 81–96.

Gregory, A. (1997). An Examination of the Long Run Performance of UK Acquiring Firms. *Journal of Business Finance and Accounting, 24,* 971–1002.

Grinblatt, M., & Titman, S. D. (1988). The Evaluation of Mutual Fund Performance: An Analysis of Monthly Returns. University of California at Los Angeles Working Paper.

Grinblatt, M., & Titman, S. D. (1989). Mutual Fund Performance: An Analysis of Quarterly Portfolio Holdings. *Journal of Business, 62,* 393–416.

Ibbotson, R. G. (1975). Price Performance of Common Stock New Issues. *Journal of Financial Economics, 2,* 235–272.

Jensen, M. C., & Ruback, R. S. (1983). The Market for Corporate Control: The Scientific Evidence. *Journal of Financial Economics, 11,* 5–50.

Kennedy, V.A., & Limmack, R. J. (1996). Takeover Activity, CEO Turnover, and the Market for Corporate Control. *Journal of Business Finance and Accounting, 23,* 267–285.

Kothari, S.P., & Warner, J. B. (1997). Measuring Long-Horizon Security Price Performance. *Journal of Financial Economics, 43,* 301–340.

Lakonishok, J., Shleifer, A., & Vishny, R. W. (1994). Contrarian Investment, Extrapolation, and Risk. *Journal of Finance, 49,* 1541–1578.

Lang, L., Stulz R., & Walking R. (1989). Managerial Performance, Tobin's Q and the Gains from Successful Tender Offers. *Journal of Financial Economics, 24,* 137–154.

Langetieg, T. C. (1978). An Application of a Three-Factor Performance Index to Measure Stockholder Gains from Merger. *Journal of Financial Economics, 6,* 365–383.

Lehmann, B. N., & Modest, D. M. (1987). Mutual Fund Performance Evaluation: A Comparison of Benchmarks and Benchmark Comparisons. *Journal of Finance, 42,* 233–265.

Limmack, R. J. (1991). Corporate Mergers and Shareholder Wealth Effects: 1977–1986. *Accounting and Business Research, 21,* 239–251.

Loderer, C., & Martin, K. (1992). Postacquisition Performance of Acquiring Firms. *Financial Management, 21(3),* 69–79.

Loughran, T., & Ritter, J. R. (1995). The New Issues Puzzle. *Journal of Finance, 50,* 23–51.

Loughran, T., & Vijh, A. M. (1997). Do Long-Term Shareholders Benefit from Corporate Acquisitions. *Journal of Finance, 52,* 1765–1790.

Lyon, J. D., Barber B M., & Tsai, C-L. (1999). Improved Methods for Tests of Long-Run Abnormal Stock Returns. *Journal of Finance, 54,* 165–201.

Magenheim, E. B., & Mueller, D.C. (1988). Are Acquiring-Firm Shareholders Better off after an Acquisition. In: J. C. Coffee, Jr., L. Lowenstein, and S. Rose-Ackerman, (Eds.), *Knights, Raiders and Targets: The Impact of the Hostile Takeover.* New York: Oxford University Press.

Malatesta, P. H. (1983). The Wealth Effect of Merger Activity and the Objective Functions of Merging Firms. *Journal of Financial Economics, 11,* 155–181.

Mandelker, G. 1974. Risk and Return: The Case of Merging Firms. *Journal of Financial Economics, 1,* 303–335.

Martin, K. J., & McConnell, J. J. (1991). Corporate Performance, Corporate Takeovers, and Management Turnover. *Journal of Finance, 46:* 671–687.

Mitchell, M. L., & Stafford, E. (1998). Managerial Decisions and Long-Term Stock Price Performance. Working paper, Harvard Business School.

Myers, S. C., & Majluf, N. S. (1984). Corporate Financing and Investment Decisions when Firms have Information that Investors Do Not Have. *Journal of Financial Economics, 13,* 187–221.

Rau, P. R., & Vermaelen, T. (1998). Glamour, Value and the Post-Acquisition Performance of Acquiring Firms. *Journal of Financial Economics, 49,* 223–253.

Roll, R. (1986). The Hubris Hypothesis of Corporate Takeovers. *Journal of Business, 59,* 197–216.

Servaes, H. (1991). Tobin's Q and the Gains from Takeovers. *Journal of Finance, 46,* 409–419.

Vasicek, O. A. (1973). A Note on Using Cross-Sectional Information in Bayesian Estimation of Security Betas. *Journal of Finance, 28,* 1233–1239.

THE INFLUENCE OF CULTURAL COMPATIBILITY WITHIN CROSS-BORDER ACQUISITIONS: A REVIEW[1]

Richard Schoenberg

ABSTRACT

This chapter synthesises theoretical and empirical perspectives on cultural compatibility within cross-border acquisitions, drawing on both the organisational and national culture streams of acquisitions literature. The impact of cultural compatibility on subsequent acquisition performance is seen to revolve around the form of post-acquisition integration and the relative attractiveness of the acquirer's culture. For the latter, there is some evidence that attitudes towards participation, formality and risk may have a particular importance, although the relative influence between organisational and national culture remains unclear. Avenues for future research are indicated.

INTRODUCTION

Recent years have seen a marked increase in cross-border acquisition activity as firms pursue a simultaneous strategy of business consolidation and geographical diversification. Globally, cross-border acquisitions have grown to represent 25% of the annual expenditure on mergers and acquisitions, with companies committing $600 billion to this form of international expansion last year alone.

Advances in Mergers and Acquisitions, Volume 1, pages 43–59
Copyright © 2000 by Elsevier Science Inc.
All rights of reproduction in any form reserved.
ISBN: 0-7623-0683-1

Yet, despite this level of activity, empirical studies continue to draw attention to the poor performance record of such acquisitions. Although some researchers have reported that cross-border acquisitions create small positive abnormal returns for the shareholders of the acquiring firm (Markides & Oyon, 1998), others have found statistically significant evidence of negative shareholder wealth effects (Datta & Puia, 1995). Indeed, broader practitioner surveys reveal that 43% of international acquisitions fail to produce a financial return in excess of the acquirer's cost of capital (Bleeke, Isono, Ernst & Weinburg, 1993), while 45% fail to meet their initial strategic objectives (Rostand, 1994). Disturbingly, these figures show only a marginal improvement over Kitching's 1974 study, which found 46–50% of European acquisitions were considered failures, or not worth repeating, by the acquiring management.

Three main bodies of literature can be identified that discuss the determinants of acquisition performance. The 'Strategic Fit' literature focuses on the link between performance and the strategic attributes of the combining firms, in particular, the extent to which a target company's business should be related to that of the acquirer. While little consensus emerges as to the importance of relatedness and relative size between bidder and target (Kusewitt, 1985; Lubatkin, 1987; Singh & Montgomery, 1987; Seth, 1990; Flanagan, 1996; Farjoun, 1998), recent extensions to this literature stream do identify generic value creation mechanisms based on resource sharing and knowledge transfer (Brush, 1996; Capron, Dussauge & Mitchell, 1998; Capron, 1999). The 'Process' literature focuses on the important role that the choice of acquisition process, itself, can play. These scholars highlight that inappropriate decision-making, negotiation and integration processes can impede adequate consideration of strategic fit and organisational fit issues and so lead to inferior acquisition outcomes (Jemison & Sitkin, 1986; Hunt, 1990; Haspeslagh & Jemison, 1991; Pablo, Sitkin & Jemison, 1996; Singh & Zollo, 1998). A key contribution of this approach has been the contingent framework for the form of post-acquisition integration that takes into account both the strategic and organisational requirements of a particular acquisition (Haspeslagh & Jemison, 1991). The 'Organisational Fit' acquisitions literature attempts to understand how the organisational and human resource aspects of an acquisition influence the subsequent performance of the union. This literature stream has diverse origins in the human resource, organisational behaviour and strategic management disciplines that, in combination, provide both theoretical and empirical perspectives on the factors influencing organisational and cultural compatibility (Sales & Mirvis, 1984; Napier, 1989; Schweiger & Walsh, 1990; Cartwright & Cooper, 1993; Very, Lubatkin & Calori, 1996; Morosini, Shane & Singh, 1998).

Recent years have seen a growing recognition of the latter issue by practitioners. Many column inches have appeared in the recent financial press, which argue that acquiring across borders can bring clashes of different management styles, philosophies and ways of interacting with the market place. For example, the success of the Chrysler-Daimler Benz merger has been linked to its ability to marry the entrepreneurial management style of the American corporation with the more conservative and formal style of the German partner (The Economist, January 9th, 1999). Similarly, the proposed European life-sciences merger between Hoechst, of Germany, and Rhone-Poulenc, of France, has raised questions regarding the extent to which the two management styles, rooted in their different national contexts, will be compatible (Financial Times, December 2nd 1998). This concern with management style and cultural compatibility is confirmed by practitioner surveys, which have reported that up to 90% of unsuccessful cross-border acquisitions experience major, unforeseen, difficulties due to cultural differences (Norburn & Schoenberg, 1994) and that internal managerial issues are viewed as the primary cause of the higher perceived risk associated with international acquisitions (Angwin & Savill, 1997).

Against this background, this paper presents a critical review of the prior cultural compatibility research. How much do we really know about the determinants and consequences of cultural compatibility in cross-border acquisitions? The paper is presented in three sections. First, the theoretical models and empirical lessons available from the literature on organisational cultural compatibility are reviewed. The next section addresses the empirical studies that have investigated the influence of national culture compatibility in cross-border acquisitions. Finally, the results from these two literature streams are integrated to provide conclusions relevant to both practitioners and future researchers.

COMPATIBILITY OF ORGANISATIONAL CULTURES

Compatibility of Organisational Cultures: Theoretical Studies

Culture has been defined as "the beliefs and assumptions shared by members of an organisation" (Nahavandi & Malekzadeh, 1988: 80) and "the collective programming of the mind which distinguishes the members of one group or category of people from another" (Hofstede, 1991: 5). Organisational culture has been shown to be an important determinant of organisational behaviour (Johnson, 1992) and a strong and coherent culture has been linked to superior performance (Deal & Kennedy, 1982; Barney, 1986). Given that an acquisition involves the coming together of two separate organisational cultures, a large part of the 'Organisational Fit' acquisitions literature has been concerned with the issue of cultural compatibility. What factors determine cultural compatibility and how does it impact acquisition outcomes? The former question has been addressed largely by theoreticians, while the latter has been investigated in a variety of empirical studies. The theoretical contributions to this stream are described below, followed by a review of the empirical studies.

Acculturation describes the process by which members from one culture adapt to another culture. Acculturation in acquisitions has been framed in terms of the struggle between human and property rights (Walter, 1985), a force-field analysis between the forces of cultural differentiation and organisational integration (Elsass & Veiga, 1994), and, perhaps most usefully, from an anthropological perspective, which identifies four distinct modes of acculturation (Nahavandi & Malekzadeh, 1988, 1994):

Assimilation, in which the acquired firm willingly relinquishes its own culture and adopts that of the acquiring firm. Assimilation implies willingness, rather than coercion, and, therefore, is associated with low degrees of conflict.

Integration, where the basic assumptions and practices of both organisations are accepted and preserved. There is an element of both relative cultural autonomy and the exchange of selected cultural elements.

Separation occurs where the acquired firm wishes to maintain all aspects of its culture in an autonomous manner and rejects the other's culture. The desire to remain separate is likely to cause a relatively high degree of conflict and be difficult to implement.

Deculturation, in which members of the acquired company no longer value the culture of their previous organisation, but do not wish to be assimilated into that of the acquiring firm. In effect, such employees find themselves to be outcasts and deculturation is associated with the highest levels of conflict and difficulties.

Nahavandi & Malekzadeh (1988) further identify the factors that influence the choice of acculturation mode and postulate an overall model for the acculturation process in acquisitions. They argue that the level of potential post-acquisition conflict, or 'acculturative stress', rises both as a function of the acculturation mode adopted and the degree of congruence between the modes favoured by the merging firms. For the acquired firm, the favoured acculturation mode will depend on their perception of how attractive the acquirer's culture is, relative to their own. In the case of the acquiring firm, the acculturation mode will depend on the extent to which cultural diversity is tolerated and accepted within the parent company. The acquiring firm will also be influenced by its acquisition strategy, in particular the extent to which the acquirer has to impose its culture and practices on the target company in an attempt to achieve operating synergies. In their 1988 paper Nahavandi & Malekzadeh suggest acquisition relatedness as the best proxy for cultural imposition, although, in the light of the work of Haspeslagh & Jemison (1991), the form of integration is likely to describe more accurately the strategic influences on the acculturation mode. This is because the form of integration takes into account, not only the degree of strategic interdependence necessary between the firms post-acquisition, but also the degree of organisational autonomy that is to be granted to the target company.

It should be noted, also, that the acculturation process is a dynamic one and the acculturation mode and level of perceived stress may change over time, for example as a result of familiarisation with the other organisation's culture and behaviour (Nahavandi & Malekzadeh, 1994). Multiple sub-cultures may also exist within a single organisation and, therefore, more than a single mode of acculturation may be operating post-acquisition (Elsass & Veiga, 1994).

Implicit in the acculturation model is the link between acculturative stress and conflict behaviour and the eventual acquisition outcome, a link that has received wide empirical support, as detailed below. Therefore Nahavandi & Malekzadeh's (1988) model provides a useful theoretical framework to understand the factors that influence the overall relationship between cultural differences and acquisition performance.

Compatibility of Organisational Cultures: Empirical Studies

To date, there have been four major empirical contributions to the literature on acculturation in domestic acquisitions. Three of these are case study based, undertaken from a phenomenological perspective (Sales & Mirvis, 1984; Buono & Bowditch, 1989; Cartwright & Cooper, 1992) and one is based on a positivist quantitative survey (Chatterjee, Lubatkin, Schweiger & Weber, 1992).

Sales & Mirvis (1984) provide a detailed exploration of the acculturation process, in an agreed acquisition of a medium sized U.S. manufacturing firm by a large U.S. conglomerate. They detail the clear differences that existed between the philosophies and behaviours of the two companies and document the miscommunication, misunderstanding and conflict that arose, as a result of these cultural differences, during the first year. Although no attempt at performance evaluation is made, Sales & Mirvis's description reinforces the acculturation modes identified by Nahavandi & Malekzadeh (1988), as well as highlighting the dynamic nature of the process. Early actions of 'separation' were seen to give way, over a period of three years, to 'integration' of management styles and 'assimilation' of reporting and control practices.

Cartwright & Cooper (1992, 1993) also lend support to Nahavandi & Malekzadeh's (1988) framework. Their study, of four U.K. acquisitions, led them to confirm the proposition that culture clashes will be minimised when acquired employees are both willing to abandon their old culture and perceive the acquirer's culture as attractive. Cartwright & Cooper argue that this is achieved where the acquiring company has a culture that gives individuals a similar or greater degree of participation and autonomy than was granted within the acquired company's culture. Employees within the acquired company were seen to display greater commitment to achieving successful post-acquisition integration when they perceived that the acquisition would at least maintain, if not increase, their level of participation and autonomy.

Although Cartwright & Cooper suggest general applicability of their conclusion, concerns of ethnocentric interpretation can be raised, following the warnings of Adler (1983) & Ajiferuke & Boddewyn (1970). For example, the work of Hofstede (1991) points to the cultural specificity of a desire for greater participation and autonomy: such a desire is consistent with the mental programming of the average U.K. employee, but is not universally applicable across all nations. Care may be required, therefore, in extending Cartwright & Cooper's findings to cross-national acquisitions or those outside the UK.

Buono & Bowditch's (1989) longitudinal study, of three service industry acquisitions, documents the acculturative stress that can occur on the marriage of incompatible organisational cultures. In a bank merger, the planned vision of complete integration was initially reflected in the choice of the new name, locations and systems. However, within a year it had become clear that, in reality, the values, philosophy and personnel of one partner were dominating the merged organisation. This led to significant voluntary resignations, from target company employees, and resentment from those that remained, who ultimately adopted "a series of behaviours that attempted to undermine the merger…and presented a significant barrier to successful integration of the firms, during the first four years following the merger" (Buono & Bowditch, 1989: 183). Similarly, although to a lesser degree, the acquisition of a fast food chain by a large conglomerate was seen to lead to negative acculturative stress, despite being positioned as a stand alone subsidiary within the new organisation. The marked difference between the family business style, of the fast food chain, and the systematised high growth orientation, of the conglomerate parent, led to feelings of intense pressure and frustration for the senior executives of the acquired firm as they came to terms with the skills necessary to master the new formal planning systems and procedures. The result was an underachievement of the strategic growth targets set for the new subsidiary, along with the planned voluntary exit of its Chief Executive Officer.

These qualitative reports of the negative impact of cultural differences have been confirmed statistically, in a dataset of 30 U.S. acquisitions, by Chatterjee et al. (1992). These researchers found a strong negative relationship between perceived cultural differences and shareholder gains resulting from the acquisitions. Importantly, and against the prediction of Nahavandi & Malekzadeh's (1988) model, the introduction of a measure of the multicultural tolerance of the acquiring firm did not moderate the relationship. Although indicative of the negative impact that cultural differences can have on overall performance, the study is potentially constrained by the ex-ante nature of the stock price performance variable. Parallels can be drawn with the early relatedness studies in that shareholder expectations of future operating performance, here measured as the abnormal returns over the 15-day period surrounding the acquisition announcement, may not reflect accurately the ex-post reality (Nayyar, 1992).

In summary, the empirical studies confirm that differences in organisational culture can lead to acculturative stress, which results in negative human resource implications and, in turn, inferior acquisition performance. Empirical support has been forthcoming for Nahavandi & Malekzadeh's (1988) model of the acculturation process and, in particular, for how the impact of cultural diffeences can be moderated by perceptions of the relative attractiveness of the new culture and by the chosen form of integration strategy.

COMPATIBILITY OF NATIONAL CULTURES

National culture has been defined as the collective programming of the mind which distinguishes members of one nation from another (Hofstede, 1991). In contrast to organisational culture, the mental programmes that make up one's national culture are learned through early socialisation with one's family and reinforced during schooling. These 'national' mental programmes reside primarily at the level of values about what is normal versus abnormal (Hofstede, 1991) and define one's basic assumptions concerning relationships with people, time and nature (Trompenaars, 1996).

Hofstede (1980) and, more recently, Trompenaars (1993) have produced classifications of national culture, based on extensive survey data, which both define the dimensions embodied by the concept and allow a country's national culture to be operationalised in numerical form.

National culture, at least as defined by Hofstede's dimensions, has been found to influence many aspects of a firm's organisation and systems; for example, the success of organisational development interventions (Johnson & Golembiewski, 1992), managers' responses to strategic issues (Schneider & De

Meyer, 1991), their openness to strategic change (Geletkanycz, 1997), decision-making styles (Tayeb, 1988), and the choice of foreign market entry mode (Kogut & Singh, 1988; Shane, 1994). Furthermore, the existence of congruence between a firm's management practices and its national culture has been shown to provide superior financial performance (Newman & Nollen, 1996). Given these influences on organisational life and the link between organisational compatibility and acquisition performance, several authors have posited that the compatibility of national cultures between firms combining in cross-border acquisitions will be an important determinant of the eventual outcome of the union (Hofstede, 1980, 1991; Napier, Schweiger & Kosglow, 1993; Olie, 1994; Very, Lubatkin, Calori & Veiga, 1997; Morosini et al., 1998).

The cross-national acculturation process is similar to that for the intra-national circumstances (Tung, 1993). Accordingly, and in line with the results of the organisational culture studies, Olie (1994) postulates that the cultural difficulties experienced within a cross-border acquisition will be contingent upon not only the degree of differences in organisational and national cultures, but also the level of integration achieved and the perceived attractiveness of the new identity.

These concepts have been investigated in a number of empirical studies. A significant contribution has been made by the team of Calori, Lubatkin & Very, based at Groupe ESC Lyon. These researchers collected data from 117 French and British firms that had been acquired by French, British, or American companies between 1987 and 1989. The sample design provided for comparative data on cross-border and domestic acquisitions and captured acquisition performance, two to four years post-acquisition, using perceptual measures which aggregated earnings, sales and market share variables. Importantly, data was collected from top managers of the acquired firm. This raises some concerns regarding the perceptual performance measure, as the acquired firm managers will not necessarily have been in a position to accurately assess performance relative to the acquisition's original objectives, as set by the acquiring firm.

Their work provides two main empirical results. First, in line with Hofstede's (1980) national culture dimensions, French acquirers were found to exercise more centralised formal control over the strategy and operations of their acquired businesses (high Power Distance and Uncertainty Avoidance), while American acquirers relied to a greater extent on informal communication and co-operation (lower Uncertainty Avoidance). Further, aspects of these differing control mechanisms were found to correlate with acquisition performance, suggesting that the national culture of the acquirer does have an impact on the outcome of its cross-border acquisitions. Higher performance was associated with acquirers that exhibited high levels of informal personal efforts and imposed a low level of operational control (Calori, Lubatkin & Very, 1994). This result is noteworthy, in that it reinforces Cartwright & Cooper's (1992) finding on relative cultural attractiveness, even within a sample that includes France, a high Power Distance nation.

The second set of results focused on the level of acculturative stress felt by managers in target companies (Very, Calori & Lubatkin, 1993; Very et al., 1996). Cross-border and domestic acquisitions were found to cause different levels of acculturative stress, particularly where expectations differed from reality with regard to 'performance and reward objectiveness' (British targets) and 'personal and societal response' (French targets). Greater levels of acculturative stress along these dimensions were associated with inferior acquisition performance. However, the cross-border acquisitions did not always result in higher acculturative stress than their domestic counterparts. The latter result suggests that national cultural differences may elicit perceptions of attraction, as well as stress, in acquired firms, although it also raises questions concerning the relative influence of organisational culture differences over national culture differences.

In a later extension to their work, Very et al. (1997) further explored the issue of relative cultural attractiveness. They established a measure of cultural attractiveness, within 106 of the European cross-border acquisitions, by comparing how acquired firm managers perceived the company's culture, both before and after the acquisition, relative to their normative beliefs as to what the culture ought to be. The results indicated that, the more the cultural values of the buying firm were in line with the normative values of the target firm managers, the higher the resulting performance of the acquisition. Conversely, inferior acquisition performance was reported where the manager's normative values were closer to the culture that existed before the merger, than that which transpired post-acquisition. Overall, the study suggests that differences in national culture, between bidder and target, should not automatically be associated with negative consequences. Rather, where the bidder's culture is perceived to exhibit relative attractiveness, the combination of dissimilar cultures may be beneficial to post-acquisition performance.

These conclusions are supported in separate work carried out by Morosini, Shane & Singh (1998). In a sample of 52 Italian cross-border acquisitions, national cultural distance, measured using a composite index of Hofstede's (1980) scores, was seen to be positively related to post-acquisition performance, after controlling for a variety of strategic and environmental factors. Specifically, the greater the national cultural distance between the bidder and target, the higher the sales growth within the acquired firm was found to be, for a two year period following acquisition. Detailed case studies, undertaken within four of the acquisitions, confirmed that the acquirers were positively motivated by the opportunity to acquire 'organisational repertoires and routines' embedded in the target company's national culture. For example, interviewees from the Electrolux-Zanussi acquisition highlighted that the Italian traits of creativity and flexibility were highly desired by the Swedish acquirer, to provide an improved joint research and development function (Morosini et al., 1998).

It must be noted, however, that the empirical evidence does not universally support the positive impact which differences in national culture may bring. Datta & Puia (1995) examined shareholder value creation in 112 large cross-border acquisitions, undertaken by U.S. firms, and found that acquisitions characterised by high national cultural distance (again measured using a composite index of Hofstede's (1980) scores) were associated with lower abnormal returns for acquiring firm shareholders. Clearly, further research must be awaited before definite conclusions can be reached in this area.

These empirical studies have also provided insights into the interaction between national cultural compatibility and post-acquisition integration strategy. Very et al.'s (1997) research took account of the degree of post-acquisition autonomy granted to the acquired firm and found that, where the firm's autonomy was reduced following acquisition, this heightened the negative consequences of any cultural incompatibilities. Similarly, case-study evidence suggests that successful cross-border acquirers may rely on high degrees of autonomy to promote acculturation, whilst simultaneously pursuing staff rotation programmes and global co-ordination policies to achieve the desired skills transfer and value creation (Morosini et al., 1998). Insofar as autonomy for the acquired firm is consistent with low levels of integration, these results imply that the impact of national cultural differences may be moderated by the choice of post-acquisition integration strategy.

Related work by Morosini & Singh (1994) has investigated how target firm national culture influences the success of different post-acquisition integration strategies. Their sample, of 65 Italian cross-border acquisitions, was classified according to three classes of post-acquisition strategy: integration (cf. absorption), independence (cf. preservation), and restructuring (cf. holding/symbiosis). The interaction between the strategy adopted and Hofstede's (1980) national culture scores was regressed against changes in acquired firm performance, controlling for relatedness and relative size. The findings revealed that the performance of a particular strategy was related to Hofstede's Uncertainty Avoidance score for the target firm. Targets in high Uncertainty Avoidance nations gave the highest one year profit margin increase when an independence strategy was adopted, while a full integration strategy led to highly favourable results in countries with low Uncertainty Avoidance (Morosini & Singh, 1994). Of interest is that no statistically significant results are reported for Hofstede's other three dimensions of national culture, pointing to the particular influence of the Uncertainty Avoidance dimension. However, it is also noteworthy that two-year performance measures did not show the same strength of relationship, which suggests that further study is warranted on the time dependence of any national culture effect. Finally, some caution may be needed in interpreting these particular results, as the performance measure, again, focused specifically on the acquired firm, with the added complication here of accurate disaggregation in the full integration cases.

The studies reviewed thus far have confirmed theoretical reasoning that links the relative national cultures of buyers and sellers to the eventual outcome of an international acquisition. Yet, the majority of these studies also note strongly, in their conclusions, that the interaction between national and organisational culture must not be ignored. Indeed, Very et al. (1993: 343) conclude: "cross-national mergers are a complex phenomenon, sometimes influenced by national cultural differences, sometimes by organisational influences, sometimes by both and sometimes by neither". Management style is a central element of a firm's culture, which simultaneously reflects the influence of both organisational culture (Sathe, 1983; Sales & Mirvis, 1984) and national culture (Tayeb, 1988; Hofstede, 1991; Smith, 1992). In a recent extension of the cultural compatibility work on international acquisitions, Schoenberg & Norburn (1998) have investigated how differences within specific dimensions of management style impact on acquisition outcome, within a sample of 129 European cross-border acquisitions. Of the six components of management style difference identified, only differences in the attitude towards risk were found to exhibit a statistically significant influence on performance; the greater the difference in the risk orientations of the bidder and target, the lower the performance of the acquisition. Differences within the five other components of management style showed no impact on performance. Interestingly, and in apparent contrast to some of the prior research outlined above, differences in risk orientation were found to exert a negative influence, even when the acquired firm was granted a high degree of autonomy within a preservation type post-acquisition strategy. These results, concerning the role of the form of integration, parallel those of an earlier study that examined the influence of aggregate management style differences within a sample of domestic US acquisitions (Datta, 1991).

CONCLUSION

Although cultural differences have sometimes been seen as a second order effect, the academic literature reviewed above shows that their impact is both measurable and meaningful. Cultural differences, both organisational and national, can lead to difficulties in the post-acquisition period, which in turn can reduce acquisition performance. However, cultural differences should not automatically be associated with negative consequences. In acquisitions where the bidder's culture is perceived to exhibit relative attractiveness, the combination of dissimilar cultures has been found to exert a positive influence on performance.

These broad conclusions confirm the, often cited, need for practitioners to make a detailed assessment of cultural compatibility as part of their pre-bid planning and evaluation activities. Yet, the issue remains as to which particular factors should be the focus of attention in such an assessment. It is here that our present body of knowledge is not so definite. Theoretical models predict that the underlying determinants of cultural compatibility will be the acquirer's tolerance of multiculturalism, the relative attractiveness of the acquirer's culture and the post-acquisition integration strategy (Nahavandi & Malekzadeh, 1988; Olie, 1994). The actual influence of each of these factors has been tested separately, in one or more empirical studies, but with varied results.

The tolerance for multiculturalism has been found not to moderate the impact of organisational cultural differences (Chatterjee et al., 1992). This result might be explained as follows. The tolerance for multiculturalism has been seen as an individual, rather than organisational, trait (Adler, 1986) and an international acquirer frequently will allocate responsibility for the integration of each of its acquisitions to a different manager or set of managers. Thus, there may be wide variations in the tolerance for multiculturalism present within any given acquirer, making this a problematical variable to operationalise and use in a predictive mode at the organisational level. In the absence of further research, the implication for practitioners is that, if anything, an assessment should be made of the fit between the individual managers' tolerance for multiculturalism and the cultural dynamics of the particular acquisition for which they will be responsible.

The influence of the form of integration has received mixed empirical support. While several studies have reported that the integration approach may moderate the negative impacts of any cultural differences present (Morosini & Singh, 1994; Very et al., 1997; Morosini et al., 1998), others have concluded that the relationship between cultural differences and acquisition performance is independent of the form of integration (Buono & Bowditch, 1989; Datta, 1991; Schoenberg & Norburn, 1998). Further research is undoubtedly needed in this area, but the implication for practitioners is that it may be dangerous to assume that managing an international acquisition at arm's length (preservation integration) will necessarily soften the negative impact of any cultural differences.

The relative attractiveness of the acquirer's culture is supported as a key determinant of how readily two cultures will merge following acquisition (Very et al., 1997). Superior acquisition performance has been reported, in two studies, to occur where the bidder's culture endorses a higher level of delegated autonomy and participation, relative to that of the target (Cartwright & Cooper, 1992; Calori et al., 1994). Other studies point also to the particular influence of the firms' relative attitudes towards informality and risk (Calori et al., 1994; Morosini & Singh, 1994; Schoenberg & Norburn, 1998). These results suggest that prospective acquirers should focus particularly on the combining firms' relative attitudes towards participation, formality and risk.

Unfortunately, it is difficult to differentiate whether these attributes are based in the organisational or national cultures of the firms concerned, given the established methodological problems of separating the individual contribution of national and organisational culture within a given firm (Hofstede, 1991; Very et al., 1993; Olie, 1994). Certainly, the attributes do correspond to Hofstede's national culture dimensions of Power Distance and Uncertainty Avoidance, which suggests that a generic country effect may play a role in determining cultural compatibility in cross-border acquisitions. Yet, these two dimensions are closely associated with decision-making routines and choices of organisational structure (Hofstede, 1980) that are open also to the influence of organisational culture. Establishing the size and importance of any purely national effect is likely to prove difficult, in practice.

It is interesting to note, however, that there is some emerging evidence that Uncertainty Avoidance may have a particular role to play in the determination of national cultural compatibility. Morosini et al. (1998) included Uncertainty Avoidance scores as a control variable in their research on the impact of national cultural distance and found that the acquirer's Uncertainty Avoidance score had a small, but statistically significant, impact on post-acquisition performance. In their earlier study, Morosini & Singh (1994) reported that Uncertainty Avoidance, alone amongst Hofstede's dimensions of national culture, exerted an influence on the success of integration strategies within international acquisitions. Similarly, the related construct of risk orientation (Hofstede, 1991) was the sole dimension of management style compatibility seen to influence cross-border acquisition performance in Schoenberg & Norburn's (1998) study. Certainly, the notion of the particular influence of Uncertainty Avoidance is supported within the strategic alliances literature, where differences in Uncertainty Avoidance between partner firms have been found to exert a particularly detrimental effect on the performance (survival) of international joint ventures (Barkema & Vermeulen, 1997).

Finally, the issue of relative cultural attractiveness raises the question as to whether attractiveness should be viewed in terms of cultural similarities or cultural differences. Researchers have differed in their position on this issue, with some reporting that cultural differences are positively associated with performance (Morosini et al., 1998), whilst others link cultural similarity to superior outcomes (Chaterjee et al., 1992; Datta & Puia, 1995). However, these large sample empirical studies have tended to employ absolute measures of cultural distance between the combining firms as their independent variable. A way forward on this issue may be offered by the methodology of Very et al. (1997), who view cultural distance in terms that are relative to the normative cultural values of the acquired firm. Their results support the key notion that it is perceived relative cultural attractiveness that operates as the performance determinant, rather than absolute differences or similarities per se.

Overall, the lack of consensus that emerges from the studies reviewed in this paper points to the potential value of further research in the area. The paucity of firm conclusions, to date, on the influence of the form of integration and the exact dimensions of culture that exert a critical influence on eventual performance suggest fruitful avenues for future quantitative studies. Researchers should also continue to investigate the presence of any country specific patterns within the results of such studies, to establish the precise influence of national culture over organisational culture and any particular role played by Uncertainty Avoidance.

Qualitative researchers might pursue the direction established by Morosini et al (1998: 155) and "explore the specific mechanisms through which cultural factors influence performance." For example, can generic processes be identified, from successful acquirers, that aid implementation of the opportunities offered by cultural differences, whilst simultaneously minimising any adverse impacts? Continued research on this important topic will assist future cross-border acquirers to focus on the key dimensions of cultural compatibility and to understand the circumstances and mechanisms by which they exert an influence on ultimate acquisition outcomes.

NOTES

1 This paper is an extended and revised version of an earlier paper presented to the Academy of International Business 24th Annual UK Conference, Leeds, April 1997 and subsequently published in the conference volume Burton, F., Chapman, M. & Cross, A., (Eds.), 1999. International Business Organization: Subsidiary Management, Entry Strategies and Emerging Markets, Basingstoke: Macmillan, pp. 294–306. The permission of Macmillan Press Ltd to reproduce sections of the earlier paper is gratefully acknowledged.

REFERENCES

Adler, N. (1983). A Typology of Management Studies Involving Culture. *Journal of International Business Studies, 14,* 29–47.

Adler, N. (1986). International Dimensions of Organisational Behaviour. Boston, MA: Kent Publishing.

Ajiferuke, M., & Boddewyn, J. (1970). Culture and Other Explanatory Variables in Comparative Management Studies. *Academy of Management Journal, 13,* 153–156.

Angwin, D., & Savill, B. (1997). Perspectives on European Cross-Border Acquisitions: A View From European Executives. *European Management Journal, 15,* 423–435.

Barkema, H., & Vermeulen, F. (1997). What Differences in the Cultural Backgrounds of Partners are Detrimental for International Joint Ventures? *Journal of International Business Studies, 28,* 845–864.

Barney, J. (1986). Organisational Culture: Can it be a Source of Sustained Competitive Advantage? *Academy of Management Review, 11,* 656–665.

Bleeke, J., Isono, J., Ernst, D., & Weinburg, D. (1993). Succeeding at Cross-Border M&A. In: J. Bleeke, & D. Ernst, (Eds), Collaborating to Compete: Using Strategic Alliances and Acquisitions in the Global Marketplace. New York: J Wiley & Sons.

Brush, T. (1996). Predicted Change in Operational Synergy and Post-Acquisition Performance of Acquired Businesses. *Strategic Management Journal, 17,* 1–24.

Buono, A., & Bowditch, J. (1989). The Human Side of Mergers and Acquisitions. San Francisco: Jossey-Bass.

Calori, R., Lubatkin, M., & Very, P. (1994). Control Mechanisms in Cross-Border Acquisitions: An International Comparison. *Organisation Studies, 15,* 361–379.

Capron, L. (1999). The Long Term Performance of Horizontal Acquisitions. *Strategic Management Journal, 20,* 987–1018.

Capron, L., Dussauge, P., & Mitchell, W. (1998). Resource Redeployment Following Horizontal Acquisitions in Europe and North America 1988–1992. *Strategic Management Journal, 19,* 631–661

Cartwright, S., & Cooper, C. (1992). Mergers and Acquisitions: The Human Factor. Oxford: Butterworth-Heinemann.

Cartwright, S., & Cooper, C. (1993). The Role of Culture Compatibility in Successful Organizational Marriage. *Academy of Management Executive, 7,* 57–70.

Chatterjee, S., Lubatkin, M., Schweiger, D., & Weber, Y. (1992). Cultural Differences and Shareholder Value in Related Mergers: Linking Equity and Human Capital. *Strategic Management Journal, 13,* 319–334.

Datta, D. (1991). Organisational Fit and Acquisition Performance: Effects of Post-Acquisition Integration. *Strategic Management Journal, 12,* 281–297.

Datta, D., & Puia, G. (1995). Cross-Border Acquisitions: An Examination of the Influence of Relatedness and Cultural Fit on Shareholder Value Creation in US Acquiring Firms. *Management International Review, 35,* 337–359.

Deal,T., & Kennedy, A. (1982). Corporate Cultures: The Rites and Rituals of Corporate Life. Mass.: Addison-Wesley.

Elsass, P., & Veiga, J. (1994). Acculturation in Acquired Organisations: A Force-Field Perspective. *Human Relations, 47,* 431–453.

Farjoun, M. (1998). The Independent and Joint Effects of the Skill and Physical Bases of Relatedness in Diversification. *Strategic Management Journal, 19,* 611–630.

Flanagan, D. (1996). Announcements of Purely Related and Purely Unrelated Mergers and Shareholder Returns: Reconciling the Relatedness Paradox. *Journal of Management, 22*, 823–835.

Geletkanycz, M. (1997). The Salience of Culture's Consequences: The Effects of Cultural Values on Top Executive Commitment to the Status Quo. *Strategic Management Journal, 18*, 615–634.

Haspeslagh, P., & Jemison, D. (1991) Managing Acquisitions. New York: Free Press.

Hofstede, G. (1980). Culture's Consequences. London: Sage.

Hofstede, G. (1991). Cultures and Organisations, London: McGraw-Hill.

Hunt, J. (1990). Changing Pattern of Acquisition Behaviour In Takeovers and the Consequences for Acquisition Processes. *Strategic Management Journal, 11*, 69–77.

Jemison, D., & Sitkin, S. (1986). Corporate Acquisitions: A Process Perspective. *Academy of Management Review, 11*, 145–163.

Johnson, G. (1992). Managing Strategic Change: Strategy, Culture and Action. *Long Range Planning, 25*, 28–36.

Johnson, K., & Golembiewski, R. (1992). National Culture in Organizational Development: A Conceptual and Empirical Analysis. *International Journal of Human Resource Management, 3*, 71–84.

Kitching, J. (1974). Winning and Losing with European Acquisitions. *Harvard Business Review, 52*, 124–136.

Kogut, B., & Singh, H. (1988). The Effect of National Culture on the Choice of Entry Mode. *Journal of International Business Studies, 19*, 413–431.

Kusewitt, J. (1985). An Exploratory Study of Strategic Acquisition Factors Relating to Performance. *Strategic Management Journal, 6*, 151–169.

Lubatkin, M. (1987) Merger Strategies and Stockholder Value. *Strategic Management Journal, 8*, 39–53.

Markides, C., & Oyon, D. (1998). International Acquisitions: Do They Create Value for Shareholders? *European Management Journal, 16*, 125–135.

Morosini, P., Shane, S., & Singh, H. (1998). National Cultural Distance and Cross-Border Acquisition Performance. *Journal of International Business Studies, 29*, 137–158.

Morosini, P., & Singh, H. (1994). Post Cross-Border Acquisitions: Implementing National Culture Compatible Strategies to Improve Performance. *European Management Journal, 12*, 390–400.

Nahavandi, A., & Malekzadeh, A. (1988). Acculturation in Mergers and Acquisitions. *Academy of Management Review, 13*, 79–90.

Nahavandi, A., & Malekzadeh, A. (1994). Successful Mergers Through Acculturation. In: G. von Krogh, A. Sinatra, & H.Singh, (Eds.), *The Management of Corporate Acquisitions*, (293–306). London: Macmillan.

Napier, N. (1989). Mergers and Acquisitions, Human Resource Issues and Outcomes: A Review and Suggested Typology. *Journal of Management Studies, 21*, 271–289.

Napier, N., Schweiger, D., & Kosglow, J. (1993). Managing Organizational Diversity: Observations from Cross-Border Acquisitions. *Human Resources Management, 32*, 505–523.

Nayyar, P. (1992). On The Measurement of Corporate Diversification Strategy: Evidence From Large US Service Firms. *Strategic Management Journal, 13*, 219–235.

Newman, K., & Nollen, S. (1996). Culture and Congruence: The Fit Between Management Practices and National Culture. *Journal of International Business Studies, 27*, 753–779.

Norburn, D., & Schoenberg, R. (1994). European Cross-Border Acquisition: How Was It for You? *Long Range Planning, 27*, 25–34.

Olie, R. (1994). Shades of Culture and Institutions in International Mergers. *Organisation Studies, 15*, 381–405.

Pablo, A., Sitkin, S., & Jemison, D. (1996). Acquisition Decision-Making Processes: the Central Role of Risk. *Journal of Management, 22,* 723–746.

Rostand, A. (1994). Optimizing Managerial Decisions during the Acquisition Integration Process. Paper presented to 14th Annual Strategic Management Society International Conference, Paris.

Sales, A., & Mirvis, P. (1984). When Cultures Collide: Issues in Acquisition. In: J. Kimberly, & R. Quinn (Eds.), New Futures: *The Challenge of Managing Corporate Transition,*(107–133). Homewood, IL: Irwin.

Sathe, V. (1983). Some Action Implications of Corporate Culture: A Manager's Guide to Action. *Organisational Dynamics, 11,* 4–23.

Schneider, S., & De Meyer, A. (1991). Interpreting and Responding to Strategic Issues: The impact of National Culture. *Strategic Management Journal, 12*: 307–320.

Schoenberg, R., & Norburn, D. (1998). Leadership Compatibility and Cross-Border Acquisition Outcome. Paper presented to 18th Annual Strategic Management Society International Conference, Orlando.

Schweiger, D., & Walsh, J. (1990). Mergers and Acquisitions: An Interdisciplinary View. *Research in Personnel and Human Resource Management, 8,* 41–107.

Seth, A. (1990). Value Creation in Acquisitions: A Re-examination of Performance Issues. *Strategic Management Journal, 11,* 99–116.

Shane,S. (1994). The Effect of National Culture on the Choice Between Licensing and Direct Foreign Investment. *Strategic Management Journal, 15,* 627–642.

Singh, H., & Montgomery, C. (1987). Corporate Acquisition Strategies and Economic Performance. *Strategic Management Journal, 8,* 377–386.

Singh, H., & Zollo., M. (1998). The Impact of Knowledge Codification, Experience Trajectories and Integration Strategies on the Performance of Corporate Acquisitions. Academy of Management Annual Conference Best Papers Proceedings. San Diego.

Smith, P. (1992). Organisational Behaviour and National Cultures. *British Journal of Management, 3,* 39–51.

Tayeb, M. (1988). Organisations and National Culture: A Comparative Analysis. London: Sage.

Trompenaars, F. (1993). Riding the Waves of Culture. London: Economist Books.

Trompenaars, F. (1996). Resolving International Conflict: Culture and Business Strategy. *Business Strategy Review, 7,* 51–68.

Tung, R. (1993). Managing Cross-National and Intra-National Diversity. *Human Resource Management, 32,* 461–477.

Very, P., Calori, R., & Lubatkin, M. (1993). An Investigation of National and Organisational Cultural Influences in Recent European Mergers. *Advances in Strategic Management, 9,* 323–346.

Very, P., Lubatkin, M., & Calori, R. (1996). A Cross-National Assessment of Acculturative Stress in Recent European Mergers. *International Studies of Management and Organizations, 26,* 59–86.

Very, P., Lubatkin, M., Calori, R., & Veiga, J. (1997). Relative Standing and the Performance of Recently Acquired European Firms. *Strategic Management Journal, 18,* 593–614.

Walter, G. (1985). Culture Collisions in Mergers and Acquisitions. In: P. Frost, et al. (Eds.), *Organisational Culture,* (301–314). Beverly Hills: Sage Publications.

INTEGRATING MERGERS AND ACQUISITIONS: AN INTERNATIONAL RESEARCH REVIEW[1]

David M. Schweiger and Philip K. Goulet

INTRODUCTION

As the 20th century opened there was a wave of mergers and acquisitions (M&As), characterized by horizontal consolidation. Since then, M&A activity has remained a consistent and growing part of the business landscape, characterized by a number of major and differing waves.

As we begin the 21st century, we are again facing another major wave. This one is the largest in history and is being driven by globalization, technological change and deregulation. Unlike the conglomeration movement of the 1960s, the latest wave appears to be quite strategic. Companies are attempting to improve their current and future strategic positions, domestically, regionally and globally, and are doing so by acquiring new technologies, products and services, increasing geographic presence and consolidating within the markets they compete or hope to compete in. Critical to the success of these deals will be management's ability to integrate the combining companies, especially in cases where the prices paid were based on synergy values.

That acquisitions are so pervasive is best reflected in the fact that, in 1998, there were 11,655 domestic deals, worth $1.6 trillion, transacted (Securities Data Corporation, 1999). This reflects a doubling in the number of deals since 1990. Growth, in both number and value of deals, set record levels in both

Advances in Mergers and Acquisitions, Volume 1, pages 61–91.
2000 by Elsevier Science Inc.
ISBN: 0–7623–0683–1

Asia and Europe as well. Worldwide, the total value of deals reported was $2.489 trillion, up 54% from 1997. Moreover, the number and value of cross-border deals has consistently increased during the last 10 years. In July 1999 the Conference Board (July 13, 1999) reported that 70% of senior executives surveyed indicated that they expected M&A activity to increase within their industry; 77% expected that cross-border deals would increase.

Given the pervasiveness and growth of M&A activity and the volume of capital involved, it is critical that we understand as much as we can about the dynamics underlying M&As and what contributes to their effectiveness.

Numerous studies have investigated the relationship between M&As and financial performance. Using a variety of financial measures (e.g. profit, stock price) and timeframes (e.g. pre- and post-measurement) these studies continue to demonstrate that, on average, M&As benefit the target's shareholders, but not the buyer's shareholders. In fact, there are varying results with respect to buying firms' performance (see Lajoux, 1998, for an extensive review of this literature).

Although many reasons have been advanced for these results (e.g. see Sirower, 1997), a number point to aspects of M&A integration as a major contributing factor (Schweiger & Walsh, 1990; Csiszar & Schweiger, 1994). That this is the case is reflected in a recent survey of Forbes 500 CEOs (Schmidt, 1999) that identified post acquisition factors as contributing to merger failure. Using a 7-point scale, where higher scores indicate a greater contribution to failure, the survey found that incompatible cultures (5.60), inability to manage target (5.39), unable to implement change, clash of management styles/egos (5.11), and incompatible marketing systems (4.01) were among the top 10 reasons cited.

In this chapter we will review what is known about one major area that has been identified as contributing to M&A effectiveness, organizational integration.

For sake of brevity, this review will be restricted as follows. First, since there are numerous studies that have addressed employee reactions to M&As (e.g. Marks & Mirvis, 1998; Schweiger & Walsh, 1990) they will not be reviewed here. However, it should be noted that these studies are important, in that employee reactions affect outcomes (e.g. performance, turnover, absenteeism) that can have a bearing on the success of the integration process (Cartwright & Cooper, 1996). Second, although there are numerous practitioner articles, books and cases on integration, we will focus only on research articles, books and cases. Third, we will include only research published in English language journals and books.

This chapter will be divided into three Sections. In Section one, we will focus on the concept of integration. In Section two, we will review research that deals with integration. In Section three, we will discuss questions that remain in the literature and future research opportunities.

THE INTEGRATION CONCEPT

Integration Defined

Surprisingly, very little literature directly defines integration. Although most authors acknowledge that integration involves some form of combining the assets and people of the buyer and the target, in general, the term is used quite loosely. Moreover, as is noted in our review of the research below, it is typically not used as a dependent measure.

The limited literature that has emerged on this topic does recognize that there are different ways in which assets and people can be combined (i.e. integrated) in an acquisition and that each type has different organizational challenges associated with it. Several integration frameworks are presented below.

Using the concept of capability transfer between an acquirer and acquired firm, Haspeslagh & Jemison (1991) define four types of integration, based on two dimensions: Need for Strategic Interdependence and Need for Organizational Autonomy. According to the authors:

> Some acquisitions have a high need for strategic interdependence, and a low need for organizational autonomy. These acquisitions call for what we label an absorption approach to integration. Other acquisitions, to the contrary, present a low need for strategic interdependence, but a high need for organizational autonomy. We will call the integration approach associated with these acquisitions preservation. Other acquisitions are characterized by high needs for interdependence and high needs for organizational autonomy. We will use the term symbiosis to describe the integration approach called for in such acquisitions…[The fourth type] would be acquisitions where the firm has no intention of integrating and creating value through anything except financial transfers, risk-sharing, or general management capability … The only integration in such acquisitions would, in a sense, be a mere holding activity (pp.146–147).

Marks & Mirvis (1998) also take a multi-dimensional view of integration, "…. ranging from full consolidation to near separation of the companies …" (p.68). They see this range as including such forms as separate holding company, strategic control, managed subsidiary, operational control and merged and consolidated. The order is presented in increasing levels of consolidation of the acquiring and acquired firms. Marks & Mirvis also view integration from the perspective of degree of change made in either the buyer, the target, or in both firms. Similarly to Haspeslagh & Jemison, they identify five approaches, absorption, preservation, best of both, transformation and reverse merger.

Whereas Haspeslagh & Jemison, and Marks & Mirvis, view each acquisition as representing a different type of integration, Schweiger (1999) notes that, within an acquisition, different types of approaches may be used, based on functions, geographical areas and product lines. He notes that there are four types of approaches that might be used within an acquisition.

(1) **Combination** – The extent to which the separate functions and activities of both the acquirer and the target firms are physically consolidated into one.
(2) **Standardization** – The extent to which the separate functions and activities of both firms are standardized and formalized, but not physically consolidated (e.g. separate operations may be maintained, but the operations are made identical). This is typical when acquirers formally transfer best practices across firms.
(3) **Coordination** – The extent to which functions and activities of both firms are coordinated (e.g., one firm's products are sold through the other firm's distribution channels).
(4) **Intervention** – The extent to which interventions are made in the acquired firm to turnaround poor cash flow or operating profits, regardless of any inherent sources of combination value (e.g. replace management, drop unprofitable products).

Drawing upon anthropology and cross-cultural psychology, Nahavandi & Malekzedah (1988) define integration from the perspective of acculturation. They define four modes:

(1) **Integration** – Where two organizations are structurally integrated, but there is little cultural and behavioral assimilation.
(2) **Assimilation** – A unilateral process in which one organization (typically the acquired firm) willingly adopts the identity and culture of the other.
(3) **Separation** – Where an organization (typically the acquired firm) attempts to maintain and preserve its culture and refuses to become assimilated.
(4) **Deculturation** – Where members of an organization do not value their culture and do not want to be assimilated into that of another.

In particular they focus on integration as a process of changing one or both cultures in the merging organizations. They also identify four approaches to integration that might be employed by an acquirer based on the degree of relatedness of the combining firms and the degree of multiculturalism tolerated by the buyer.

A variety of other integration frameworks have also been identified (Bastien & Van de Ven, 1986; Haspeslagh & Farquar, 1987; Schweiger & Ivancevich, 1987; Shrivastava, 1986; Shanley, 1988; Buono & Bowditch, 1989; Napier, 1989; Lubatkin, Calori, Very & Veiga, 1998). For sake of brevity we will not review all of them here. With some exceptions, all frameworks are quite similar, in that integration can be captured, based on the degree of independence and autonomy between the buyer and seller. Different types of integration appear to present different types of organizational challenges, which in turn suggest different types of impacts and warrant different types of interventions for successful performance.

Stages of the Integration Process

Another interesting question concerns the scope of the integration process. Specifically, when does the process begin? With some exceptions (Haspeslagh & Jemison, 1991; Csiszar & Schweiger, 1994; Marks & Mirvis, 1998; Schweiger, 1999), the literature does not formally address this issue. Integration is often viewed as beginning after closing. A number of authors believe, however, that the process begins at the point at which a target is selected and continues through due diligence, negotiations, closing and post-closing. Schweiger (1999) labels these stages as transaction, transition and integration. Marks & Mirvis (1998) define these as pre-combination, combination and post-combination. The importance of these distinctions is that the process of integration and activities that influence the success of the integration begin long before the closing, at the point when companies first make contact. Unfortunately, there is little empirical research that has systematically examined the relationships among the stages and how activities conducted during them affect the success of the integration process.

INTEGRATION RESEARCH

In this section of the paper we review research focused on the M&A integration process. The section is divided into three broad research areas: National and Organizational Culture, Integration Implementation Process, and Integration Decision Process. These areas were based on a thematic assessment of the literature, rather than on clear streams of programmatic research. With the exception of research on the antecedents and outcomes of top management turnover following acquisition, the integration research has not been programmatic.

National and Organizational Culture

An area of M&A research receiving significant attention, especially during the 1990s, is that of culture. An objective in studying culture has been to examine how national culture affects acquirer's integration practices and how similarity and dissimilarity between cultures of combining entities effects post-acquisition integration and performance. Culture has been generally described as the norms, values, beliefs, and attitudes of a group of people. These characteristics of culture may be broadly based in societies (Hofstede, 1980), or in organizations (Schein, 1985).

Consequently, the M&A integration literature has addressed culture at two levels, the national level and organizational level. The next section will be divided into two parts. Part one presents studies involving national culture, whereas part two presents studies involving organizational culture.

National Cultures

According to Hofstede (1980), national culture is the collective programming of the human mind and is operationalized using four cultural dimensions: power distance, uncertainty avoidance, masculinity/femininity and individualism/collectivism. Hofstede has found that national cultures vary significantly across these four dimensions. Power distance is the degree to which power differences are expected and preferred by a society. Uncertainty avoidance is the extent to which a society feels threatened by uncertain and ambiguous situations. Masculinity, versus femininity, expresses the extent to which the dominant values in a society are 'masculine' (i.e. competitiveness, assertiveness, ambition, and the acquisition of money). Individualism, versus collectivism, refers to the degree to which a society emphasizes the role of the individual versus the role of the group (Hofstede, 1980: 45–46). The greater the discrepancy between nations, on one or more of these four dimensions, the greater their national cultural distance. Two groups of studies have been conducted on national culture. The first group examines the relationship between culture and integration practices used. The second examines the direct impact of cultural differences on integration and performance

National culture and integration practices.

Several studies have examined the influence of national culture on M&A integration practices. Research by Morosini & Singh (1994) examined the relationship between the degree of cultural distance between acquirers and acquired firms and the degree of integration and its effect on organizational performance. Their longitudinal study, of 65 western European and U.S. firms involved in cross-border acquisitions, used Hofstede's uncertainty avoidance and individualism/collectivism dimensions to characterize national culture. Organizational performance was operationalized by profitability growth (change in net income to net sales) and productivity growth (change in sales and number of employees).

The results indicated that the higher the uncertainty avoidance of the acquired company's national culture, the stronger the relationship between an independence strategy (of the acquired firm) and profitability one year after acquisition. Conversely, in countries with lower uncertainty avoidance, integration was significantly related to profitability; no effect was found relating uncertainty avoidance to productivity growth.

Morosini & Singh also found that in highly individualistic societies a lower level of post-acquisition integration appeared to lead to higher productivity growth one year after acquisition. On the other hand, the relationship between individualism and integration was not found to influence profitability growth.

Another study, of 75 acquisitions, by Calori, Lubatkin & Very (1994), examined the integration procedures practiced by U.S., British, and French acquirers of both British and French acquired firms. Their findings tend to support the significance of Hofstede's cultural dimensions, and indicate that differences exist among integration measures practiced by national heritage of acquirer. For instance, their study found that French acquirers tend to exercise higher formal control than do U.S. and British acquirers. This is consistent with Hofstede's cultural dimension of uncertainty avoidance, in which France is known to score higher than both the U.S. and U.K.

Other results indicated that U.S. acquiring firms relied more on informal communication and cooperation than the French, while relying more on formal control by procedures than the British. In addition, U.S. managers tend to provide a higher level of personal effort to ensure that the merger is successful; they become more involved with target people than do the British. This 'hands-off' attitude of acquiring managers was found to be typically British.

Furthermore, the types of integration measures practiced were significantly related to post-acquisition performance. Informal communication and cooperation, along with informal personal efforts from managers of the acquiring firm, were positively correlated with improvements in attitudinal performance of the acquired firm.

The study also found that the higher the informal personal efforts of the managers of the buying firm, the higher the economic performance of the acquired firm and, conversely, the level of control exercised by the acquirer over the acquired firm's operations is negatively correlated with economic performance. These results indicate that for British and French acquired firms the use of informal integration mechanisms yields higher post-acquisition performance. Acquirers must therefore be aware of how they may be culturally predisposed to approach integration of acquired firms in an effort to maximize M&A performance.

Lubatkin, et al. (1998) extended the above findings in a subsequent study. Their study of 83 French and British domestic and cross-border acquisitions found a significant relationship between national heritage of acquirers and the administrative approaches used by managers during merger integration. The French express a greater acceptance of power distance and have a greater need for uncertainty avoidance than do the British. As a result, French acquirers were found to rely more on centralized headquarters-subsidiary controls, so that power and influence resides at the hierarchical top, than were the British. The research findings are consistent; national differences do in fact exist, and they are significantly related to post-acquisition integration procedures employed by the acquirer.

Impact of national cultural differences.

The following studies examine the impact that cultural differences have on M&A integration. Although national cultural distance adds to the complexity of understanding an acquisition partner and creates the potential for 'culture clash', such distance may not be an automatic antecedent of poor performance. This was exactly the case in a study of 52 European and U.S. cross-border acquisitions, conducted by Morosini, Shane and Singh (1998). They found that the cross-border acquisitions that tended to perform better, as defined by sales growth, were those in which the acquirer and the target firm were, on average, more distant in routines and repertories that were embedded in national culture.

However, the issue of culture is a complex one. Differences in organizational culture between combining firms can have differential effects on integration, depending upon whether the acquisitions are cross-border or not. For example, Weber, Shenkar & Raveh (1996) found, in an exploratory study of 52 acquisitions of U.S. firms, that the relationship between differences in organizational culture and attitudinal and behavioral measures for international M&As is inverse to that found in domestic M&As. The study indicates that the degree of differences in organizational culture was negatively related to autonomy removal of the target in domestic M&As, whereas it was positively related in international M&As. They also found that in domestic M&As differences in organizational culture had a negative effect, in the post-acquisition period, on attitudinal and behavioral variables that are believed to lead to conflict and reduced synergy realization. On the other hand, in international M&As, differences in organizational culture had a positive effect on variables believed to aid in achieving synergies realization.

Further issues, regarding the complexities of culture, were identified by Very, Lubatkin & Calori (1996) in a study of 106 acquisitions of French and British firms by French, British, and U.S. acquirers. Their study addressed the issue of acculturative stress, defined as the disruptive tension that is felt by members of one culture when they are required to interact with and adopt the ways of a second culture. Results indicate that, depending on the dimension of acculturative stress and the home countries of the acquirer and acquired firms, some dimensions of cultural differences elicited perceptions of attraction rather than stress. For example, for the French, the salient dimension of acculturative stress appeared to be personal and societal responsibility, which the authors believe is due to the high premium the French place on the national culture dimension of collectivism. However, an unexpected finding of the study was that French firms acquired by other French firms experienced a higher degree of acculturative stress regarding the acquirer's personal and societal responsibility, while expressing attraction to that dimension for American acquirers. The results of this study indicate that some cultural problems associated with combining organizations are more amplified in domestic rather than in cross-national settings.

A subsequent study, using the same sample, by Very, Lubatkin, Calori & Veiga (1997) tended to support these findings, by indicating that cross-national mergers were not associated with higher levels of cultural difficulties, performance problems and autonomy removal.

The finding that cultural problems may be more salient in domestic, rather than in cross-national, settings was further supported in a study of 61 case studies by Larsson & Finkelstein (1999). Their research found that cross-border M&As marginally reduced employee resistance. The authors provide two possible reasons for this finding. First, combination potential may be more complementary and, thus, less threatening in cross-border combinations than in domestic M&As with overlapping operations. Second, cultural differences that can negatively affect integration in domestic M&As may be more carefully attended to in cross-border combinations.

Conversely, though, research has also related negative post-acquisition results to national culture differences. Krug & Hegarty (1997), in their study of 270 acquisitions of U.S. firms, found that acquired top management team (TMT) turnover was higher for foreign acquisitions of U.S. firms than for domestic acquisitions. Their study indicated that beyond the third year after acquisition, acquired TMT turnover in domestic acquisitions began mirroring turnover of non-acquired firms, whereas turnover remained significantly higher in the foreign acquisitions in the fourth and fifth years after acquisition. Surprisingly, though, the study did not find a significant difference in U.S. acquired TMT turnover between Anglo and non-Anglo foreign acquirers.

These results led Krug & Hegarty to suggest that integration may be a longer process in foreign acquisitions and that differing measures need to be designed to account for cultural differences between the combining firms that may not manifest themselves until the later stages of the post-acquisition process.

Krug & Nigh (1998) found national culture differences to play an even stronger role in TMT turnover in a cross-border study of 103 acquisitions of U.S. manufacturing firms. They found that TMT departures in U.S. companies acquired by a non-U.S. firm are positively associated with the cultural distance between the U.S. and home country of the foreign multinational. In addition, they found that the level of international integration among subunits of multi-national firms within the target industry and the foreign acquirer's U.S. acquisition experience were also positively related to TMT turnover. These findings indicate the complex nature of TMT turnover, which involves an acquirer's judgment of its experiences and capabilities, as well as those of the target's, in achieving cross-border post-acquisition integration and operational performance.

Organizational Cultures

Similar to national culture, organizational culture has also been found to affect the nature of integration practices. Research indicates that organizational culture dissimilarity, between combining organizations, and its effects on post-acquisitions performance tend to be underestimated by acquirers.

An early anthropological study by Sales & Mirvis (1984) illustrated the impact of cultural differences on the integration process over a three-year period. They found that differences in culture (philosophy, values, norms of interpersonal behavior, and business related behaviors) led to polarization, negative evaluations of counterparts, anxiety and ethnocentrism between members of the acquiring and acquired TMT, during the first year after the closing of the deal. After three years, most hostile behaviors diminished, although differences in philosophy, values and norms of interpersonal behaviors remained. Differences in business related behaviors diminished as the acquired TMT assimilated into the new company.

The salience of organizational culture is also evident in a case study by Greenwood, Hinings & Brown (1994) that studied the merger process between two professional service firms. Their study indicated that even with proper consideration for organizational fit, during the courtship phase of the M&A process, cultural differences between the two firms inevitably lead to conflict during post-acquisition integration. Their findings suggest that firms may become enamoured by strategic fit, thus resulting in a relatively superficial examination of organizational compatibility. Or, perhaps, strategic fit blinds the parties to cultural dissimilarities, during the courtship phase of the M&A process, thus causing an underestimation of the magnitude of the integration issues at hand.

The difficulties inherent in integrating firms with differing organizational cultures has led some researchers to suggest that M&As be confined to organizations with similar cultures. Several studies indicate that M&As among firms with similar cultures result in more effective merger performance.

A study of 52 related acquisitions by Chatterjee, Lubatkin, Schweiger & Weber (1992) was the first to examine the relationship between differences in acquiring and acquired TMT cultures and the post-acquisition stock market performance of related acquisitions. Using event study methodology, they found a strong relationship between cultural differences and stock market performance. An extension of that study (Lubatkin, Schweiger & Weber, 1999), using 36 related acquisitions, found that cultural differences were significantly related to TMT turnover in the first year after the acquisition, for a combined sample of manufacturing firms and banks, but not in the fourth year. However, cultural differences were marginally related to turnover for banks in the fourth year.

Weber & Pliskin (1996), in a study of 69 acquisitions, investigated the effectiveness of integrating information systems of merged organizations that were information technology intensive. Their study found that the information systems integration and merger effectiveness, which were based on several organizational dimensions, were superior for firms with more similar cultures.

A study by van Oudenhoven & de Boerovin (1995) clearly indicates that managers are aware of the problems that cultural differences can create. In a laboratory experiment, they found that 90 managers of a Dutch organization preferred acquiring a firm with a similar culture, and that cultural similarity is positively related to degree of integration. Managers show a greater willingness to merge with a similar partner, estimate the chance of success to be higher and expect less resistance to the merger within their own company. The authors suggest, from these findings, that acquirers perceive being different as manageable, as long as the partners to the combination do not require a high level of integration.

The results of the studies cited indicate cultural differences have a significant and positive impact on acquired TMT turnover and a negative impact on subsequent financial performance. Surprisingly, in the case of cross-border deals, the results are varied. Several studies have attempted to explain these findings. They have alluded to, but have not directly examined, the role that expectations, interventions and time play in managing the effects of culture. This is certainly a ripe area for research.

Integration Implementation Process

Another important area of research concerns the management of the integration process and its impact on the success of the integration. Included in this area are issues regarding autonomy, learning and involvement, communications, incentive structures and speed of integration. These categories have been chosen based on their ability to capture the research conducted, while providing unique perspectives on the complexity of the integration process.

Autonomy

Research has focused on the level of autonomy given to acquired TMTs after the deal is made. Research has described autonomy removal as a characteristic of relative standing, a condition contributing towards acquired executives' feelings of inferiority relative to acquiring executives, or acquiring executives viewing themselves as superior. The implications of this research are that maintaining relative standing of acquired executives, and even providing status bestowal (e.g. a role for acquired executives in the acquiring firm), enhances acquired executive retention. Retention, in turn, leads to a more successful integration and, thus, higher post-acquisition performance.

A case study of two merging firms by Shirley & Peters (1976) found that centralization of functions (i.e. a loss of autonomy) after the merger created motivational problems for the faculty of the smaller university. Centralization, which changed the culture of the smaller university from small and informal to large and bureaucratic, led to defensiveness and frustration by the faculty. It also led to a loss of control over events by, and diminution of status of, the acquired faculty.

A study by Bohl (1989) also found that of all changes made following an acquisition, centralization of activities created the most organizational problems. The number of problems, in descending order of frequency, were greatest for those acquisitions that centralized, eliminated management layers or made no changes in the autonomous organizational structure.

Cannella & Hambrick (1993), in a sample of 97 U.S. acquisitions, found that removal of autonomy from individuals, especially in the case of the senior-most executives, during the first two years after the acquisition was associated with executive departure. Moreover, those acquired executives who were given status (i.e. became an officer or director in the acquiring firm) were less likely to leave. Surprisingly, the relationships were reversed in the fourth year after the acquisition. Based on the findings, the authors suggest that the removal of autonomy signals a loss to the acquired executives, compounded by increased coordination requirements between acquirer and acquired executives that in turn results in antagonism between the two groups. However, the reversal after four years indicates that acquisitions create ongoing social dynamics that continue to change well after the closing.

Cannella & Hambrick also found that the departure of acquired executives from acquired firms leads to lower financial performance of the acquiring firm. The granting of status to at least one acquired executive was related to positive profitability. The results were more profound for the senior-most executives.

The negative findings of autonomy removal were also confirmed in a European study by Very et al. (1997). Their study of 106 acquisitions of French and British firms by French, British and U.S. acquirers indicated that removal of autonomy from individuals accustomed to high levels of autonomy caused performance (i.e. acquired TMT's perceptions of performance, based on earnings, sales, and market share) to deteriorate.

Research by Chatterjee et al. (1992), cited above, also found a strong relationship between autonomy removal and the post-acquisition stock performance of acquirers. An extension of this study, by Lubatkin, et al. (1999), specifically studied the fourth year turnover results of acquired executives. Their study indicates that autonomy removal was related to TMT turnover in the first year after the acquisition. It did not explain turnover in years two and three. However, the relationship was again significant in year four, with autonomy removal having a significantly greater effect on manufacturing firms than on banks.

While all the research cited above suggests that autonomy removal may be dysfunctional, Weber (1996) suggests that it does not necessarily follow that autonomy should be provided to the acquired management, to ensure M&A performance. In a study of 73 acquisitions of service and manufacturing firms, Weber found that autonomy removal was positively related to the performance (i.e. rate of increase in ROA) of M&As involving manufacturing firms, whereas it was negatively related for M&As involving banks. He explained these results by concluding that the negative effects of autonomy removal in less human-intensive industries may be more than offset by the synergy gains received from the higher level of integration.

Although not directly related to autonomy, one study of 230 acquisitions of manufacturing and mining firms, by Choi (1993), examined the relationship between merger type and post-merger organizational structure. The study found that a lateral managerial organizational structure (i.e. acquired firm's managers join the newly merged firm's top management) was used more often for horizontal mergers than for conglomerate mergers. On the other hand, a vertical structure (i.e. acquired firm's managers become subordinates of the acquiring firm's managers, or are replaced) is used more often in conglomerate mergers.

These findings make sense since, in a horizontal merger, the businesses being combined are similar and can be managed through a single TMT. In a conglomerate, the diversity of businesses requires separate management teams to run each business, but requires vertical control mechanisms to ensure that each business' managers interests are aligned with those of the corporation. Although not directly examined, the author notes that more focus needs to be given to post-merger compensation systems and the impact that they have in influencing the behavior of acquired managers.

Learning and Involvement

The management of the integration transition process can significantly affect the success of the subsequent integration (Marks & Mirvis, 1998). The objective of this process is to ensure that conditions for cooperation, commitment and learning, among people from merging firms, are created and that decisions on how to combine the firms are based on sound information (Schweiger, 1999). To that end, several studies have examined the integration transition process. Studies have broadly examined two issues, involvement of acquired people in the integration process and approaches for facilitating learning between the combining firms.

Fostering involvement.

In a case study of three cross-border Dutch and German international mergers, Olie (1994) observed an effort to preserve parity (i.e., the balancing of positions assigned to acquiring and acquired firm's managers) between the merging firms. This was accomplished through a transition structure of equal representation, from both firms, on the board of directors and in other key management positions. Although this structure was found to initially eliminate conflict, it did not lead to a true integration of the two firms. The study found that this structure did not reconcile the different styles of management between the Dutch (congenial and informal) and German (autocratic and formal) firms, and distrust between certain departments was never reconciled (i.e. sales departments retained their pre-merger perceptions as competitors). In addition, board members felt a greater attachment to their respective home structures than to the newly combined firm. Integration did not take hold until the parity of power, responsibility and authority, between the Dutch and German firms, was abandoned and board members and managers in key positions were primarily selected on the basis of managerial capability. Only under this structure were the combined firms able to shape a common identity that allowed for the benefits of integration.

The post-acquisition structure of the successful International Computers Ltd (ICL) acquisition of Nokia-Data (ND) in 1991 (Mayo & Hadaway, 1994) supports the Olie findings. This combination created managerial positions that were granted based on capability, rather than parity, with the acquired firm overseeing a majority of the combined firm's operations in Europe.

In addition, the ICL-ND combination utilized in-house integration teams, consisting of managers from both companies, to reach conclusions together on proposals regarding organization, process and people. Training in national inter-cultural understanding between the U.K. and Finnish firms, respectively, and persuading managers deemed critical to the integration process to stay, aided the integration process. Moreover, an integration director position in headquarters was created to assist and support (not direct) the integration process, and full-time local integration managers were appointed to coordinate various integration activities at the local level. This transition structure exhibited that integration was a serious exercise, requiring dedicated resources and involvement of all participants, and, as such, the combined firm was able to understand the importance of shared education to build shared visions and values.

Research by Gerpott (1995), involving 96 acquisitions between German manufacturing firms, studied the relationship between the degree of involvement and the post-acquisition success of integrating firms' R&D functions. Results indicate that interventions, fostering open information exchange between both partners and ensuring that decision-making responsibilities for strategic R&D issues are clearly taken over by the acquirer's top management, seem to be particularly effective in promoting R&D integration success in the first three years after a deal. In addition to finding that a high degree of involvement aided the integration of R&D functions, integration success was also found to be significantly influenced by acquisition management interventions both before and after a deal is formally closed.

Also supporting a high degree of involvement in integrating combining organizations is a study of synergy realization, involving 61 domestic and cross-border acquisitions, by Larsson & Finkelstein (1997). They found that the extent of interaction and coordination during the organizational integration process was the strongest predictor of synergy realization. The authors argue that it may not be enough for a merger or acquisition to have potential synergies to exploit. Structural and process changes must be undertaken that allow those synergies to be realized.

Promoting learning.

A number of studies have focused on promoting learning during the integration process. It is argued that by facilitating interaction and the sharing of information and feelings, conflict between people of combining companies will be more effectively managed, and better solutions for the 'new' organization will be reached. These then will result in a more effective integration process.

A study by Blumberg & Weiner (1971), of two geographically separate units of a voluntary community organization, found that inter-group mirroring workshops, between merging management teams, facilitated the integration.

Blake & Mouton (1984), in a study of a chemical company acquired by another chemical company, found that collaborative problem solving and inter-group mirroring workshops, between the top management teams, reduced misperceptions and inter-group conflict and facilitated the implementation of the integration. Marks & Mirvis (1985) found that when two management teams of a hospital merger reconciled interpersonal issues (e.g. values, philosophy, perceptions of one another) first, they were better able to manage technical issues.

In a merger of two banks, Buono & Bowditch (1989) found that when the management teams of both banks focused only on the task issues associated with integration, early in the integration process, ethnocentric attitudes and defensiveness developed. These in turn contributed to the failure of transition teams. Teams that were formed later in the merger, and that addressed both interpersonal and technical issues, performed well.

Leroy & Ramanantsoa (1997), in a study involving the merger of two previously acquired companies into the same division of a French organization, found that learning was the result of a systematic comparison of organizational differences between merging firms. Moreover, they found that the post-acquisition phase is a complex learning process that is enhanced by merger workshops. These workshops reduced negative feelings, resulting from the merger, by engaging employees in understanding the logic or rationale of the merger. The employees jointly participated in determining best practices to be used in the combined firm. These workshops resulted in enhanced employee teamwork, cooperation and commitment to cultural change and integration.

The Leroy & Ramanantsoa findings are consistent with that of the study involving the ICL acquisition of ND, discussed earlier. ICL clearly stated that its desire was not to destroy, but to learn from, cultural differences between the two firms that would have a positive effect on the management of the new business (Mayo & Hadaway, 1994). Both studies indicate the importance of creating a 'win-win' context, by promoting learning between the two combining organizations and by avoiding the supremacy of the acquirer over the acquired firm.

Organizational learning, resulting from dissimilarities between combining firms, was also supported by a study of 147 acquisitions, conducted by Krishnan,

Miller & Judge (1997). Their study found that organizational learning resulted from merging dissimilar TMTs and that differences in functional backgrounds of TMT members had a positive effect on post-acquisition performance. This ability of merging firms to learn from different TMTs was supported by the additional finding that differences in functional backgrounds are more easily integrated into the new organization while similarities led to redundancy and conflict.

Research has also addressed the process of learning in cross-border acquisitions. In a study of 35 acquisitions of Central East European companies, by western companies, Villinger (1996) found that both Western and Central Eastern European firms placed greater value on managers' general business skills than on their cross-border management skills (e.g. understanding of the partner's language, general sensitivity to the merger partner). Paradoxically, though, the author also found that these same cross-border skills proved to be more important in facilitating learning and successful integration. These findings led the author to suggest that, following an international acquisition, language training and cultural awareness workshops should become a main focus of employee development, to facilitate learning and the consequent transfer of business-related skills.

Hakanson (1995) examined the integration of R&D units in three cross-border acquisitions by three Swedish multinational companies. He found that managerial, sociocultural, technical and procedural issues were critical to successful integration, especially in symbiotic acquisitions (see Haspeslagh & Jemison, 1991). With respect to managerial and sociocultural integration, communication, leadership, involvement of acquired people and face-to-face personal relationships among people from both organizations were important to facilitate partnerships and collaborative working environments.

A study by Haleblian & Finkelstein (1999) addressed another aspect of learning. Rather than focusing on the process of learning, among counterparts of combining companies, they focused on whether companies learn and improve their acquisition performance with experience. In a study involving 449 acquisitions of manufacturers, they found that relatively inexperienced acquirers, after making their first acquisition, inappropriately generalize to the next acquisition. More experienced acquirers, however, appropriately distinguish between their acquisitions. The results suggest that, with increased experience, acquirers do indeed learn what does and does not apply from previous contexts and utilize that information to improve the subsequent performance of acquisitions. Moreover, performance is greater in cases where firms make acquisitions similar to those that they made in the past.

Communications

Communications has been identified as the major intervention for reducing the uncertainty of people going through a merger and acquisition. It has been argued that such uncertainty can create numerous dysfunctional effects for employees and undermine the integration process. A number of studies have examined the impact of communications.

A three-case study by Bastien (1987) examined the impact of acquisition on 21 acquired managers. He found that formal communications appeared to be associated with both positive reactions toward the acquirer, stabilization of volatile situations and minimization of management resignations. Regardless of the form of communication, honesty was found to be important.

Napier (1989) studied the communication process in two merging banks. Based on 24 interviews and survey data from 103 others, she found that lack of communications was related to decreased trust and increased anxiety on the part of employees.

In a study of 51 firms, Shanley (1988) examined the effects of communication on perceived acquisition performance. There were significant positive relationships between the use of training or information programs and the placement of acquiring corporate personnel at the acquired firm's site.

Bohl (1989), in a study of 109 firms, found that there was less productivity loss and employee turnover for acquiring firms that communicated with employees about developments associated with the merger. There was, however, no impact on financial performance.

Schweiger & DeNisi (1991) examined the impact of communication during a merger on a number of employee reactions, all of which are believed to affect the success of the integration process. Using a longitudinal field experiment, with a control and experimental communication intervention, the authors found that employee reactions declined after the announcement of a merger. Moreover, they found that, in the control plant, these reactions continued to deteriorate over time. In the experimental plant (i.e. the communication intervention plant), employee reactions stabilized, but did not return to pre-announcement levels over time.

Incentive Structures

Acquired TMT members are believed to play a critical role in the post-acquisition transfer of knowledge and capabilities from acquired firms to acquirers. Given the value of these employees to the combined organization, measures, such as incentive structures, to retain acquired TMT members can play a key role in post-acquisition performance. Unfortunately, little research has been conducted in this area.

One such study by Ghosh & Ruland (1998), involving 212 large U.S. acquisitions, found that ownership sharing was a legitimate incentive to retain acquired top managers. They found that managers of an acquired firm are more likely to remain in the combined firm when they receive shares in the new firm, as payment for their ownership interests in the acquired firm. In fact, the findings indicate that jobs were not retained, following payments with stock, in only 10 percent of the acquisitions. However, their study also indicates that acquiring managers, who value continued control of the acquiring company, prefer to pay cash to avoid diluting their existing holdings. As a result, this study suggests that a conscious effort, to integrate acquired management into the combined organization, must be made by the acquirer and the sharing of ownership control appears to be an incentive structure that aids in this process, by reducing acquired TMT turnover.

Speed of Integration

There is plenty of conventional wisdom concerning the speed of the integration process (Schweiger & Walsh, 1990). Speed can best be defined as the time it takes to make changes in the buyer, seller, or both and thus integrate the firms. There are two camps of thought on the issue of speed. The first camp suggests that targets be integrated slowly. The buyer should take time to get to know the target firm, its people, culture, operations, markets, etc. before making changes. This is probably due to the lack of completeness of the due diligence or pre-closing acquisition integration planning process. The second camp suggests that the integration process should move quickly. Quickness avoids periods of uncertainty in direction, both in the organization and in the marketplace. It also sets an early expectation that changes will be made and mitigates some of the buildup of political resistance to change.

To date, there has been little research to answer this question. A recent study by PricewaterhouseCoopers (1997), of 124 medium to large companies that executed a merger or acquisition within the last three years, provides some evidence on this issue. They found that companies that managed the transition faster had more favorable gross margins, cash flows, productivity, profitability and speed to market; 89% of those surveyed felt that they should have managed the transition even more quickly. Unfortunately, there is not much precision in the definition of speed. Respondents indicated whether the transition was managed more or less quickly than their normal pace of work. Speed of integration of operating policies was also reported to have an effect on employee reactions. More rapid integration led to greater confidence in company direction, clarity of company direction, product focus and speed of decision making. Moreover, more rapid integration was associated with acceptance of new vision, employee commitment and motivation, customer relations and communications to employees and customers. It should be noted that the study reports frequency data, no inferential statistical tests between fast and slow integrators are reported.

Secondary findings of several other studies do provide some indication of the virtues of a fast versus slow integration process and the context in which one or the other may be expected to lead to greater post-acquisition performance. In a case study of three international mergers by Olie (1994), a slow integration process was used to minimize conflict between the merging partners. Parity (i.e., balancing of management positions between the two companies), for example, was instituted between the power, responsibility, and authority positions of combining firms' management teams. However, this process was later blamed for the combined firm's inability to develop cooperation within the board and management levels, along with a common identity necessary for post-acquisition performance. The slow integration process used by these firms was actually found to inhibit, rather than enhance, integration.

On the other hand, Mayo & Hadaway (1994) found that the successful acquisition of ND, by ICL, was the result of selectively and simultaneously utilizing both slow and fast approaches to integration. They indicate that a key to the success of the merger was allowing time for each partner to learn about each other and for ICL to identify merger priorities. Change was phased in over time, without stripping either company of the areas it valued most. On the other hand, the two companies decided to begin to work on a new range of products, which appealed to the acquired employees who were weary of the acquirer's bureaucracy and potential inability to maintain the acquired firm's responsive decision making practices. Furthermore, the decision was made to change every ND sign in its home country of Finland to an ICL sign on the date of acquisition approval and to engage in press and other media campaigns to leave no doubt about the acquisition. This study clearly indicates that the speed of integration is complex, in that some facets of integration may be best suited for slow speed, while others for fast.

Based on his research findings regarding the integration of R&D functions among combining manufacturing firms, Gerpott (1995) also suggests that speed is a complex issue. He found that human resource-focused integration plans and actions that help to promote a gradual process in which individuals from two organizations learn to work together and cooperate in the transfer of strategic capabilities improve post-acquisition performance. He also found that the centralization of R&D within the acquirer appeared to quickly provide clear strategic

R&D objectives for the combined organization, resolute implementation of burdensome organizational changes and avoidance of endless discussions on a joint R&D strategy. Speed, thereby, substantially reduced the uncertainty among acquired firms' R&D professionals.

From a process perspective, Leroy & Ramanantsoa (1997) found that the speed at which integration occurred depends upon whether people were involved in a merger workshop. Employees engaged in the workshops were able to develop a shared diagnosis or vision of an improved combined entity. This created increased organizational commitment and openness to post-acquisition integration and, consequently, quicker integration. In addition, the authors argued that encouraging learning between the merging firms which combines both cognitive learning, based on rational processes, and behavioral learning, based on experimental learning, also improves the speed of integration.

Integration Decision Process

A variety of acquisition characteristics have been studied and found to have a significant effect on the integration decision process. The results of this research has provided an understanding of not only those characteristics that influence the integration process, but also under what conditions those characteristics become most salient.

Haspeslagh & Jemison (1991) examine how decisions and actions throughout the acquisition process affect integration. Although the issues discussed fall into many of the categories in this section, we review their work for sake of brevity. They observed that many managers fail to consider how their decision-making process affects their decision or the acquisition outcome. Managers tend to define the value of acquisitions from a financial perspective, as opposed to a strategic and organization one. Haspeslagh & Jemison point out that often firms forfeit the benefits of acquisitions by insisting on compliance with a predetermined path or by avoiding changes all together in an effort to minimize resistance and change. Key to integration is obtaining the participation of the people involved, without compromising the strategic task. Their research found that acquisition integration involved adapting pre-acquisition views to embrace reality, an ability to create the atmosphere necessary for capability transfer, the leadership to provide a common vision, and careful management of the interactions between the organizations (1991: 11). The success of a particular acquisition depends on the managers' ability to reconcile the need for strategic interdependence between the two firms that is required to transfer strategic capabilities and the need for organizational autonomy of the acquired firm that is required to preserve the acquired strategic capabilities. However, because there are many purposes for acquisitions, there is no one best way to integrate.

Haspeslagh & Jemison view integration as an interactive and gradual process in which individuals from two organizations learn to work together and cooperate in the transfer of strategic capabilities. "Creating an atmosphere that can support the integration process is the real challenge" (1991: 106). Their research suggests that this atmosphere has five key ingredients: a reciprocal understanding of each firm's organization and culture, the willingness of people in both firms to work together after the acquisition, the capacity to transfer and receive the capability, discretionary resources to help foster the atmosphere needed to support the transfer, and a cause-effect understanding of the benefits expected from the acquisition (1991: 110–111).

They argue that acquisition integration should be seen as a two-phase process. The first phase sets the stage for the actual integration, largely by addressing the interaction issues that determine the atmosphere and shape the context in the period immediately following an acquisition. Only in the second phase should managers pursue the realization of synergies across organizations. The successful acquirers they studied tackled the stage-setting phase by pursuing seven key tasks: establishing interface management, putting operations on an even keel, instilling a new sense of purpose, taking stock and establishing control, strengthening the acquired organization, developing mutual understanding, and building credibility (1991:173).

In a study by Pablo (1994), of executives of 56 acquiring organizations, task, cultural and political characteristics of acquisitions were studied to determine their influence on decisions regarding levels of integration (i.e., the degree of post-acquisition change in an organization's technical, administrative, and cultural configuration). The study found that task-related criteria were the dominant characteristics associated with managers' integration decisions, accounting for nearly 75% of the total explained variance. Of this, nearly two-thirds was explained by organizational task needs, which reflected the desire to maintain some level of structural differentiation between the combining organizations, and one-third by strategic task needs, which reflected the need to develop links between combining firms' value activities.

Pablo's study also indicated that multiculturalism, or the degree to which the management of the acquiring firm tolerates and values a diversity of values, philosophies and beliefs, is negatively related to the level of integration chosen. Interestingly, industry classification was found to influence integration decision policies. Managers in service industries were more heavily influenced by information about multiculturalism than were managers in manufacturing industries. This led Pablo to suggest that culture is a more salient issue in acquisitions of service organizations, since such organizations compete largely on the basis of relationships among organizational actors – thus making culture a key success factor.

The study also indicated that a lack of compatibility of acquisition visions between the combining firms elicited higher levels of integration, suggesting that perhaps incongruent goals may provoke the acquirer to increase hierarchical control mechanisms over the acquired firm, in an effort to reduce agency problems. On the other hand, power differentials were negatively related to the level of integration chosen. This suggests that relative size of an acquired firm is not perceived as a basis of power, but rather as a factor influencing management attention to an acquisition, with relatively small acquired firms remaining virtually autonomous because they do not attract a high level of management attention.

As noted earlier, van Oudenhoven & de Boerovin (1995) found that managers are more willing to merge with a firm that has a similar culture, in addition to expecting a greater chance for success and less resistance to the merger within their own company. Further, they found that if the required level of integration is to be low, cultural differences seem to matter less. Consequently, van Oudenhoven & de Boerovin suggest that if there is a large cultural gap between the merging parties, they should strive for a less intensive form of integration, or degree of involvement, between the combining entities. Other findings of this study indicate that managers are more willing to merge, and expect more success, with a firm that has a similar strategic profile, when the departments within the combining organizations are only slightly discrepant in capability. Otherwise, partners with dissimilar strategic profiles are preferred. The authors suggest that these findings indicate that managers react to the appeal of a strategically different (complementary) partner because it can compensate for the mediocre or poor strategic aspects of their own company. Therefore, degree of integration would appear to be positively related to perceptions of rewards achieved through either similarity or dissimilarity of a given partner.

Capron & Hulland (1999), in their research involving 253 acquisitions of manufacturing firms, studied the effect of relative size of the acquired company on the integration decision process. Their study examined the redeployment of key marketing resources following horizontal acquisitions. It was found that although general marketing expertise is redeployed from the acquirer to the acquired firm, it was not frequently redeployed from the target to the acquirer, except when the served markets of the two firms were very similar or the acquired firm's resource strength (relative size) was high. This relationship existed even though longer-term advantages appeared to accrue to those firms willing to redeploy marketing expertise bi-directionally. These results tend to confirm Pablo's findings and explanation that relatively small acquired firms may be subject to a lower degree of integration than larger ones, simply because they do not attract the same level of acquirer management attention.

QUESTIONS THAT REMAIN: RESEARCH OPPORTUNITIES

As noted in this review, there has been significant research on areas related to M&A integration during the past 15 years. Unfortunately, most of this research, with the exception of culture and acquired firm TMT turnover, has not been systematic and linked to any comprehensive theory.

The accumulated evidence, however, does suggest that both national and organizational culture, the management of the integration process and integration decisions play an important role in influencing a variety of outcome measures, including the financial performance of M&As.

In spite of this research there remain many unanswered questions on what contributes to M&A integration effectiveness and, thus, many opportunities exist for future theory development and research. It is important to note that many of the opportunities we identify are derived from both our observations of the integration problems and challenges that executives face today and the research literature. These are presented below.

Linking Other M&A Activities with Integration

With the exception of the work by Haspeslagh & Jemison (1991) and Jemison & Sitkin (1986a, b) there is little empirical research that has systematically examined the extent to which continuity/fragmentation, among those who value and price deals, conduct due diligence and integrate M&As, impacts value creation. For example, 89% of companies use some form of discounted cash flow (DCF) to value investment opportunities, such as acquisitions (Brunner, Eades, Harris, & Higgins, 1998). DCF depends upon the accuracy of revenue, cost, and investment projections, all of which are realized after a deal has been closed. If projections are not realistic or do not accurately account for the ability of the acquirer to make necessary changes in either the target or buyer after the deal is closed, the acquirer is likely to overpay for the target and, thus, value creation will suffer (Csiszar & Schweiger, 1994). Further, if the price paid for the target includes a premium for which synergies are estimated, the likelihood of value creation is even lower (Sirower, 1997).

This line of reasoning suggests that continuity, communication and the sharing of information among those involved in all aspects of the M&A process is essential for value creation. Those valuing and pricing deals need to communicate with those integrating targets, so that realistic forecasts are developed prior to closing and that realistic goals are focused on during integration. Those conducting due diligence must communicate with those integrating targets so that the latter are aware of all issues identified early (e.g. culture, management talent) that might affect integration success. Clearly research linking the pre- and post-closing stages of acquisitions is needed.

As importantly, research needs to examine the full scope of the integration process and determine the extent to which activities throughout the entire process (e.g. cultural due diligence, initial contact with the target) impact integration, synergy realization and financial performance of the acquisition. For example, are companies that conduct cultural due diligence more successful than companies that do not?

There is a ripe opportunity for researchers to examine the extent to which project management methodologies can be employed to enhance continuity of the process and to ensure that integration is managed in a timely manner. Many companies today, especially those that are very acquisitive, have developed somewhat standardized project management templates and processes.

Another interesting area of exploration is based on Haleblian & Finkelstein's (1999) findings that companies improve their acquisition performance with experience. While the finding is interesting, it leaves many questions as to how experience converts to learning and improvements in the way acquisitions are managed. Research focused on what managers learn from experience, and how they convert (i.e. institutionalize) that learning into new and improved practices, would be quite useful.

Culture

No research has addressed the possibility of an industry (as opposed to national or organizational) level of culture that may affect the integration process. Although research addresses some effects that human-intensive industries versus capital-intensive industries appear to have on the integration process, it does not address characteristics, such as an industry's rate of consolidation, that could affect an organization's norms, values, and beliefs. For example, would an acquired organization be less resistant to post-acquisition change if its industry were experiencing a high rate of consolidation; i.e. would the level of acquisition activity in an industry set norms of behavior that would enable acquired firms to be more accepting of integration measures? Research needs to be performed in this area to determine the true complexities of culture and its impact on the integration process and post-acquisition performance.

Although implied by the literature, research is yet to verify that national cultural differences are more salient, during the acquisition process, than are organizational or functional cultural differences. It has been suggested that perhaps acquirers are more sensitive to national cultural differences and that this heightened sensitivity leads to more comprehensive assessments of dissimilarities between the combining organizations. This heightened attention to issues affecting integration results in more effective integration procedures and post-acquisition outcomes. Empirical research needs to verify the existence of this phenomenon and the extent of its effect on the integration decision process. Understanding the dimensions of cultural differences between combining firms that elicit management attention would provide a greater insight into the reasons why some seemingly similar organizations may fail at the integration process while others, which are quite different, may succeed.

Moreover, it would be useful to learn more about functional area cultures and integration, since specific functions, rather than entire organizations, are often integrated (Schweiger, 1999). That such functional area cultures may have an impact on integration is suggested by the work of Lawrence & Lorsch (1967). Their seminal research clearly established that different functional areas have different orientations that impact their relations with each other. Taken one step further, it is plausible that different functional cultures exist within the same function across different merging organizations. In a recent acquisition, two research and development units, with completely different orientations, were combined. One unit was very academic and the other very commercially focused.

Management of the Integration Process

To date, very little is still known about the management of the integration process itself, although research has provided support for the value of involving acquired company people in the integration process and interventions to facilitate learning. Although these findings are interesting, research needs to examine conditions under which involvement may not be warranted. In particular, there is an extensive body of research on managerial discipline that suggests that takeovers may be used to rid a company of poor management, based on prior poor performance (Schweiger & Walsh, 1990). Thus involvement may be beneficial when those included have been successful and their retention is important to the success of the merger.

Many practitioners (e.g. Galpin & Herndon, 2000; Marks & Mirvis, 1998) recommend the use of transition structures as a means of integrating M&As. These include the use of transition and integration teams. In fact, their use has become conventional wisdom. However, little research has systematically examined whether such structures are effective or whether other structures or approaches would be more effective. Moreover, there have been no studies that have addressed whether one type of structure suits all M&As or whether different structures should be used depending upon the relative size of the acquired company (e.g. small acquisition vs. equal sized merger) or the integration approach desired.

Additional descriptive and normative research needs to examine how integration is and should be managed across different organizational contexts. For example, are there differences in how companies manage and integrate small versus large acquired firms or mega-mergers? Are there differences in companies that have divisional and corporate people involved in the acquisition process? How should these people coordinate to ensure that the integration process remains systematic and integrated with front-end valuations? Are there differences in the integration process for firms that are highly acquisitive (e.g. to consolidate a fragmented industry) versus those where acquisition is an occasional activity? Are there differences, other than cultural ones (e.g. access to information, legal requirements), that affect the integration process of domestic versus international companies? These are just a few of the many questions that, if answered, would help improve the effectiveness of acquisition integration.

Research on Interventions

More integration research, systematically linked to different frameworks of integration, would be helpful. Although researchers have utilized different contextual variables, such as the relatedness of the acquisition, the relative size of the acquired firm and the hostile nature of the deal, there has been little examination of the impact that approaches to integration have. Does physical consolidation of assets and people require the same interventions as does autonomy or standardization with physical independence? How do firms pursuing different approaches successfully achieve integration or synergy? For example, a large bank may acquire a small bank in a new geographic market. It may choose to physically consolidate information systems into a single geographical location, but choose to standardize branch operations and leave them physically separate.

Need for a Comprehensive Theory

Although many aspects of integration have been addressed by research, there exists a need to consolidate the findings of these studies in an effort to significantly advance M&A theory and practice. As noted throughout this review there is a general lack of programmatic research on integration. Antecedents of, and the context surrounding, M&As need to be simultaneously and parsimoniously linked to integration processes and procedures that will lead to post-acquisition performance. Specifically, research needs to more effectively determine to what degree integration is firm specific. A comprehensive understanding of integration issues that can be generalized across acquisitions must be obtained before theory can be developed and extended in a meaningful way.

A Note on Methodology

It is encouraging to see the balance of methodologies that have been employed by researchers in studying integration. Case studies have been very helpful in identifying critical issues. Larger sample studies, particularly longitudinal studies, have also been helpful in understanding the generalizability of findings. The continuous interplay between these methods is critical to advancing our understanding of this complex phenomenon.

With some exceptions (e.g. Schweiger & DeNisi, 1991), however, there have been very few field experiments. Such studies would provide us with a better understanding of causality, especially with regard to practices and interventions that can facilitate the integration process. We do note, however, that access to organizations to conduct such studies is extremely difficult and presents a major challenge to significantly advancing research in this area.

Finally, research must broaden the sample of M&As examined. Future case studies and large sample research should systematically include, but not be limited to, a broad variety of acquisitions with different objectives, relative sizes of acquired companies, integration approaches, and historical performances of acquiring and acquired firms. Only by broadening the context of M&As can we truly understand those factors that contribute to integration and financial success.

NOTES

1 The authors would like to thank Philippe Very for his insightful comments on an earlier version of this paper.

REFERENCES

Bastien, D. T. (1987). Common patterns of behavior and communication in corporate mergers and acquisitions. *Human Resource Management, 26*, 17–34.
Bastien, D. T., & Van de Ven, A. W. (1986). Managerial and organizational dynamics of mergers and acquisitions. *SMRC Discussion Paper No. 46*. University of Minnesota, Strategic Management Research Center.

Blake, R. R., & Mouton, J. S. (1984). Solving costly organizational conflicts: Achieving intergroup trust, cooperation, and teamwork. San Francisco: Jossey-Bass.

Blumberg, A., & Wiener, W. (1971). One from two: Facilitating an organizational merger. *Journal of Applied Behavioral Science, 7,* 87–102.

Bohl, D. L. (19890. Tying the corporate knot. New York: American Management Association.

Bruner, R. F., Eades, K. M., Harris, R. S., & Higgins, R. C. (1998). Best practices in estimating the cost of capital: Survey and synthesis. *Financial Practice and Education, 8,* 13–28

Buono, A. F. & Bowditch, J. L. (1989). The human side of mergers and acquisitions. San Francisco, CA: Jossey-Bass.

Calori, R., Lubatkin, M. & Very, P. (1994). Control mechanisms in cross-border acquisitions: An international comparison. *Organization Studies, 15*(3), 361–379.

Cannella, A. A., Jr., & Hambrick, D. C. (1993). Effects of executive departures on the performance of acquired firms. *Strategic Management Journal, 14,* 137–152.

Capron, L., & Hulland, J. (1999). Redeployment of brands, sales forces, and general marketing management expertise following horizontal acquisitions: A resource-based view. *Journal of Marketing, 63*(4), 41–54.

Cartwright, S., & Cooper, C. L. (1996). Managing Mergers, Acquisitions and Strategic Alliances: Integrating People and Cultures. Oxford: Butterworth-Heinemann Ltd.

Chatterjee, S., M.H. Lubatkin, Schweiger, D.M., & Weber, Y. (1992). Cultural differences and shareholder value in related mergers: Linking equity and human capital. *Strategic Management Journal, 13,* 319–334.

Choi, Y. K. 1993. The choice of organizational form: The case of post-merger managerial incentive structure. *Financial Management* (winter), 69–81.

Conference Board. July 13, (1999). Pulse Survey. The Conference Board's 1999 Post-Merger Integration Conference.

Csiszar, E. N., & Schweiger, D. M. (1994). An integrative framework for creating value through acquisition. In: H. E. Glass & B.N. Craven (Eds.), *Handbook of Business Strategy,* (93–115). New York, Warren, Gorham and Lamont.

Galpin, T. J., & Herndon. M. (2000). The complete guide to mergers and acquisitions. San Francisco: Jossey Bass.

Gerpott, T. J. 1995. Successful integration of R&D functions after acquisitions: An exploratory empirical study. *R&D Management, 25*(2), 161–178.

Ghosh, A., & Ruland, W. (1998). Managerial ownership, the method of payment for acquisitions, and executive job retention. *The Journal of Finance, 53*(2), 785–798.

Greenwood, R., Hinings, C. R., & Brown, J. (1994). Merging professional service firms. Organization Science, 5(2), 239–257.

Hakanson, L. (1995). Learning through acquisition: Management and integration of foreign R&D laboratories. *International Studies of Management and Organization, 25,* 121–157.

Haleblian, J., & Finkelstein, S. (1999). The influence of organizational acquisition experience on acquisition performance: A behavioral learning perspective. *Administrative Science Quarterly, 44,* 29–56.

Haspeslagh, P. C., & Farquhar, A. B. (1987). The acquisition integration process: A contingent framework. Paper presented at the meeting of the Strategic Management Society, Boston.

Haspeslagh, P. C., & Jemison, D. B. (1991). Managing acquisitions: Creating value through corporate renewal. New York: The Free Press.

Hofstede, G. (1980). Culture's Consequences: International Differences In Work-Related Values. Beverley Hills: Sage Publications.

Jemison, D. B., & Sitkin, S. B. (1986a). Corporate acquisitions: A process perspective. *Academy of Management Review*, 11, 145–163.

Jemison, D. B., & Sitkin, S. B. (1986b). Acquisitions: The process can be the problem. *Harvard Business Review*, *64*, 107–116.

Krishnan, H. A., Miller, A. & Judge, W. Q. (1997). Diversification and top management team complementarity: Is performance improved by merging similar or dissimilar teams? *Strategic Management Journal, 18*(5), 361–374.

Krug, J. A., & Nigh, D. (1998). Top management departures in cross-border acquisitions: Governance issues in an international context. *Journal of International Management, 4*, 267–287.

Krug, J. A., & Hegarty, W. H. (1997). Postacquisition turnover among U.S. top management teams: An analysis of the effects of foreign vs. domestic acquisitions of U.S. targets. *Strategic Management Journal, 18*(8), 667–675.

Lajoux, A. R. (1998). The art of M&A integration. New York: McGraw Hill.

Larsson, R., & Finkelstein, S. (1999). Integrating strategic, organizational and human resource perspectives on mergers and acquisitions: A case survey of synergy realization. *Organization Science, 10*(1), 1–26.

Lawrence, P. R., & Lorsch, J. W. 1967. Organization and environment. Boston, MA: Division of Research, Graduate School of Business Administration, Harvard University.

Leroy, F., & Ramanantsoa, B. (1997). The cognitive and behavioural dimensions of organizational learning in a merger: An empirical study. *Journal of Management Studies, 34*(6), 871–894.

Lubatkin, M., Calori, R., Very, P., & Veiga, J. (1998). Managing mergers across borders: A two-nation exploration of a nationally bound administrative heritage. *Organization Science, 9*(6), 670–684.

Lubatkin, M., Schweiger, D., & Weber, Y. (1999). Top management turnover in related M&As: An additional test of the theory of relative standing. *Journal of Management, 25*(1), 55–67.

Marks, M. L., & Mirvis, P. H. (1998). Joining forces. San Francisco: Jossey-Bass.

Marks, M. L., & Mirvis, P. H. (1985). Merger syndrome: Stress and uncertainty. *Mergers and Acquisitions, 20*, 50–55.

Mayo, A., & Hadaway, T. (1994). Cultural adaptation – the ICL-Nokia-Data merger 1991–92. *Journal of Management Development, 13*(2), 59–71.

Morosini, P., Shane, S., & Singh, H. (1998). National cultural distance and cross-border acquisition performance. *Journal of International Business Studies, 29*(1), 137–158.

Morosini, P., & Singh, H. (1994). Post-cross-border acquisitions: Implementing 'national culture-compatible' strategies to improve performance. *European Management Journal, 12*(4), 390–400.

Nahavandi, A., & Malekzedah, A. R. (1988). Acculturation in mergers and acquisitions. *Academy of Management Review, 13*, 79–90.

Napier, N. K. (1989). Mergers and acquisitions, human resource issues and outcomes: A review and suggested typology. *Journal of Management Studies, 26*, 271–289.

Olie, R. (1994). Shades of culture and institutions in international mergers. *Organization Studies, 15*(3), 381–405.

Pablo, A. L. (1994). Determinants of acquisition integration level: A decision-making perspective. *Academy of Management Journal, 37*(4), 803–836.

PricewaterhouseCoopers. (1997). A survey of mergers and acquisitions.

Sales, A. L.,& Mirvis, P. H. (1984). When cultures collide: Issues in acquisition. In: J. R. Kimberly & R. E. Quinn (Eds.), *Managing Organizational Transitions* (pp. 107–133). Homewood, IL: Irwin.

Schein, E. H. (1985). Organizational Culture and Leadership: A Dynamic View. San Francisco: Jossey-Bass.

Schmidt. J. A. (1999). Realizing the full value of a merger or acquisition: A risk management perspective. Towers Perrin.

Schweiger, D. M. (1999). Creating value through successfully integrating acquisitions. Unpublished manuscript.

Schweiger, D. M., & DeNisi, A. S. (1991). Communication with employees following a merger: A longitudinal field experiment, *Academy of Management Journal 34*(1), 110–135.

Schweiger, D. M., & Ivancevich, J. M. (1987). The effects of mergers and acquisitions on organizations and employees: A contingency view. Paper presented at the meeting of the Strategic Management Society, Boston.

Schweiger, D. M., & Walsh, J. P. (1990). Mergers and acquisitions: An interdisciplinary view. In: K. Rowland & G. Ferris (Eds.), *Research in Personnel and Human Resources Management, 8*, (41–107). Greenwich, CT: JAI Press Inc.

Securities Data Corporation. (1999). Contract research data.

Shanley, M. T. (1988). Reconciling the rock and the hard place: Management control versus human resource accommodation in acquisition integration. Unpublished paper, Graduate School of Business, University of Chicago.

Shirley, R. C., & Peters, M. H. (1976). University merger: A case of organizational change. *College and University*, (winter) 142–151.

Shrivastava, P. (1986). Postmerger integration. *Journal of Business Strategy, 7*, 65–76.

Sirower, M. L. (1997). The synergy trap. New York: The Free Press.

van Oudenhoven, J. P., & de Boer, T. (1995). Complementarity and similarity of partners in international mergers. *Basic and Applied Social Psychology, 17*(3), 343–356.

Very, P., Lubatkin, M., & Calori, R. (1996). A cross-national assessment of acculturative stress in recent European mergers. *International Studies of Management & Organizations, 26*(1), 59–86.

Very, P., Lubatkin, M., Calori, R., & Veiga, J. (1997). Relative standing and the performance of recently acquired European firms. *Strategic Management Journal, 18*(8), 593–614.

Villinger, R. (1996). Post-acquisition managerial learning in Central East Europe. *Organization Studies, 17*(2), 181–206.

Weber, Y. (1996). Corporate cultural fit and performance in mergers and acquisitions. *Human Relations, 49*(9), 1181–1202.

Weber, Y., & Pliskin, N. (1996). The effects of information systems integration and organizational culture on a firm's effectiveness. *Information & Management, 30*, 81–90.

Weber, Y., Shenkar, O., & Raveh, A. (1996). National and corporate cultural fit in mergers/acquisitions: An exploratory study. *Management Science, 42*(8), 1215–1227.

TAKEOVERS[1] AS A DISCIPLINARY MECHANISM?

R. J. Limmack

INTRODUCTION

The aim of the current chapter is to provide a review of the literature relating to the disciplinary role of takeovers. A major problem in attempting to achieve this aim is that while there is an abundance of literature that indirectly addresses this issue, few papers have specifically addressed it. As will be seen from the discussion below, many papers examine profitability or wealth changes arising following takeovers and only indirectly address the source of these changes. Others attempt to test other motives for takeovers and, by a process of elimination, impute efficiency (or rather synergistic) sources for the gains. A further body of literature examines other governance aspects and finds a relationship between a number of these and takeover threats. Readers will also discover a surprising lack of agreement over the conclusions reached from one of the most extensively researched aspects of corporate decision making. Disagreements exist over the methodologies adopted, samples investigated and even the questions addressed. Perhaps the lack of agreement is to be expected. Takeover activity is big business, not only for those involved in the activity itself but also for those who undertake research.

One of the dominant themes in the analysis of corporate activity has been the means by which it may be possible to resolve the agency problem caused by the separation of ownership and control. In the first (and revised) edition of their now-classic work Berle and Means identified the role of profits in both

Advances in Mergers and Acquisitions, Volume 1, pages 93–118 providing the inducement to individuals to undertake risky investments and also as the "spur ... to exercise his utmost skill in making his enterprise profitable" (Berle & Means, 1968, p. 300). They then proceed to point out that "only as profits are diverted into the pockets of control" (ibid p. 307) do they perform their second function. While most finance researchers would substitute the concept of wealth for that of profits, the sentiment remains the same. Given the separation of ownership and control, there needs to be incentives in the modern corporation to encourage managers to make decisions that are in the interests of owners. The implications of the above were further developed in the articulation of Agency Theory by Jensen & Meckling (1976) and, within a slightly different framework, by researchers into behavioural theories of the firm (Cyert & March, 1971). For this reason, modern corporate governance mechanisms include emphasis on the sharing of corporate wealth increases between owners and managers. Current emphasis on share option schemes is one example of how this may be achieved. It is of interest to note that, although share option schemes were also available in the 1950s and 1960s, these were not seen to have a long term future (Marris, 1971). Instead, some commentators placed more emphasis on the potential disciplinary nature of the takeover market on poorly performing firms and management. Others suggest that, at the least, takeovers can provide an external control device, if internal mechanisms are not sufficient (Manne, 1965).[2] It is also important to note that the takeover mechanism is often seen as complementary to, and not a substitute for, alternative governance mechanisms.

The disciplinary role of takeovers may be viewed as a mechanism for the transfer of control of resources in a target company either by means of an acquisition or, in the USA, by means of a proxy contest. Only in the former case will an actual ownership change take place. In the latter case it is sufficient for dissident shareholders to obtain partial control of the board of directors. Thus Jensen & Ruback (1983) described the takeover market, or market for corporate control, as "the market in which alternative management teams compete for the rights to manage corporate resources" (p.6). It is often predicted that, if the market for corporate control operates efficiently, poorly performing companies will be targets of takeover bids or proxy contests. If successful, then proxy contests can lead to changes in board policies. Indeed, even failed proxy contests and takeovers can lead to a shake up of management and an improvement in performance (Bradley, Desai & Kim, 1983, Limmack, 1991, 1994, Parkinson & Dobbins, 1993). In other cases, proxy contests can themselves lead to a full takeover bid (DeAngelo & DeAngelo, 1989).

In order for the market for corporate control to operate efficiently, in the manner described above, it is necessary for market participants to possess the ability to identify poorly performing companies. It is also important that a minimum of barriers exist to prevent the transfer of control. One aspect of published literature on takeover activity has been the number of studies that have questioned, either directly or otherwise, whether market participants are able to identify such companies. These studies have also used a variety of performance measures including accounting measures, security returns and, more recently, cash flow measures. There has, however, been much less attention given explicitly to studies that have examined the impact of potential (and actual) barriers to transfer of control, including regulatory barriers, defensive tactics by targets and financial barriers.

Initial studies of the financial impact of takeover activity often concentrated on the measurement of prior performance characteristics of the companies involved. Other studies, in a similar tradition, attempted to identify those characteristics that may have distinguished takeover targets from other companies.[3] Many of these studies used accounting data to define the above characteristics. Later studies, which developed from a perspective of efficient securities markets, measured the share price reaction of companies involved in takeovers, in an attempt to identify the distribution of any wealth changes. Studies rarely attempted to directly identify the source of any wealth changes, for example whether they were due to synergistic aspects of the takeover, exercise of monopoly power, or efficiency gains.[4] In later studies, increased recognition was given to potential managerial motives for takeovers. Some of the motivation for these later studies was the perceived negative long run wealth effects that earlier research had identified, for shareholders of bidding companies. A body of literature has emerged that suggested, rather than being a solution to the agency problem and a possible disciplinary mechanism, takeovers may actually be part of the problem itself. This literature may also be seen as one of the developments of the managerial theory of the firm expressed by earlier researchers, including Marris (1964) & Mueller (1969). There has therefore been a wide variation in views expressed on the potential disciplinary role of takeovers. Thus, while Posner (1976) claimed that there are beneficial effects for the U.S. economy from mergers, Scherer (1977) argued that they represented a 'sterile game' which "diverts management attention from running existing operations well." A number of other studies have suggested that recent takeover activity has provided 'an adaptive response' to changes in world market conditions and that these changes could not easily have been produced without the threat (or actuality) of takeover.[5] In the review article cited at the beginning of this paper Jensen & Ruback (1983) suggest that corporate takeovers provide positive gains and that these gains are not the result of the exercise of monopoly power (p. 47). Later studies have questioned the conclusion of positive gains, not least because of the identification of long run negative returns to shareholders of acquiring companies (see, for example, Ruback, 1988, Limmack, 1991, Agrawal, Jaffe & Mandelker, 1992, Gregory 1997, Loughran & Vijh, 1997). While the jury may still be out on this particular issue, it is clear that many early studies contained, what are now perceived to be, methodological errors, which either account for their results or at least for the variation in results across studies.

As well as the direct influence that takeovers may have there is also the possibility that the threat of takeover may itself be a spur to further action, resulting in improved performance. Pickering (1983) for example suggests that, for some firms that had previously experienced poor performance, the "sense of crisis at the receipt of an unwanted takeover bid had created a favourable opportunity for internal change" (p. 275). Recent literature, on various aspects of corporate restructuring, has often found that the restructuring arrangements are conducted as a response to the threat of takeover. A related strand of literature is that which has attempted to place the role of takeovers within the context of alternative corporate governance mechanisms. In this latter stream, the takeover market is often seen as the market of last resort, if all other mechanisms fail.

The current chapter will identify the major approaches that have been adopted, in addressing the question as to whether takeovers are an effective disciplinary mechanism, and will also review the major findings to date. The structure of the remainder of the chapter is as follows:

In Section (ii), a brief review is provided of papers that have attempted to use accounting performance measures in an attempt to assess the disciplinary nature of takeovers. Section (iii) includes a review of studies that have used security market analysis to assess the wealth changes associated with takeovers. Section (iv) includes a review of studies relating to forms of corporate restructuring that were either associated with, or a reaction to, takeover threats. The special nature of conglomerate acquisitions is also considered in this section. In section (v), indirect evidence of the disciplinary role of takeovers is provided, through an examination of studies that have examined top management compensation packages and executive turnover, in response to takeovers. The final Section provides a summary of the evidence and some suggestions for further research.

(ii) Accounting performance

For those who view takeovers as providing a disciplinary role in the economy, it is often assumed that the bidders will be drawn from those companies that already achieve a 'superior' level of performance prior to the bid.[6] This line of argument also predicts that acquired firms would be less profitable than both non-acquired and acquiring firms. One of the first approaches used to assess the disciplinary role of takeovers was to examine the relative profitability of the companies involved. Hence a number of early studies of takeover activity, particularly in the U.K., focused either on the relative profitability characteristics of the various companies involved or else on the change in profitability of the acquiring firm subsequent to the takeover. One of the main limitations of such studies, however, is the implied assumption that the main motive for takeovers is the disciplinary one and that the major source of gain is to be found in improved efficiency (see Appleyard, 1996). There are unfortunately very few papers that have addressed the above limitations, although a study by Maloney & McCormick (1988) found that 'intermittent excess capacity' can provide a motive for merger even in the absence of managerial inefficiencies. In addition, Sudarsanam, Holl & Salami (1996) reported that "marriage between companies with a complementary fit, in terms of liquidity slack, and surplus investment opportunities is value creating for both groups of shareholders" (ibid p. 692). Researchers into the strategic aspects of acquisitions have also suggested that a contingency framework should be adopted, in studies of post-acquisition performance, in order to allow for factors that may explain the degree of strategic fit between acquirer and acquired (Lubatkin, 1983, Fowler & Schmidt, 1989).

One of the first attempts to test whether takeovers in the U.K. provide a disciplinary role was the study by Singh (1971) of the characteristics of companies involved in takeovers over the period 1954 to 1960. Singh reported that, on average, U.K. acquirers experienced a decline in profitability subsequent to the takeover. Subsequently Utton (1974) examined the profitability of 39 companies that were described as merger-intensive over the period 1954 to 1965. He found no evidence that merger intensive firms performed significantly better than the average for their particular industry. In addition Utton reported that firms which relied on internal growth performed significantly better, on average, than his merger intensive sample.

In a follow up to his earlier study, Singh (1975) examined the financial characteristics of surviving, acquiring and acquired companies over the period 1967 to 1970. He found that acquired firms were, on average, less profitable than surviving firms, thus providing some support for the disciplinary role of takeovers. However, he also suggested that size, rather than profitability, was a more important factor in identifying the probability of being taken over. Singh also found that acquiring firms were slightly more profitable than acquired companies, although the former demonstrated an increase in profitability prior to acquisition, while the latter showed a decline in profitability. His results, while confirming some aspects of the disciplinary role of takeovers, also suggested that it was an imprecise tool and that size was an effective defence, at least in the 1960s.[7]

One of the features of many of the early studies, other than that of Utton (1974), is that they concentrated on single acquirers, rather than multiple acquirers. Thus Meeks (1977) examined 233 companies which made one single acquisition over the period 1964 to 1972. He reports a slight improvement in profitability in the year of the merger, followed by a decline in the following seven years. However his sample selection criteria excludes those bidders which are most likely to have achieved positive benefits from takeover activity and concentrates on those for which the outcome may have biased them against further takeovers. While this approach may have some justification in terms of methodological problems in adopting an alternative approach (see Meeks, p. 26.), it does reduce, somewhat, the validity of any conclusions that may be drawn from these studies, about the disciplinary role of takeovers.

One of the first accounting-based studies of takeover performance in the USA was that by Kelly (1967). Kelly compared the financial performance of 21 merger intensive companies with 21 companies matched in terms of industry and size.[8] Although the merger intensive companies had higher growth rates and Price to Earnings ratios he found no difference in profitability between the two groups over an eleven year period, centred on the takeover year. A more comprehensive study was that by Reid (1968), who investigated the financial characteristics of 478 large U.S. industrial companies, which had themselves acquired over 3300 other companies over the period 1951 to 1961. Reid found that, while acquisition active firms had higher levels of growth over the period, they performed less well using variables chosen to represent shareholder interests. Reid concluded that "managers of merging firms are, on average, not primarily profit maximisers" (p. 194), and that "they tend to serve managers' interests, and goals, independent of those of the stockholders" (p. 4).

Reid's study was, however, heavily criticised by Weston and Mansingka (1971), both for the interpretation placed on his results and also for the variables selected to represent shareholder interests.[9]

A study by Lev & Mandelker (1972) of the relative profitability of a matched sample of acquiring and non acquiring US firms concluded that "the five year return to stockholders of acquiring firms was probably higher than the return to stockholders of comparable non-merged firms" (p. 102). The authors also rejected the hypothesis that improved performance for acquirers was a result either of accounting manipulations, or merger accounting methods.

A related series of studies to the above are those that have attempted to identify the financial characteristics of likely takeover targets. Given the lack of clear understanding of the motives for takeover, it is not surprising that these studies have achieved only limited success. A number of these studies have produced relatively high levels of discrimination between acquired and non-acquired companies using publicly available financial data.[10] However, they have been criticised for using inappropriate research designs (Palepu, 1986). Palepu identifies the following three design errors, in these studies, leading to overestimation of the predictive power of the model: (i) the use of equal number samples (of acquired and non-acquired companies) in the model estimation period, without modification to the estimators; (ii) use of equal number samples in the prediction period; and (iii) the use of arbitrary cutoff probabilities without specifying the costs of incorrect decisions. Palepu reports a low predictive power for his model when correcting for these problems. Although researchers appear to be able to classify targets and non-targets ex-post, from samples consisting of equal proportions of each, they appear unable to do so when the samples are more representative of the population of potential targets (Krinsky, Rotenberg & Thornton, 1988).

   In summary, the early accounting-based studies provided mixed results, with some reporting improvements in profitability and others reporting a decline (Singh, 1971). Methodological problems were also associated with many of these studies, including those relating to accounting issues (see Appleyard, 1980) and sample choice (many studies deliberately excluded merger active firms or retained a survivorship bias, for example, Singh, 1971, Utton, 1974, Meeks, 1977). As Scherer (1977) notes, there is only weak evidence, from the early accounting-based studies, that takeovers punish inefficient managers. Rather, these studies demonstrate that size, rather than efficiency, was the main defence against a hostile bid. However, changes in the economic environment over the last thirty years, including the increased availability of new forms of finance, have reduced, if not eliminated, this form of defence. More recently a number of studies have used cash flow measures of operating performance in an attempt to avoid some of the problems in accrual accounting measures.[11] These studies have generally identified small improvements in operating performance post-bid, although it is not clear that these improvements have been sufficient to justify the premiums paid on acquisition. At present, however, the samples used have been relatively small with the consequent difficulty in generalising from these results.

(iii) Studies of share price performance:

One of the problems with studies of acquisition activity is to determine how to measure improvements in economic efficiency that may arise from the disciplinary aspects of the takeover. There are at least two reasons for this, the first being the difficulty in disentangling the changes due to improvements in efficiency from those relating to other causes, including the exercise of monopoly power. The second problem, however, relates to uncertainty as to when the efficiency gains will arise. One possible solution to the second of these two problems was obtained through relying on the basic assumptions of the Efficient Markets Hypothesis, namely that share prices would react in a timely and unbiased manner to new information. This reliance allowed researchers to measure the share price reaction around the takeover and, subject to controls for other factors, use this share price reaction to identify the expected present value of the change in cash flows resulting from the takeover. Thus, a number of the early stock market based studies of takeover activity measured average adjusted share price returns, around the takeover period, in order to identify the expected long term impact. Subsequently, researchers began to question whether the short term reaction was an unbiased predictor of the long run economic impact of the takeover. As these later studies, by implication, question the efficiency of securities markets, they also raise questions about the validity of the methodology, whereby the economic impact of an event is capable of being assessed by examination of security returns. As will be seen in the following review, there are considerable doubts over the reliability of long run measures of security return behaviour. It is still an unresolved question as to whether shareholders of the companies involved (and in particular of the acquiring company) gain or lose from takeover activity.[12]

In a number of the studies reviewed in this section, the authors have examined the share price behaviour of bidding companies, normally with the aim of identifying whether shareholders in these companies experience wealth gains or losses from takeover activity. While this approach has some merit, it cannot, by itself, determine whether takeovers exercise a disciplinary influence. In part, this is because the source of any wealth change is rarely identified. In addition, however, in a perfectly competitive acquisitions market, all the gains from acquisition would instead accrue to the shareholders of the acquired firm. If, as is likely, the acquisitions market is less than perfectly competitive, then it may be that shareholders of acquiring firms will share in some of the gains. However, it is also possible that 'successful' acquirers may end up paying more for the target than is warranted by the expected economic benefits (the so called 'winners curse').[13] Only if the overall wealth effects of the takeover are measured, for both acquiring and acquired firm shareholders, can any conclusions be made about the possible presence of efficiency gains. This is not, in itself, sufficient evidence to conclude that acquisitions perform a disciplinary role as other possible causes of wealth gains, including monopoly profits and transfers from other stakeholders, must first be eliminated. Relatively few studies have either measured the total wealth effects or attempted to identify the source of these. Most have, instead, followed along similar lines to the previously reported accounting studies and attempted to identify whether targets had previously under performed relative to a predetermined benchmark and whether bidders had exceeded benchmark performance. A few studies, including those by Eckbo (1983, 1985) and Stillman (1983), attempted to eliminate monopoly power as the potential source of wealth gains and infer that these are then due to improved efficiency. Others have attempted a similar approach in relation to potential financial gains or redistribution effects between different groups of capital providers (Asquith & Kim, 1982).

One of the first studies of share price performance of acquiring firms was that undertaken by Hogarty (1970). Hogarty studied shareholder returns for a sample of 43 U.S. companies that had been identified as active acquirers over the period 1953 to 1964. Hogarty's results suggested that "the investment performance of heavily merging firms is significantly worse than the average performance of firms in their respective industries" (p. 323). Hogarty's paper was one of the first to suggest that managers were attracted to takeovers by the possibility of very high returns in a small number of cases. This hypothesis was, however, rejected in a subsequent paper by Gort & Hogarty (1970), which suggested that managers would have to be excessively optimistic for these probabilities to have influenced their acquisition decisions. The latter paper also suggested that, while acquiring firm shareholders lost, on average, and target shareholders gained, there was an overall zero wealth effect.

A subsequent paper by Weston, Smith & Shrieves (1972) suggested that the above results were partly influenced by inadequate methodology (ignoring dividend effects) and by the inclusion of a number of mergers that they described as 'marriages of necessity' (footnote 3, p. 358). Further evidence was provided, by Melicher & Harter (1972), which contradicted the finding of poor investment performance of acquiring firms. The latter authors found that the share price performance of 158 large industrial companies, which made acquisitions during the period 1961 to 1968, was equal to, or better than, that of the Standard and Poor's Index of 425 industrial companies.[14] In addition Melicher & Harter reported that active acquirers achieved superior performance to non-active acquirers.

Research by Mandelker (1974) also suggested that US takeovers, undertaken in the period 1941 to 1962, produced positive returns to shareholders of bidding companies. Mandelker's conclusions were, however, based on analysis for a period beginning 40 months prior to a merger and ending 40 months after and included evidence of a post outcome downward revision in share prices, a phenomena that was to re-occur in more recent studies of long run post acquisition bidder performance. A similar result to that obtained by Mandelker was reported by Halpen (1973), in a study of 77 NYSE listed companies that made acquisitions of other listed companies, over the period 1950 to 1965. Halpern reported net gains overall from the mergers, leading him to conclude that the takeover market leads to real gains, either through removal of ineffective management or through the combination of 'unique factors' (p. 572). His analysis was, however, restricted to the period up to and including the takeover and excluded the post takeover period.

Evidence on the pre-bid performance of target and bidding companies has been provided in a number of studies. For example, Asquith (1983) reported negative cumulative abnormal returns, averaging around 14%, to target company shareholders, over a period beginning 480 trading days prior to the bid and ending 20 days prior to the bid. A similar pattern, to that reported by Asquith, was also observed by Smiley (1976) and Malatesta (1983), but not by Dodd & Ruback (1977). A number of studies have also identified an improvement in target company performance in the six months prior to the bid, a result which may reflect either bid anticipation or the market reaction to improvements that management had recently initiated. Asquith (1983) reported that successful bidding firms, on the other hand, achieved significantly positive abnormal returns of around 13% over the same period. By contrast Malatesta (1983) reports wealth losses to acquiring firms in the pre bid period, although his results are not strictly comparable as he uses what is, in effect, a value weighted performance measure. Malatesta's results, therefore, suggest that large acquirers perform relatively less well in the pre acquisition period. A pattern of long run negative returns, pre bid, to target shareholders, but positive returns to bidding company shareholders, has also been identified in other countries, including the United Kingdom (Firth, 1980, Kennedy & Limmack, 1996) and Australia, for bidding firms (Brown & Da Silva Rosa, 1998). The results provide tentative evidence that bids are made by strongly performing firms for under performing targets.

An alternative way of measuring the pre bid financial performance of targets and bidders has been to identify their Tobin's q ratio. Tobins q measures the ratio of the market value of the firm's equity to the replacement value. Advocates of the use of this measure claim that it represents the market's view of the quality of a firm's existing and future projects (Lang, Stulz & Walking, 1989). Lang et al., classify bidding and target companies, in US tender offers, according to this ratio and then compare their post acquisition performance. The authors find that bidders, typically, have been low q ratio firms for a number of years prior to the acquisition, while the q ratio of targets has recently declined. In addition, bidders with low q ratios generally experience negative abnormal returns following the completed tender, while bidders with high pre-tender q ratios generally experience positive abnormal returns. The results provide evidence of the ability of the market to distinguish between those bidding firms that are likely to benefit from takeover activity and those that are likely to lose. Bidding firms with a good history and future prospects appear to make good acquisitions.

Asquith (1983) identified significantly negative returns over the 240 days following bid outcome, a result similar to that also reported by Langetieg (1979). What is particularly surprising about this result is that the negative share price reaction appears to be delayed initially, until 60 days after the outcome, but then to continue for an extended period of time. As discussed above, the price reaction and delay are both inconsistent with the research paradigm adopted in these studies, that of the efficient markets, but this result has been a feature of many of the later studies. The long run negative post outcome pattern of returns, to shareholders of U.K. acquiring companies, has also been reported by Barnes (1984), Dodds & Quek (1985), Firth (1979, 1980), Franks & Harris (1989), Gregory (1997), and Limmack (1991), among others.[15] Papers which found no evidence of long run negative post outcome returns, to shareholders of acquiring firms, include those by Franks, Broyles & Hecht (1977), for a sample of U.K. acquirers in the brewing industry and Franks, Harris & Titman (1991), for U.S. acquisitions. The latter study was, however, criticised by Agrawal et al. (1992) as being both sample specific and also failing to distinguish between the returns from mergers and tender offers. Using a larger set of acquisitions, obtained over a longer period of time, Agrawal et al. found that the results reported by Franks et al. (1991) were mainly driven by positive returns obtained by acquirers in the period 1975 to 1979. Agrawal et al. also reported insignificant post outcome returns in tender offers, but significantly negative returns in mergers. A later paper, by Loughran & Vijh (1997), reported that tender offers were likely to be financed by cash, while merger offers were more likely to be financed by equity. Tender offers are generally viewed as hostile bids, with disciplinary/efficiency motives. Cash is often used as the medium of payment in hostile bids in order to avoid the statutory delays that arise in equity offers. The paper by Loughran & Vijh, therefore, provides a clear example of evidence that disciplinary bids are viewed more favourably, by the market, than 'friendly' bids.

A number of studies have attempted to measure the combined wealth effects of takeovers, partly to identify whether there are net gains, rather than simply a transfer of wealth from acquiring firm shareholders' to those of the target firm. Dodd (1980) and Bradley, Desai & Kim (1987) report an insignificant combined wealth increase from U.S. tender offers undertaken over the period 1962 to 1980. Malatesta (1983) reports combined wealth losses as a result of mergers, from 1969 to 1974, between U.S. companies with market values in excess of $10 million. Denis & McConnell (1986), however, reported significant combined wealth increases, measured over the 40 day period surrounding the bid announcement date, for mergers in the USA, undertaken over the years 1962 to 1980. Similar analysis by Firth (1980) shows a small, but insignificant average combined wealth loss for U.K. acquisitions over the period 1969 to 1975. In a later study of U.K. acquisitions, over the period 1977 to 1986, Limmack (1991) found a small but insignificant wealth gain. The lack of significant wealth change reported by most of the studies suggests that, on average, takeovers do not lead to an improvement in profitability of the firms, once they have combined. It appears, rather, that many takeovers involve, at best, a transfer of wealth from shareholders of the acquiring firm to shareholders of the acquired firm.

An alternative approach to testing for possible synergistic gains from acquisitions is to study the share price behaviour of targets in unsuccessful bids.[16] If the source of gain relates to synergistic benefits, then failure of the bid is likely to cause the target's share price to return to its pre-bid level, unless there is a chance of further bids. Dodd & Ruback (1977) reported that the abnormal returns, to shareholders of target companies in unsuccessful tender offers, were not wholly eliminated following abandonment of the bid. They conclude that this result is consistent with a more efficient utilisation of the assets of the target following the bid. By contrast, Dodd (1980) found that target company shareholders suffered a significantly negative abnormal return at the announcement of termination of merger negotiations. However, when termination is because of veto by target management, the wealth loss on announcement of termination was not sufficient to eliminate the gains due to the merger offer. Asquith (1983) also found that the post outcome share price behaviour of targets in unsuccessful bids was negative and reversed the gains made previously during the bid period. While Bradley et al. (1983) found that targets in unsuccessful bids retained a significant portion of the bid premium following bid abandonment, this was mainly due to the anticipation of further bids. In a study of targets in unsuccessful bids in the U.K., Limmack (1994) found that, while some of the retention of bid premium was due to the possibility of further bids, there was evidence that some targets had improved their accounting performance following the bid abandonment. Supporting evidence for the disciplinary nature of the bid process was provided by Parkinson (1989), who reported an improvement in the accounting performance of targets in abandoned bids.

(iv) *Takeovers, diversifying acquisitions and corporate restructuring activities*

Conglomerate acquirers have a special place in the discussion as to whether takeovers are an example of the agency problem or a solution to it. Early proponents of the disciplinary role of takeovers suggested that the managers of conglomerates possessed superior managerial skills, which allowed them to acquire and turn around the performance of previously under performing companies in a variety of industries. Opponents have instead suggested that diversifying takeovers provide an easy road to growth that is unencumbered with the same issues of market power encountered in related acquisitions.

In a study of U.S. corporate performance in the period 1951 to 1961, Reid (1968) reported that conglomerate acquirers had higher levels of profitability than other types of acquirer. Weston & Mansingka, (1971) found that conglomerate firms had lower operating profit margins during the early part of the 1960s, but that profitability improved during the later half of that decade. Weston & Mansingka concluded that conglomerates were achieving a policy of 'defensive diversification' that was designed both "to preserve the values of ongoing organisations as well as restoring the earnings power of the entities" (p. 928). In a follow up to his earlier study, Reid (1971) suggested that the improvements in profitability, for conglomerate companies over the period, were caused by higher levels of gearing, rather than improvements in performance.[17] The same point was also made by Mueller (1977), who suggested that the improvements in performance, reported by conglomerate firms, were not surprising if the conglomerates were simply acquiring companies that were more profitable than themselves (p. 322). However, the possibility of the above form of 'profit averaging' was rejected in a study, by Conn (1973), of conglomerates acquisitions over the period 1954 to 1969. Conn found no difference in profitability between acquirer and acquired firm. However, he did find that, while active acquirers outperformed single acquirers in the early part of the period studied (1954 to 1965), in the latter part of the period (1966 to 1969) multiple acquirers had significantly lower profitability than single acquirers. Further rejection of Muellers 'profit averaging' hypothesis was provided in a study, by Melicher & Rush (1974), that investigated the performance of companies involved in acquisitions during the period 1960 to 1969. The authors reported that conglomerate acquirers were less profitable than non-conglomerates, pre-acquisition, but that there was no significant difference in pre-acquisition profitability of the two groups of target firms.

Elgers & Clark, (1980) also report that diversifying acquisitions achieve higher returns than non diversifying mergers. Schipper & Thompson, (1983) found that the stock market reacts in a positive manner to the announcement of the beginning of an acquisition campaign by diversified firms. Asquith, Bruner & Mullins (1983) later reported that not all these gains were captured at the commencement of the merger programme. The latter authors also report that, while these gains are larger prior to 1969, they are also present in mergers over the period up to 1979.[18] Lewellen (1971) proposes that diversified firms can achieve a higher gearing level and, thus, reduce capital costs (through tax shields), due to reduced earnings variability. Shleifer & Vishny (1992) suggest that a higher gearing potential may also be obtained by conglomerates, due to the increased likelihood that they will be able to identify marketable assets for disposal when faced with liquidity problems. Asquith & Kim (1982), however, report that, while target shareholders obtain gains from diversifying acquisitions, it is not at the expense of bondholders. Thus, while most of the studies identified above suggest positive market reaction to diversifying takeovers by conglomerates, it is not clear whether the gains obtained were due to improved efficiency or other factors.

By contrast to the above, a number of authors have suggested that firms diversify to protect their human capital (Amihud & Lev, 1981), or to make their own services more indispensable (Shleifer & Vishny, 1989). A number of studies have also documented that diversification leads to value loss for investors. For example, Berger & Ofek (1995) report that, during the period 1986 to 1991, diversified firms are valued at a discount of approximately 15% to the value of each segment, if operated as a stand alone business.

One motive for diversifying acquisitions, that is consistent with shareholder wealth maximisation, is the notion that firms create internal capital markets when there are major information asymmetries with the external finance providers. The information advantage that internal managers possess over external providers of finance is well known and has been described by Alchian (1969) and Williamson (1970), among others. Myers & Majluf (1984) describe the loss of positive net present value projects that can result from the information asymmetry. More recently, Matsusaka & Nanda (1996) suggest that, if the external financing costs are significantly high, then it may be more efficient for a multi-segment firm to reallocate funds to divisions which are more profitable. Hubbard & Palia (1999) suggest that information asymmetries were sufficiently large, in the 1960s, to provide a value maximising role for diversification. In a study of diversifying acquisitions in the USA, in the 1960s, they reported significantly positive abnormal returns for shareholders of bidding firms. They also identified that the positive abnormal returns were more likely to be obtained when financially constrained firms were acquired by those firms with a financial surplus.

The absence of a disciplinary role for conglomerate acquisitions of the late 1960s and early 1970s is implied in the finding by Matsusaka (1990) that the largest benefits to diversifying companies were obtained by those companies which acquired strongly performing targets and retained target management. This result suggests that the benefits of the internal market may have been more important than improved operating efficiencies, although it does not preclude the application of more advanced management control techniques, as reported by Baker (1992).[19] Baker also suggested that the development of a well organised bond market, in the 1970s, provided access to growth finance for smaller companies and consequently reduced the benefits of the internal market. Other authors have also suggested that the information asymmetries, which existed in the 1960s, are no longer present and that the losses suffered, from pursuit of managerial motives for diversification, outweigh the benefits, if any, of the internal market (Bhide, 1990, Stultz, 1990). The study by Baker, of Beatrice Company, provides a rich illustration of an activity (diversified acquisitions) which was value creating in one time period and with one set of organisational structures (decentralised), but which became value reducing in a later time period and with a different organisational structure (highly centralised).

A recent paper by Servaes (1996) provides evidence that contradicts the finding of a decline in the benefits of diversifying activities in recent years. Servaes reports that diversified firms were valued at a discount even during the 1960s and that it is only in the 1970s when this discount begins to disappear. He further reports that managerial share ownership was lower for diversified firms in the 1960s but increased relative to single segment firms during the 1970s, at which time the degree of diversification also increased. However Morck, Shleifer & Vishny (1990) reported that unrelated acquisitions significantly under performed, by comparison with related bidders, in both the 1970s and the 1980s. Morck et al. concluded that their results are consistent with the notion that the source of 'bust-up' gains in the 1980s is the reversal of unrelated diversification of the 1960s and 1970s.

The value loss which, on average, appears to be associated with diversification has led to a number of firms increasing corporate focus in recent years (Comment & Jarrell, 1995). In general, this refocussing has led to significant increases in shareholder wealth. However, this increase in focus has not necessarily been achieved on a voluntary basis. The literature on leveraged buyouts (LBO's) and management buyouts (MBO's) has documented these aspects of corporate restructuring as mechanisms to reduce the agency problem and restore the alignment of interests for senior managers and shareholders. Restructuring activities, at times, occur as a response to unwelcome takeover bids or at least in the period surrounding the bid announcement. Thus Denis (1994) describes the leveraged buy out of Safeway Stores Inc., in the USA, by Kohlberg, Kravis & Roberts (KKR), following an unsuccessful takeover bid from the Dart Group. The LBO ultimately resulted in the company being taken private and major restructuring activities being initiated that lead to a $2,000 million increase[20] in shareholders' wealth. In the same paper, Denis contrasts the fortunes of Kroger Co., also of the USA, whose directors resisted a takeover bid from Dart and a LBO approach from KKR, in order to initiate their own capital restructuring programme. While Kroger also managed to generate significant value increases to shareholders, following its own restructuring, these were significantly less than the amount that was available in the LBO offer.

A similar picture to the above is provided in Baker's (1992) analysis of the rise and decline of Beatrice Companies (USA). Baker described Beatrice as the most active acquirer, in terms of transactions, from 1955 to 1979 and the most active divestor, in the USA, from 1979 to 1987. Following a period of poor performance and apparent loss in investor confidence, Beatrice became the subject of a takeover bid from the Dart Group. The company eventually accepted a leveraged buy out offer from KKR which restored "virtually all of the value lost" during the previous 8 to 10 years (ibid p. 1104). Restructuring activities do not appear to be confined to leverage buy outs. A study of hostile takeovers by Bhagat, Shleifer & Vishny (1990) also reports that a substantial proportion of the acquired assets are subsequently sold to management in divisional LBO's.

(v) Executive compensation and takeover activity

A growing body of research has examined the relationship between management compensation packages and shareholder interests. A number of studies, published in the late 1950s or early 1960s, reported the close relationship between sales and executive salaries and the lack of relationship between profits and executive salaries (McGuire, Chiu & Ebling, 1962, Roberts, 1959, Patton, 1965). More recently, studies have investigated the relationship between managerial share ownership, structured compensation schemes, and takeover performance. Evidence in support of managerial theories of the firm have tended to infer that if a decision was detrimental to shareholders interests, then it must have been taken in the interests of managers. However, as Mikkelson & Ruback (1985) point out, this does not necessarily follow: the decision may simply reflect an error of judgment or the possession of information by one party that is not available to the other. A more appropriate test of the effectiveness of governance mechanisms, including compensation schemes, is to identify situations in which both managers and owners benefit. Lewellen, Loderer & Rosenfeld (1985) use a model that identifies the characteristics of management compensation packages as a variable to represent the degree to which management interests are aligned with those of the owners. They reported a persistent, positive (although not always statistically significant), relationship between abnormal returns to bidding firms in completed mergers and the percentage of ordinary shares held by senior management. The results provide tentative support for the hypothesis that managers are less likely to undertake value-reducing takeovers when they share in the financial loss.

The role of takeovers in replacing senior management of the acquired company has also been documented in a number of studies. Thus, Walsh (1989) reported a 61% rate of turnover of senior management in U.S. target companies over the five years post takeover. As he also identified that hostility to the bid increased the rate of subsequent turnover, it is not clear whether the turnover reflects replacement of inefficient managers or simply their unwillingness to work with the new management team. In a related study, Walsh & Elwood (1991) reported a higher than normal proportion of top managers leaving the target, in the two years after acquisition. A contrary finding, of no increase in senior management turnover, was reported in a study by Griffin & Wiggins (1992), of takeovers in the petroleum industry. However, the specific features of the industry selected (over capacity), suggests that the latter study may not have involved disciplinary takeovers.

Mulherin & Poulsen (1998) find that, when a proxy contest was accompanied by a successful takeover, then shareholders experience wealth increases. If the bid failed, then a wealth loss occured. However, when a proxy contest is not accompanied by a takeover bid, then the key factor in determining whether shareholders gain or lose is whether the senior executive is replaced. In 71% of those cases in which the senior executive was replaced, the company initiated a major restructuring programme that led to an improvement in performance. By contrast, a major restructuring programme was initiated in only 41% of firms subject to a proxy contest following which the senior executive was not replaced. The authors concluded that the proxy contest appears to have been used in a complementary role, in those situations where it was necessary to remove management who would otherwise block a takeover or a restructuring programme.

One development of the above strand of research is to test the relationship between the prior performance of target companies and subsequent management turnover. Thus, Martin & McConnell (1991) examined target CEO turnover, for a sample of 253 takeovers, in the period 1958 to 1984. Although they reported that there was an increase in CEO turnover post-acquisition, they were only able to report a weak relationship between prior performance and subsequent CEO turnover. Hambrick & Cannell (1993) also found a relationship between senior management turnover post acquisition and poor pre acquisition target performance. The authors also reported that the greater the difference between bidder and target performance, pre acquisition, the greater the rate of target senior management turnover, post acquisition. This result suggests that the benchmark against which target management is judged is that of the bidder management, rather than that of the market. Kennedy and Limmack (1996) also reported a significant increase in post acquisition turnover of senior executives in U.K. targets, in takeover bids completed in the 1980s, while Franks & Mayer (1996) identify a similar pattern for 1985 and 1986. Although the two studies use different criteria to classify bids as hostile and accepted, they both find little evidence to distinguish pre bid performance. The latter study also finds little evidence that pre bid performance of targets in hostile bids is inferior to that of non-acquired companies. Franks & Mayer conclude that their results are not consistent with the hypothesis that hostile takeovers are associated with a disciplinary role in the U.K., at least for the period that they studied.

A study by Denis & Denis (1995) also established a relationship between the threat of takeover and forced resignation of top managers. They first identified a link between poor prior performance and forced resignations of senior executives. The authors then reported that forced resignations occurred in only a small proportion of their sample (approximately 13% of the cases), but were followed by significant down-sizing of operations. Finally, they identify that, in a large number of these cases, the forced resignation happens after the firm has been the target of some form of corporate control contest. It appears that the external threat is the catalyst for change in under-performing companies. Further evidence in support of this relationship was provided in the study, by Denis & Serrano (1996), of top management turnover in targets of unsuccessful control contests initiated between 1983 and 1989. The authors report that 34% of target companies replaced top management in the two years following unsuccessful contests. Many of these companies had previously experienced poor performance, but became involved in a restructuring programme, subsequently, which generated improved operating performance and led to increases in shareholder wealth. Denis & Serrano also found that the presence of a large blockholder was an important factor in determining whether a restructuring programme was likely to take place.

Finally, a study by Mikkleson & Partch (1997) reported that a decline in takeover activity in the USA, from the period 1984 through 1988 to 1989 through 1994, was also accompanied by a reduced level of, what the authors described as, 'disciplinary pressure' on top managers. In particular, they found that the inverse relationship between firm performance and management turnover, reported in other studies, had disappeared during the later period.

Although it is not possible to prove a causal relationship, the authors suggest that regulatory and defensive mechanisms against takeovers in the USA have reduced their disciplinary impact.

(vi) *Summary and conclusions*

It is not surprising that the above review has been unable to provide a definitive answer as to whether the takeover market acts as an effective disciplinary mechanism. Problems encountered in research programmes that have attempted to address this issue include the possible presence of conflicting takeover motives and methodological issues relating to the various performance matrices used. In addition it is clear that studies which produced results that were appropriate to one data set and time period are no longer relevant to the current global economic environment. The use of size as a defence mechanism (as discussed by Singh, 1971) is clearly no longer available in an environment in which hostile bids in excess of £1 billion are becoming more common. The benefits, from an internal capital market and managerial expertise, that partly motivated many conglomerate acquisitions in the 1950s and 1960s are also no longer available to counterbalance the potentially harmful aspect. However, many of the issues, identified by early researchers, still remain. Over-optimism and managerial (and sponsor) self interest do appear to be factors that either produce value destroying acquisitions or at least those in which acquirers overpay. At the same time, there is also evidence that takeovers (and the threat of takeover) serve as a force in modernising and restructuring some industries in a way that existing mangers are unable to do. There is also evidence that other governance mechanisms can serve to mitigate some of the unfavourable aspects of takeovers. In particular, the structuring of remuneration packages through option schemes appears to reduce the likelihood that managers will undertake value-destroying acquisitions. Future research is required, to investigate how these schemes ought to be structured. It may also be the case that the extension of delayed share option schemes, to the fee structure of merger and acquisition sponsors, would reduce the incidence of overoptimistic bids. It is also likely that new organisational forms will arise to overcome any increase in government legislation and intervention in takeover activity. One new form that is already emerging, that of the strategic alliance, may also be replacing ownership alliances, according to Chan, Kensinger, Keown & Martin (1997). The latter authors find that strategic alliances, which they define to include contractual relationships as well as more formal joint ventures, give rise to wealth increases for both parties.

NOTES

1. The choice of terminology to describe this aspect of the market for corporate control (Jensen & Ruback, 1983) is unfortunately inconsistent in the literature, especially in the early years. Studies have often used the terms *takeover, acquisition* and *merger* inter-changeably. For the purpose of this paper the term used by the authors of the original paper will be used. No distinction will be made between the terms, except in those cases in which a merger between 'equal parties' is referred to, rather than an *acquisition* by one party of another.

2. At least not in the stock market conditions prevailing at the time of his writing (preface p. xxi).

3. A related strand of research has also attempted to identify the predictability of takeover targets.

4. There have been a number of notable exceptions to this generalisation, including papers by Bradley, Desai & Kim (1983, 1985), Eckbo (1983, 1985).

5. See for example Pound, Lehn & Jarrell (1986)

6. There are two problems with this assumption including both the definition of superior performance and the notion that bidders should be earning such a level.

7. This defence, while still available, has been reduced to a certain extent by the development of new financial instruments in the last 30 years.

8. A merger intensive company was defined as one that had achieved sales growth of at least 20% by external acquisition.

9. Reid used the following variables to represent shareholder interests: growth in (adjusted) market value, growth in profits relative to (i) total assets, and (ii) total sales.

10. For example Simkowitz & Monroe (1971), Stevens, (1973), Castagna & Matolcsy (1976), Belkoui, 1978, Dietrich & Sorensen (1984).

11. Healy, Palepu & Ruback (1992) for the USA, Manson, Stark & Thomas (1994) and Burt & Limmack (1999), for the U.K., and Abdul Rahman & Limmack (1999), for Malaysia.

12. At the time of writing, a newspaper report appeared in the Financial Times of a study into cross-border mergers which concluded that a majority of cross-border acquisitions 'destroyed shareholder value' (Financial Times, Monday November 29, 1999). Further reference to the report appeared in the Guardian on the following day.

13. For reference to tests of the 'winners curse' in sealed-bid acquisitions see Giliberto & Varaiya (1989). A similar explanation is also described in Roll (1986) but based on an open bidding system.

14. Note, however, the use of a different control index to that of Hogarty.

15. In a number of the papers, the authors also commented that the conclusion of negative long-run post-outcome returns was partly dependent on the choice of control model (Franks & Harris, 1989, Limmack, 1991).

16. Strictly speaking, what generally motivated these studies was to test two competing bid motives, the synergistic motive and the new information (i.e. target under-valuation) motive.

17. See also Melicher & Rush (1974)

18. It should be noted that the period investigated was restricted to 20 days following the bid announcement day.

19. See also reference to the subsequent problems of Beatrice later in this section.

20. After adjusting for general market movements.

REFERENCES

[Note references are listed for the section of the paper in which they were first cited].

(i) Introduction

Agrawal, A., Jaffe, J. F., & Mandelker G. N. (1992). The post–merger performance of acquiring firms: a re examination of an anomaly'. *The Journal of Finance, 47(4)*, 1605–1621.

Berle, A. A., & Means, G. C. (1968). The Modern Corporation and Private Property, [Revised Edition]. Harcourt, Brace and World, Inc., New York.

Bradley, M., Desai, A., Kim, E. H. (1983). The rationale behind interfirm tender offers: information or synergy? *Journal of Financial Economics, 11*, 183–206.

Bradley, M., Desai, A., Kim, E. H. (1987). Synergistic gains from corporate acquisitions and their division between the stockholders of target and acquiring firms. *Journal of Financial Economics, 21*, 3–40.

Cyert, R. M., & March, J. G. (1971). A behavioural theory of the firm, Prentice Hall, Englewood Cliffs, N.J.

DeAngelo, H., & De Angelo, L. (1989). Proxy contests and the governance of publicly held corporations. *Journal of Financial Economics, 23*, 29–59.

Denis, D. K., & McConnell, J. (1986). Corporate mergers and security returns. *Journal of Financial Economics, 16*, 143–187.

Eckbo, B. E. (1983). Horizontal mergers, collusion, and shareholder wealth. *Journal of Financial Economics, 11*, 241–273.

Eckbo, B. E. (1985). Merger and the market concentration doctrine. *Journal of Business, 58*, 325–349.

Jensen, M. C., & Meckling, W. (1976). Theory of the firm: managerial behavior, agency costs and ownership structure. *Journal of Financial Economics 3*, 305–360

Jensen, M. C., & Ruback, R. S. (1983). The market for corporate control: the scientific evidence. *Journal of Financial Economics, 11*, 5–50.

Jensen, M. C. (1988). Takeovers: their causes and consequences. *Journal of Economic Perspectives, 2*, 21–48.

Lang, L. H. P., Stulz, R. M., & Walkling, R. A. (1989). Managerial performance, Tobin's Q, and the gains from successful tender offers. *Journal of Financial Economics, 24*, 137–154.

Limmack, R. J. (1991). Corporate mergers and shareholder wealth effects: 1977 to 1986. *Accounting and Business Research, 21*, 239–251.

Limmack, R. J. (1994). Synergy or new information as a source of wealth change in acquisitions: the case of abandoned bids. *Accounting and Business Research, 24*, 255–265.

Loughran, T., & Vijh, A. M. (1997). Do long term shareholders benefit from corporate acquisitions? *The Journal of Finance, 52*, 1765–1790.

Manne, H. G. (1965). Mergers and the market for corporate control. *Journal of Political Economy, 73*, 110–120.

Marris, R. (1964) The economic theory of 'managerial' capitalism. Macmillan, London.

Marris, R., & Wood, A. (1971). The corporate economy: growth, competition, and innovation potential. Macmillan, London.

Maloney, M. T., & McCormick, R. E. (1988). Excess capacity, cyclical production, and merger motives: some evidence from the capital markets. *Journal of Law and Economics, 31*, 321–350.

Mueller, D. C. (1969). A theory of conglomerate mergers. *Quarterly Journal of Economics, 83,* 643–659.

Parkinson, C., & Dobbins, R. (1993). Returns to shareholders in successfully defended takeover bids: U.K. evidence 1975 to 1984. *Journal of Business Finance and Accounting, 20,* 501–520.

Pickering, J. F. (1983). The causes and consequences of abandoned mergers. *Journal of Industrial Economics, 31,* 267–281.

Posner, R. A. (1976). Anti-trust law: an economic perspective. University of Chicago Press, Chicago, Illinois.

Pound, J., Lehn, K., & Jarrell, G. (1986). Are takeovers hostile to economic performance? *Regulation,* (September/October) 25–56.

Ruback, R. M. (1988). Comment. In: A. J. Auerbach, (Ed.), *Corporate Takeovers: Causes and Consequences.* University of Chicago Press, Chicago, Illinois.

Scherer, F. M. (1977). The Posnerian harvest: separating wheat from the chaff. *The Yale Law Review, 86,* 974–1002.

Weston, J. F., Chung, K. S., & Hoag, S. E. (1990). Mergers, Restructuring and Corporate Control. Prentice Hall, Englewood Cliffs, New Jersey.

(ii) Accounting Performance

Abdul Rahman, R., & Limmack, R. J. (1999). Corporate acquisitions and the operating performance of Malaysian companies. *Working Paper,* 12/99. University of Stirling, Department of Accounting, Finance and Law.

Appleyard, A. R. (1980). Takeovers: accounting policy, financial policy and the case against accounting measures of performance. *Journal of Business Finance and Accounting, 7,* 541–554.

Belkoui, A. (1978). Financial ratios as predictors of Canadian takeovers. *Journal of Business Finance and Accounting, 5,* 93–107.

Burt, S., & Limmack, R. J. (1999). The operating performance of companies involved in acquisitions in the UK retailing sector, 1977 to 1992. *Working Paper,* 11/99 University of Stirling, Department of Accounting, Finance and Law.

Castagna, A. D., & Matolcsy, Z. P. (1976). Financial ratios as predictors of company acquisitions. *Journal of the Securities Institute of Australia,* (December), 6–10.

Dietrich, J. K., & Sorensen, E. (1984). An application of logit analysis to prediction of merger targets. *Journal of Business Research, 12,* 393–402.

Fowler, K. L., & Schmidt, D. S. (1989). Determinants of tender offer post acquisition performance. *Strategic Management Journal, 10,* 339–350.

Healy, P. M., Palepu, K. G., & Ruback, R. S. (1992). Does corporate performance improve after mergers? *Journal of Financial Economics, 31,* 135–175.

Kelly, E. M. (1967). The profitability of growth through merger. University Park, P.A.

Krinsky, I., Rotenberg, W. D., & Thornton, D. B. (1988). Takeovers – a synthesis. *Journal of Accounting Literature, 7,* 243–259.

Lev, B., & Mandelker, G. (1972). The microeconomic consequences of corporate mergers. *Journal of Business, 45*(1), 85–104.

Lubatkin, M. (1983). Mergers and the performance of the acquiring firm. *Academy of Management Review, 8,* 218–225.

Manson, S., Stark, A. W., & Thomas, H. M. (1994). A cash flow analysis of the operational gains from takeovers. *Certified Research Report 35,* Certified Accountants Educational Trust, London.

Meeks, G. (1977). Disappointing marriage: a study of the gains from mergers, Cambridge University Press, Occasional Paper 51.

Newbould, G. D., Stray, S. J., & Wilson, K. W. (1976) Shareholders' interests and acquisition activity, *Accounting and Business Research, 23,* 201–213.

Palepu, K. (1986). Predicting takeover targets: a methodological and empirical analysis. *Journal of Accounting and Economics, 8,* 3–36.

Ravenscraft, D. J., & Scherer, F. M. (1987). Life after takeover. The Journal of Industrial Economics, 36, 147–236.

Reid, S. R. (1968). Mergers, managers and the economy. McGraw Hill, New York.

Scherer, F. M. (1977). The Posnerian harvest: separating the wheat from the chaff. *The Yale Law Journal, 86,* 974–1002.

Simkowitz, M., & Monroe, R. J. (1971). A discriminant analysis function for conglomerate targets. *Southern Journal of Business,* Nov. 1–16.

Singh, A. (1971). Takeovers: their relevance to the stock market and the theory of the firm. Cambridge University Press, Cambridge.

Singh, A. (1975). Takeovers, economic natural selection and the theory of the firm: evidence from the postwar United Kingdom experience. *Economic Journal, 85,* 497–515.

Stevens, D. L. (1973). Financial characteristics of merged firms: a multivariate analysis. *Journal of Financial and Quantitative Analysis, 8,* 149–165.

Sudarsanam, S., Holl, P., & Salami, A. (1996). Shareholder wealth gains in mergers: effects of synergy and ownership structure. *Journal of Business Finance and Accounting, 23,* 673–698.

Utton, M. A. (1974). On measuring the effects of industrial mergers. *Scottish Journal of Political Economy, 21*(1), 13–28.

Weston, J. F., & Mansinghka, S. K. (1971). Tests of the efficiency performance of conglomerate firms. *Journal of Finance, 26,* 919–936.

(iii) Share Price Performance

Asquith, P. (1983). Merger bids, uncertainty, and stockholder returns. *Journal of Financial Economics, 11,* 51–83.

Barnes, P. (1984). The effects of a merger on the share price of the attacker, revisited. *Accounting and Business Research, 15,* 45–49.

Bhagat, S., Shleifer, A., & Vishny, R. (1990). The aftermath of hostile takeovers. *Brookings Papers on Economic Activity: Microeconomics:* The Brookings Institution, Washington D.C.) 1–64.

Brown, P., & Da Silva Rosa, R. (1998). Research method and the long run performance of acquiring firms. *Australian Journal of Management, 23,* 23–38.

Dodd, P., & Ruback, R. (1977). Tender offers and stockholder returns: an empirical analysis. *Journal of Financial Economics, 5,* 351–373.

Dodd, P. (1980). Merger proposals, management discretion and stockholder wealth. *Journal of Financial Economics, 8,* 105–137.

Dodds, J., & Quek, J. (1985). Effects of mergers on the share price movement of the acquiring firms: a UK study. *Journal of Business Finance and Accounting, 12,* 285–296.

Firth, M. (1979). The profitability of takeovers and mergers in the UK. *Economic Journal, 89,* 316–328.

Firth, M. (1980). Takeovers, shareholder returns and the theory of the firm. Quarterly *Journal of Economics, 94,* 235–260.

Franks, J. R., Broyles, J. E., & Hecht, M. J. (1977). An Industry Study of the Profitability of Mergers in the United Kingdom. *Journal of Finance, 32,* 1513–1525.

Frank, J. R., & Harris, R. S. (1989). Shareholder Wealth Effects of Corporate Takeovers: The UK experience 1955 to 85. *Journal of Financial Economics, 23,* 225–249.

Franks, J. R., Harris, R. S., & Titman, S. (1991). The Post merger share price performance of acquiring firms. *Journal of Financial Economics, 29,* 81–96.

Giliberto, S. M., & Varaiya, N. P. (1989). The winner's curse and bidder competition in acquisitions: evidence from failed bank auctions. *The Journal of Finance, 44,* 59–75.

Gort M., & Hogarty, T. (1970). New evidence on mergers', *Journal of Law and Economics, 13*(1), 167–184.

Gregory, A. (1997). An examination of the long run performance of UK acquiring firms. *Journal of Business Finance and Accounting, 7 & 8,* 971–1002.

Halpen, P. J. (1973). Empirical estimates of the amount and distribution of gains to companies in mergers. *Journal of Business, 46*(4), 554–575.

Hogarty, T. F. (1970). The profitability of corporate mergers. *Journal of Business, 43*(3), 317–327.

Langetieg, T. C. (1979). An application of a three factor performance index to measure stock gains from merger. *Journal of Financial Economics, 6,* 365–384.

Malatesta, P. H. (1983). The wealth effect of merger activity and the objective functions of merging firms. *Journal of Financial Economics, 11,* 155–181.

Mandelker, G. (1974). Risk and return: the case of merging firms. *Journal of Financial Economics, 1*(4), 303–335.

Melicher, R. W., & Harter, T. H. (1972). Abstract: stock price movement of firms engaged in large acquisitions. *Journal of Financial and Quantitative Economics, 7*(2), 1469–1475.

Parkinson, C. (1989). The performance of UK companies involved in the successful defence of hostile takeover bids. *University of Bradford Working Paper.*

Roll, R. (1986). The hubris hypothesis of corporate takeovers. *Journal of Business, 59,* 197–216.

Smiley, R. (1976). Tender offers, transaction's costs, and the theory of the firm. *Review of Economics and Statistics, 58,* 22–32.

Stillman, R. S. (1983). Examining anti trust policy towards horizontal mergers. *Journal of Financial Economics, 11,* 225–240.

The Financial Times (1999). KPMG withdraws merger study. *Companies and Markets,* Monday 29 November, page 1.

The Guardian (1999). Whisper it...takeovers don't pay. Tuesday November 30, page 27.

Weston, J. F., Smith K. V., & Shrieves, R. E. (1972). Conglomerate performance using the capital asset pricing model. *The Review of Economics and Statistics, 54,* 357–363.

(iv) Conglomerates and Restructuring Activities

Alchian, A. (1969). Corporate Management and Property Rights. In: H. Manne (Ed.), *Economic Policy and the Regulation of Corporate Securities,* American Enterprise Institute, Washington D.C.

Amihud, Y., & Lev, B. (1981). Risk reduction as a managerial motive for conglomerate mergers. *The Bell Journal of Economics, 12,* 605–617.

Asquith, P., Bruner, R. F., & Mullins, D. W. (1983). The gains to bidding firms from merger. *Journal of Financial Economics, 11,* 121–139.

Asquith, P., & Kim, E. H. (1982). The impact of merger bids on the participating firms' security holders. *The Journal of Finance, 37*(5), 1209–1228.

Baker, G. (1992). Beatrice: A study in the creation and destruction of value. *The Journal of Finance, 47,* 1081–1119.

Benston, G. J. (1985). The self serving management hypothesis: some evidence. *Journal of Financial Economics, 7,* 67–84.

Berger, P. G., & Ofek, E. (1995). Diversification's effect on firm value.*Journal of Financial Economics, 37,* 39–65.

Berger, P. G., & Ofek, E. (1996). Bustup takeovers of value destroying firms. *The Journal of Finance, 51*(4), September, 1175–1200.

Bhide A. (1990). Reversing corporate diversification, *Journal of Applied Corporate Finance, 3*, 70–81.

Comment, R., & Jarrell, G. (1995). Corporate focus and stock returns. *Journal of Financial Economics, 37*, 67–87.

Conn, R. L. (1973). Performance of conglomerate firms: comment. *The Journal of Finance, 28*(3), 754–758.

Denis, D. J. (1994). Organizational form and the consequences of highly leveraged transactions. Kroger's recapitalization and Safeway's LBO. *Journal of Financial Economics, 36*, 193–224.

Denis, D. J., Denis, D. K., & Sarin, A. (1997). Agency Problems, Equity Ownership, and Corporate Diversification. *The Journal of Finance, 52*(1), March, 135–160.

Elgers, P. T., & Clark, J. J. (1980), Merger types and shareholder returns: Additional Evidence. *Financial Management, 9*, 66–72.

Hubbard, R. G., & Palia, D. (1999). A Re examination of the Conglomerate Merger Wave in the 1960's: An Internal Capital Markets View. *The Journal of Finance, 54*(3), June, 1131–1152.

Lewellen, W. (1971). A pure financial rationale for the conglomerate merger. *The Journal of Finance, 26*, 521–537.

Matsusaka, J. G. (1990). Takeover motives during the conglomerate merger wave. *Rand Journal of Economics, 24*, 357–379.

Matsusaka, J. G., & Nanda, V. (1996). Internal Capital Markets and Corporate Refocussing. *Working Paper*, University of South California.

Melicher, R. W., & Rush, D. F. (1973). The performance of conglomerate firms: recent risk and return experience. *The Journal of Finance, 28*(2), 381–388.

Morck, R., Schleifer, A., & Vishny, R. W. (1990). Do Managerial Objectives Drive Bad Acquisitions? *The Journal of Finance, 45*, 31–48.

Mueller, D. C. (1977). The effects of conglomerate mergers: a survey of the empirical evidence. *Journal of Banking and Finance, 1*(4), 315–347.

Myers, S., & Majluf, N. (1984). Corporate financing and investment decisions when firms have information that investors do not have. *Journal of Financial Economics, 13*, 187–221.

Reid, S. R. (1971). A reply to the Weston/Mansinghka criticisms dealing with conglomerate mergers. *The Journal of Finance, 26*, 937–946.

Schipper, K., & Thompson, R. (1983). Evidence on the Capitalised Value of Merger Activity for Merging Firms. *Journal of Financial Economics, 11*, 85–119.

Servaes, H. (1996). The Value of Diversification During the Conglomerate Merger Wave. *The Journal of Finance, 51*(4), September 1996, 120–1225.

Shleifer, A., & Vishny, R. W. (1989). Management entrenchment: the case of manager specific investments. *Journal of Financial Economics, 25*, 123–140.

Shleifer, A., & Vishny, R. W. (1992). Liquidation values and debt capacity: a market equilibrium approach. *The Journal of Finance, 45*, 379–396.

Stultz, R. M. (1990). Managerial discretion and optimal financing policies. *Journal of Financial Economics, 26*, 3–27.

Williamson, O. (1970). Corporate Control and Business Behaviour. Prentice Hall, New Jersey.

(v) Executive Compensation, Management Turnover and Takeover Activity

Appleyard, A. (1996). Discussion of Takeover activity, CEO turnover, and the market for corporate control. *Journal of Business Finance and Accounting, 23*, 87–293.

Denis, D. J., & Denis, D. K. (1995). Performance changes following top management dismissals. *The Journal of Finance, 50,* 1029–1057.

Denis, D. J., & Serrano, J. (1996). Active investors and management turnover following unsuccessful control contests. *Journal of Financial Economics, 40,* 239–266.

Franks, J. R., & Mayer, C. (1996). Hostile takeovers and the correction of management failure. *Journal of Financial Economics, 40,* 163–181.

Griffin, J. M., & Wiggins, S. N. (1992). Takeovers: managerial incompetence or managerial shirking? *Economic Enquiry, 30,* 355–370.

Hambrick, D. C., & Cannella, A. A. (1993). Relative standing: a framework for understanding departures of acquired executives. *Academy of Management Journal, 36*(4), 733–762.

Kennedy, V. A., & Limmack, R. J. (1996). Takeover activity, CEO turnover, and the market for corporate control. *Journal of Business Finance and Accounting, 23,* 267–285.

Lewellen, W., Loderer, C., & Rosefeld, A. (1985). Merger decisions and executive stock ownership in acquiring firms. *Journal of Accounting and Economics, 7,* 209–231.

McGuire, J. W., Chiu, J. S. Y., & Ebling, A. O. (1962). Executive incomes, sales and profits. *American Economic Review, 52,* No. 4, 753–761.

Martin, K. J., & McConnell, J. J. (1991). Corporate performance, corporate takeovers, and management turnover. *The Journal of Finance, 46*(2), 671–687.

Mikkelson, W. H., & Ruback, R. S. (1985). Takeovers and management compensation: a discussion. *Journal of Accounting and Economics, 7,* 233–238.

Mikkleson, W. H., & Partch, M. (1997). The decline of takeovers and disciplinary managerial turnover. *Journal of Financial Economics, 44,* 205–228.

Mulherin, J. H., & Poulsen, A. B. (1998). Proxy contests and corporate change: implications for shareholder wealth. *Journal of Financial Economics, 47,* 279–313.

Patton, A. (1965). Deterioration in top executive pay. *Harvard Business Review, 43*(6), 106–118.

Roberts, D. R. (1959). Executive Compensation, The Free Press of Glencoe, New York.

Walsh, J. P. (1989). Doing a deal: merger and acquisition negotiations and their impact upon target company top management turnover. *Strategic Management Journal, 10,* 307–322.

Walsh, J. P., & Elwood, J. W. (1991). Mergers, acquisitions, and the pruning of managerial deadwood. *Strategic Management Journal, 12,* 201–217.

(vi) Summary and Conclusions

Chan, S. H., Kensinger, J. W., Keown, A. J., & Martin, J. D. (1997). Do strategic alliances create value? *Journal of Financial Economics, 46,* 199–221.

CORPORATE GOVERNANCE, CORPORATE CONTROL AND TAKEOVERS

Sudi Sudarsanam

ABSTRACT

There are a variety of monitoring and control mechanisms to resolve the agency conflict between shareholders and their agents, the managers. Given the centrality of the shareholder wealth maximisation goal in corporate finance, the function of these mechanisms is to ensure that managers pursue that goal. These mechanisms include: an independent board, outside block shareholdings including institutional shareholders, managerial ownership and incentives, lenders, the managerial labour market and the market for corporate control. We explore the inter-dependency of these control mechanisms and whether and how they complement, or substitute for, one another. The role of the market for corporate control, including proxy contests and outright takeovers, in resolving agency conflicts, the impediments to takeovers and their effectiveness are reviewed. We seek to explain the well-documented failure of acquirers to create value, in terms of the ineffectiveness of the corporate governance system in acquiring companies.

Advances in Mergers and Acquisitions, Volume 1, pages 119–155
2000 by Elsevier Science Inc.
ISBN: 0–7623–0683–1

1. INTRODUCTION

In the 1990s, we have witnessed a huge wave of mergers and acquisitions. In 1999 alone, the value of M & A in the U.S. exceeded $2,000 billions and in Europe, thanks to a number of macroeconomic, political and institutional factors, we are experiencing peak levels of M & A. The nature of M & A is also changing in continental Europe, with hostile takeovers becoming more acceptable and increasingly perceived as an effective mechanism for 'shaking up' inefficient or under-performing corporates. Amidst this tidal wave of M & A activity, there is the recurrent underlying anxiety, based on extensive empirical evidence, that many mergers and acquisitions fail to generate value for the acquirers' shareholders.

Such failure may be due to a variety of factors such as, poor strategic rationale for the merger, hubris of acquirer managers leading to excessive acquisition premium, flawed implementation of post-merger integration, faulty financial evaluation of merger benefits or just bad luck. However, the systematic nature of the evidence of failure of mergers and acquisitions to generate value suggests that the source of the problem may also be systematic if not systemic. One possibility is that poor corporate governance in the acquirer firms may have led to inadequate monitoring of the various stages of the acquisition process – pre-acquisition evaluation of target, deal structuring and negotiation, and post-acquisition integration. Poor corporate governance may also allow entrenchment of managers and prevent value maximising takeovers.

It is argued that hostile takeovers represent a disciplinary mechanism in the market for corporate control. Where the incumbent managers follow investment and financing policies that are not geared to shareholder value maximisation, competing management teams can mount hostile takeover bids for that target firm, eliminate incompetent or self-interested managers and improve the target firm's performance, to the benefit of the shareholders of both target and acquirer firms. Implicit in this disciplinary model is the assumption that the corporate governance of the target firm is seriously inadequate, thereby inviting external discipline in the form of a hostile bid.

Corporate governance has a role to play in mergers and acquisitions apart from being the key to avoiding becoming the target of a hostile bid. This lies in the monitoring of acquisition decisions by the potential and actual acquirers. Given the well-documented empirical evidence of many acquirers' failure to generate value from their acquisitions, the monitoring devices embedded in most such firms' internal corporate governance system seem to have tripped. The causes of failure of acquisitions may, thus, be traced to the causes of failure of the corporate governance system.

In this chapter, we define corporate governance and discuss its role in monitoring managerial performance. We identify a variety of dimensions that collectively constitute corporate governance. We compare internal corporate control devices with those operating through external markets. A particular focus of the chapter is the recognition of the interdependency of these alternative control devices. We set out the scope for both positive and negative interaction among them. The role of the market for corporate control, in controlling managerial discretion to follow non-value maximising strategies, is then explored. The impediments to the efficient operation of this market are discussed. We examine the relation between corporate governance and takeovers and the empirical evidence for the impact of the former on both bidding and target firms in takeovers. Throughout, the focus is on the U.S. and U.K. frameworks, which are somewhat similar, but also differ in important respects.

The chapter is organised as follows. Section 2 defines corporate governance and discusses the characteristics and dimensions of corporate governance. Section 3 examines corporate control transactions as agency control devices, focusing on large share block acquisitions, proxy contests and outright takeovers. In Section 4 we examine how corporate governance structure affects the behaviour of acquiring company and target company managers. Summary and conclusions are provided in Section 5.

2. CORPORATE GOVERNANCE AND SHAREHOLDER WEALTH

2.1 Definition of corporate governance

The Cadbury Committee was the first of several bodies entrusted with improving corporate governance in the U.K. In its Report on the Financial Aspects of Corporate Governance (1992), the committee defined corporate governance as 'the system by which companies are directed and controlled." It is also defined as "the processes of supervision and control (of 'governing') intended to ensure that the company's management acts in accordance with the interests of the shareholders" (Parkinson, 1993, p. 6). Tricker (1984, p. 6) expands this definition: "the governance role is not concerned with the running of the business of the company, per se, but with giving overall direction to the enterprise, with overseeing the executive actions of management and with satisfying legitimate expectations of accountability and interests beyond the corporate boundaries."

In the definition provided by Shleifer & Vishny (1997), corporate governance deals with "the ways in which suppliers of finance to corporations assure themselves of getting a return on their investments." This is derived from the agency model of the relation between managers, as agents, and shareholders/ creditors, as principals (Jensen & Meckling, 1976). Thus, the shareholder value increase commensurate with the risk to which equity investment is exposed is a matter of primary focus in corporate governance. Although corporate governance seeks to ensure that a firm is run in the long term interests of its shareholders, in achieving this goal the firm will need to "manage effectively relationships with its employees, suppliers, customers and with regard to the common weal" (Hermes, 1997). In this paper, we focus on the shareholder interests, i.e. the wealth effects of corporate decisions, in the context of takeovers, and how corporate governance mediates these decisions so as to ensure shareholder interests.

2.2 Corporate governance structure – internal monitors

Corporate governance structures in the U.S. and the U.K. are similar, but with important differences. In both countries, the board of directors is unitary, with the inclusion of both executive and non-executive directors on a single board. This contrasts with Germany, with a two-tier structure of a management board and a supervisory board. Insiders, i.e. executive directors, dominate the boards in the U.K., whereas boards in the U.S. have a preponderance of outside directors. The majority of boards in the U.K. have a non-executive chairman, but in the U.S. most boards have a combined CEO (Chief Executive Officer) cum Chairman. Institutional investors in the U.K. hold larger stakes in domestic equities (67%) than do U.S. institutions (47%) (Monks & Minow, 1995, p. 303).

2.2.1 The board of directors

Corporate governance has a number of dimensions that collectively can influence its effectiveness in a firm. The board of directors, as the link between shareholders and managers, has a primary responsibility to monitor the performance of management, on behalf of shareholders, and has both advisory and watchdog roles. They are elected by shareholders that have the power to remove them for negligence or unsatisfactory performance. In corporate law, directors owe a fiduciary duty, to ensure that the company is run in the interests of shareholders, and owe a duty of care and duty of loyalty to the company.

The board's role as an effective monitor and disciplinarian of executive management depends crucially upon its composition. While shareholders, in theory, elect the directors to the board of their company, in practice, elections are often thinly disguised selections, with the management selecting the directors, both executive and non-executive, and offering them for election by the shareholders. Thus the incumbent management can shape the board in their own image. Moreover, since the pool of potential directors is often limited to top management of companies, there is scope for cross-board memberships with, say, the CEO of one firm being on the board of another and vice versa. Thus non-executive directors may not be truly independent.

The size of the board as well as its composition has a bearing on the level and effectiveness of board monitoring of managers. Fama & Jensen (1983) argue that the separation of decision management and decision control, in the decision making process, can alleviate the agency problem. While inside directors are responsible for decision management, decision control should be left with outside directors. Outside directors have an incentive to monitor management actions since they have staked their reputation as professional corporate referees. For example, Kaplan & Reishus (1990) find that top executives of poorly performing firms are less likely to get additional directorships in other firms. Consequently, the larger the proportion of independent directors the more effective the monitoring is likely to be. The Cadbury Committee recommended a minimum of three non-executive directors. Of course, a simple head count may be a poor proxy for the ability and competence of the non-executives to be effective monitors. There are impediments to effective monitoring by non-executive directors. Baysinger & Hoskisson (1990) cite information asymmetry, whereby outside directors do not possess all the information that executive directors can have.

Empirically, Weisbach (1988) finds that CEO turnover is highly correlated with the proportion of outside directors to inside directors. The monitoring function of outside directors is also supported by Rosenstein & Wyatt (1990), who find a positive share price reaction to the appointment of outside directors. Further, Boeker & Goodstein (1993) report that strong insider director presence significantly influences CEO replacement decisions. In the case of poorly performing firms, Lai & Sudarsanam (1997) find that the probability of top management change increases with increasing proportion of outside directors. On the other hand, Franks, Mayer & Renneboog (1999) report little impact from a high proportion of non-executive directors in poorly performing U.K. firms.

Where one person combines the roles of board chairman and CEO (known as CEO-Chair duality or duality), his or her powers are considerable. This duality of roles can promote focused objectives and a clear line of command (Finkelstein & D'Aveni, 1994). On the other hand, duality may entrench the top management, to the detriment of shareholders, reduce the board's oversight function and weaken the governance structure. Again, the Cadbury Committee recommends splitting the two roles to improve board independence. Rechner

& Dalton (1989) find no significant difference in firm performance between dual and non-dual firms. Similarly, Baliga, Moyer & Rao (1996) find that duality does not reduce performance.

Johnson, Hoskisson & Hitt (1993) find that outside directors instigate voluntary restructuring, especially when they own stocks in the firm. Lai & Sudarsanam (1997) also report evidence that the higher the proportion of non-executive directors, the higher is the likelihood of both short term and long term restructuring. Hoskisson & Tuck (1990) argue, however, that outside directors concentrate more on financial evaluation than on strategic evaluation, because outsider-dominated boards lack the expertise and time that are needed to examine strategic directions and provide effective guidance. This may cause managers to maximise short term performance, at the expense of shareholders that may prefer long term performance. This shortcoming of outside directors is particularly relevant to acquisitions, since they are of a long term nature. The size of the board also appears to influence firm performance. Yermack (1996) finds that smaller boards are associated with superior performance.

2.2.2 Ownership structure and management monitoring

Since the scope for managerial shirking and self-interest pursuit has been increased by the separation of management and ownership, the ownership pattern of a firm can alleviate or aggravate the agency problem between the share-holders and managers. Atomistic ownership structure prevents individual shareholders from effective monitoring, because of the free rider problem. Free riding refers to some shareholders abstaining from exertions and the cost of monitoring the managers, while sharing in the benefits of such monitoring by more active shareholders. Thus, the latter bear a disproportionate cost of moni-toring and this unequal burden lessens the incentive for such shareholder activism in monitoring managerial performance.

Concentrated ownership, in the form of large block of shareholding, can lessen the cost of monitoring, thereby increasing the net payoff to such monitoring and leading to value maximising behaviour on the part of managers (Jensen & Meckling, 1976; Shleifer & Vishny, 1986). Demsetz & Lehn (1985) argue that as the size of a large shareholding increases, monitoring effectiveness also increases. The positive valuation impact of large share acquisitions has been evidenced in a number of studies. Barclay & Holderness (1991), Mikkelson & Ruback (1985), Holderness & Sheehan (1985) and Choi (1991) report, for the U.S., that block acquisitions in excess of 5% generate significant wealth gains for target shareholders. For the U.K., Sudarsanam (1996) reports similar results. Bethel & Liebeskind (1993) report that block share ownership is associated with corporate restructuring in the U.S. Hill & Snell (1989) find a positive relation between large shareholding and firm productivity.

The increasing concentration of share ownership among institutional shareholders, such as insurance companies, pension funds, mutual funds and banks, thus, can lead to better monitoring. Holland (1995), in a survey of 27 U.K. financial institutions, finds that such investors use their close relation with companies, or their position on the board, to assert their influence and control. They also pressurise companies to conform to the Cadbury Report. However, while pension funds use their relationship as above, unit and investment trusts prefer to sell shares, rather than negotiate with management.

McConnell Servaes (1990) find a significant but non-linear relation between Tobin's q (the ratio of market value to the replacement cost of a firm's assets) and the level of institutional block shareholding. Private large block shareholders, unaffiliated to management, can also exercise effective monitoring. However, the relations between institutional shareholders and corporate management can often be multidimensional and not restricted to just ownership. If they have business dealings with the investee companies, otherwise than as shareholders, their monitoring may be compromised by conflict of interest, thereby detracting from its effectiveness. Pound (1988) provides counter-argument for a less effective monitoring role for institutional and large shareholders, due to their being passive investors or having other business dealings with the company. Mallett & Fowler (1992) also report that high levels of institutional shareholdings are more positively associated with the adoption of anti-takeover poison pills, than lower levels of institutional shareholding.

In recent years, there has been a movement towards shareholder activism, led in the U.S. by institutional investors such as CalPERS (California Public Employees Retirement System) and Lens, an activist fund. In a study of 51 firms targeted by CalPERS over 1987–93, Smith (1996) finds that such firms have lower performance and higher institutional ownership than non-target firms do. Such activism leads to the target firms adopting the changes proposed by the activist shareholder or doing enough to warrant withdrawal of the proposal. Smith reports that activism is reasonably successful in getting governance structure changes adopted, but there is no marked effect on management turnover. Smith also finds that in the three years following successful activism the target firms are able to stem their poor stock price performance and that activism is value increasing for the activist shareholders. Nesbitt (1994) further confirms the significant value gains from CalPERS' activism.

On the other hand, Wahal (1996), who investigates the impact of activism by nine major US funds, concludes that the long term abnormal return to target firms is negative, prior to targeting of such firms by active pension funds, and is still negative after targeting. This failure to add value arises despite the funds' success in changing the governance structure of the target firms. Wahal's results cast doubt on the efficacy of pension fund activism in improving firm performance. In the U.K., Hermes, a major fund manager and Lens have set up an activist fund, U.K. Focus Fund, and developed strategies for 'naming and shaming' under-performing investee companies, so as to improve their shareholder value. The Focus Fund has received support and subscription from other funds (Financial Times, 17 February 2000). The support given by the institutional investors to various corporate governance regulatory initiatives, such as the Cadbury Committee and other follow-up committees in the U.K., suggests their continuing interest in improving corporate governance.

Institutional investors during takeover bids assume a particularly important role, because of their large blocks that can swing the battle either way. In the context of hostile takeover bids, there is the widely held perception that institutional investors are only too keen to sell out to the predators. However, some large institutional investors have stuck by the incumbent management in targets as a matter of policy. Takeover bids often provide large shareholders with the opportunity to offload their large blocks, without moving the market adversely.

Large shareholders may exercise their monitoring directly, by getting on the board of the investee company, or indirectly, by influencing the election of the directors who can be effective monitors. Where the incumbent board is entrenched and challenged by 'insurrectionists' in a proxy fight (see below), large block shareholders can again sway the outcome, thereby enhancing their clout over the board.

2.2.3 Aligning managerial and shareholder interests – the role of incentives

Monitoring by external stakeholders, such as shareholders and lenders, is a costly process from their points of view. An alternative approach is to provide managers with such incentives as to make their investment and financing decision behaviour congruent with the interests of shareholders. The incentives, in the form of stock options and shares based on the achievement of predetermined objectives, such as bench mark stock returns, make managers part owners of the firm, thereby potentially harmonising their and outside shareholders' interests. Hill & Snell (1989) find that both block shareholding and managerial shareholding significantly increase value added per employee, a measure of productivity.

A very high level of managerial share ownership may, however, entrench the managers. Thus, the relation between managerial ownership and alignment may be non-linear. Morck, Shleifer & Vishny (1988) report that Tobin's q rises up to 5% of managerial ownership, falls over the range 5 to 25% and then rises again. High levels of stock ownership may also mean that manager's wealth, in the form of their human and financial capital, may be held in an undiversified portfolio. As a consequence, managers may seek to reduce this undiversified risk by investing their firm's resources in unrelated activities, so as to reduce the volatility of both the firm's earnings stream and their own compensation. The firm may then follow a conglomerate diversification policy.

Larcker (1983) investigates the impact of long term incentive performance plans (LTIPs) and finds that, relative to non-adopting control firms, firms adopting LTIPs experience significant positive abnormal returns on announcement. Brickley, Bhagat & Lease (1985) also report similarly positive reaction to LTIPs. Lewellen, Loderer & Martin (1987) find that firms with a need to provide executives with a long time horizon pay a higher proportion of their pay in long term compensation. More recently, however, Gaver, Gaver & Battisel (1992) provide no evidence of significant abnormal returns when firms announce LTIP adoption, compared to non-adopting control firms. Thus, investor reaction to managerial incentive plans is not unequivocally positive. One reason may be the absence of overwhelming evidence of a positive link between managerial compensation and performance.

The empirical evidence, on the relation between managerial compensation and firm performance, does not conclusively establish a strong link. Jensen & Murphy (1990) find a statistically significant, but small, relation between CEO compensation and firm performance. Some studies have shown that such compensation may be linked to firm size or growth, rather than profitability or stock returns. From an extensive survey of both U.S. and U.K. studies, Pavlik, Scott & Tiessen (1993) conclude that there is a weaker relation between stock return performance and executive compensation than between accounting performance and such compensation. However, managers don't appear to be rewarded for increases in the size of the firm. For the U.K., Firth (1991) and Conyon & Clegg (1994) find that size of the firm, achieved through acquisitions and sales growth, is positively related to managerial remuneration.

Conyon & Peck (1998) examine the role of the board and an independent remuneration committee in determining top management compensation. They find that, for a U.K. sample spanning both pre- and post-Cadbury Report periods, management pay and company performance are more aligned when there is a higher proportion of outside directors on a main board or a high proportion serving on a remuneration committee. Thus incentive structures for managers need to be carefully policed by a vigilant board.

2.2.4 Lenders as monitors

It is not just the shareholders who have staked their wealth in the company. So have lenders. The latter are, however, protected under the law as regards payment of interest and repayment of the principal. Their ability to force the borrower firms into receivership or liquidation, by invoking their contractual rights, enables them to monitor their borrowers better. Jensen (1986) posits that lenders can force the borrowers to use their free cash flow wisely and not squander it by making value-destroying investments. Thus, shareholders benefit from the monitoring provided by lenders. Thus, lender monitoring can be complementary to, or even be a substitute for, shareholder monitoring.

On the other hand, there are potential conflicts of interests between lenders and shareholders, which mean that lender monitoring may not always be to the benefit of shareholders. Lai & Sudarsanam (1997), investigating the impact of corporate governance and lenders on the choice of turnaround strategies by U.K. firms experiencing performance decline, find that lenders and shareholders have preferences for different strategies, e.g. cash generative asset sales and rights issues.

2.3 External monitors of managerial performance

The mechanisms we have discussed so far are internal to the firm, in the sense that they may be determined or influenced by the managers, although external actors may make institutional ownership decisions. On the other hand, the managerial labour market, the stock market and the market for corporate control perform external monitoring. These, however, may differ in their performance criterion, i.e. shareholder value maximisation or other performance measures, such as profitability.

2.3.1 Managerial labour market

Since managers are likely to be evaluated and rewarded or punished by the managerial labour market, this imposes discipline on them to make decisions in the interests of the shareholders (Fama & Jensen, 1983). Where managers develop a reputation as self-dealing and negligent of the interests of the shareholders, their alternative job prospects will be diminished and their compensation will also fall.

2.3.2 The stock market

The pricing function of the stock market generates signals about the performance of a firm and can lead to changes in control through managerial displacement by the board, proxy fights for the transformation of the board or through takeover bids. The stock market exercises its monitoring, also, at the time firms seek fresh funding through new equity issues. Stock returns that are persistently below the investors' risk adjusted required returns may also trigger takeover bids, thus putting the firm 'in play' as a target in the market for corporate control.

2.3.3 The market for corporate control

The market for corporate control is characterised by management teams competing for the right to control corporate assets and the instrumentality of transfer of control is the takeover bid by one firm (the bidder) for the shares in the other (the target) (Manne, 1965). While the bid can be either friendly, i.e. made with the acquiescence and support of the incumbent target management, or hostile, i.e. made directly to the shareholders of the target over the heads of the incumbent management, it is the latter which is generally regarded as the primary manifestation of the market for corporate control, although many hostile bids can be disguised as a friendly merger.

By definition, the market for corporate control emerges as a solution to managerial failure and such failure, in turn, implies failure of the internal corporate governance mechanisms. Thus, at one level, a hostile takeover bid is a substitute for corporate governance. However, hostile takeover bids may also be reinforced by the presence of large block shareholders or the independent directors on the board, who have a fiduciary duty to act in the interests of the company and the shareholders.

The attitude of the board of directors and large, especially institutional, shareholders during hostile takeover bids will influence not only the probability of the hostile bid success, but also the takeover premium and the shareholder wealth. Board attitude, in turn, is shaped by its composition, the split between executive and independent directors, the level of independence of the non-executive directors, the stake of the directors in the ownership of their firm and the incentives for the directors to pursue shareholders' interests.

Corporate governance is relevant to both target and bidder firms. Failure of corporate governance may render a firm vulnerable to hostile takeover. In this case, a takeover corrects corporate governance failure and provides an alternative mechanism for improving corporate performance. On the other hand, failure of corporate governance may lead firms to make value-destroying acquisitions. Indeed, a consistent record of value destroying acquisitions may be a manifestation of serious breakdown of corporate governance monitoring. Over the long term, sustained corporate governance failure and a prolonged record of value-destroying acquisitions may trigger takeover bids for such firms.

2.4 Effectiveness of corporate governance

How effective are the different corporate governance structures, in terms of the shareholder value enhancement criterion? The answer is not quite straightforward since, as can be surmised from the above description of the various dimensions of corporate governance, some of them are complementary, thereby reinforcing one another. Thus, the individual effect of each is difficult to measure. For example, shareholder activism may result in a robust board, with a strong independent director presence. Similarly, block shareholders, such as institutions, may interact directly with the executive management and perform the oversight function in the absence of a strong board. In the latter case the two mechanisms are substitutes. Managerial share ownership again can complement board oversight, substitute for it or even counter it at levels where alignment gives way to retrenchment. Where lender monitoring is effective it can offset the weakness in board oversight due to the board lacking in independence.

2.5 Inter-relation among corporate control mechanisms

We have identified a range of corporate governance mechanisms. Four of them are internal and substantially influenced by the firm management – board composition, block ownership, use of debt and managerial incentives including managerial share ownership. The external monitoring mechanisms include the managerial labour market and the market for corporate control, i.e. tender offers and hostile takeover bids. These mechanisms may not, however, be independent of one another.

Many empirical studies have examined the substitution versus complementarity issue and reported evidence to support substitution as well as complementarity. Bathala & Rao (1995) have examined the inter-relation between board composition, i.e. the proportion of outside directors, and other agency monitoring variables, such as capital structure, insider ownership and institutional ownership. They find that there is an inverse relation between the proportion of outside directors and other agency monitoring devices. They conclude that different firms have different optimal governance structures and different board composition. There is, thus, some evidence of substitution among different agency monitors. Interestingly, the authors also observe that the proportion of outside directors increases with the share of institutional share ownership. This suggests that, as institutional shareholders increase their ownership, they get more serious about their monitoring role and they exercise that role by strengthening the board. This points to complementarity between the two agency monitors.

Some evidence on the substitution effect is provided by Denis & Sarin (1999), Zajac & Westphal (1994) and Peasnell, Pope & Young (1999). These studies examine the link between the level of managerial share ownership and the proportion of outside board members. Since managerial share ownership is presumed to align managerial and shareholder interests, thereby alleviating the agency problem, the need for strong monitoring by the board is reduced. This in turn reduces the need for a high proportion of independent outside directors on the board. Denis & Sarin (1999) and Zajac & Westphal (1994) both find empirical evidence of a negative relation between these two agency monitoring mechanisms, for the U.S. In contrast, Peasnell et al. (1999) argue that the relation between the two monitoring devices need not be linear. Since, at high levels of their ownership, managers may become entrenched, pursuing non-value-maximising policies, and the market discipline on such managers may be weak, the need for a robust board monitoring increases. This necessitates a strong outsider presence on the board. Peasnell et al, therefore, posit a non-linear relation between managerial ownership and the proportion of outside directors. For a sample of U.K. listed companies, they report supporting evidence.

Agrawal & Knoeber (1996) extend the interaction argument to encompass seven agency monitors.[1] Since "all of these control mechanisms are alternative ways to provide incentives to managers, each might plausibly be used instead of another." This suggests a mutually negative relation among them. However, positive relations may also exist. For example, takeovers may be facilitated, rather than hindered, by high managerial ownership, if managers stand to receive a large wealth gain. Similarly, strong outside director presence may lead to removal of anti-takeover defences by target firms and increase the chances of their being acquired. Firms may choose an optimal combination of these alternative control mechanisms, at least the internally determined ones, so as to maximise their value. An empirical implication of such a choice is that, in a cross sectional analysis of the relation between these combinations and firm performance, one may not detect any impact for individual mechanisms.

Agrawal & Knoeber (1996), therefore, measure the impact of agency control mechanisms within a simultaneous equations framework, to allow for the endogeneity of these variables. In single equation OLS regressions of firm performance, measured by Tobin's q, on one agency monitor at a time, plus control variables such as firm size, Agrawal & Knoeber find that greater insider shareholding, fewer outside directors, less corporate debt and a less active market for corporate control lead to improved performance. However, in a simultaneous model estimation insider shareholding, corporate debt and corporate control market lose significance, whereas board composition retains its negative impact. The absence of impact of the first three variables is consistent with the firm's optimal use of each control mechanism, although the persistence of the negative impact of outside director presence is a puzzle to be resolved.

Boyle, Carter & Stover (1998) argue that both insider ownership and anti-takeover provisions affect a firm's vulnerability to takeover, its value and its managers' incentives and utility. Using data from mutual savings and loan associations converting to stock form, they find that, at low levels, insider ownership is negatively related to the number of extraordinary anti-takeover provisions, emphasising the need for additional protection against takeovers. At higher levels, ownership is not related to the number of anti-takeover provisions. They conclude that this result is consistent with managerial entrenchment.

Since some of the agency monitors are endogenously determined, managers can manipulate their levels so as to strengthen their defence against potential takeover threats. For example, Garvey & Hanka (1999) argue that firms in those U.S. states that have strong anti-takeover laws (see below) have less need for debt as a defence against potential takeover threats. They find that capital structure choices reflect managerial discretion and that impediments to takeovers induce a shift from debt to equity.

These recent studies have, thus, highlighted the fruitlessness and inappropriateness of searching for a meaningful relation between individual control mechanisms and corporate performance. They have focused attention on the interaction – both substitution and complementarity – among seemingly alternative control devices. Table 1 summarises the various corporate control devices and their possible interactions. The empirical research, so far, has only explored these interactions for a small number of variables. Future research needs to identify a more exhaustive set of agency monitors and model their interactions, derive testable hypotheses and develop empirical techniques to measure their impact.

In the rest of the paper, we focus on the market for corporate control and on how this interacts with other agency control mechanisms.

3. CORPORATE CONTROL TRANSACTIONS AS AGENCY CONTROL DEVICES

Corporate control transactions include large block acquisitions, proxy contests for control of the board, tender offers and mergers. We review the empirical evidence on the impact of corporate governance on these transactions and the attendant wealth effects of such transactions.

Table 1. Alternative Corporate Control Devices and their Potential Interactions

Control device	Characteristics	Interaction	
		Positive	Negative
Board of directors	Independent board, high proportion of outside directors, no CEO-Chair duality. Nomination, remuneration and audit committees present.	Institutional activism strengthens board independence and authority. Strongly independent board facilitates takeover through more objective evaluation.	Large block ownership may reduce need for strong independent board. Strong board monitoring reduces managerial failure and need for hostile takeover.
Managerial share ownership and incentive structure	Share ownership aligns managerial and shareholder interests.	High ownership increases entrenchment and need for more independent board monitoring. May facilitate mergers due to gains on their ownership.	Ownership increases alignment and reduces need for strong board and other monitoring. Anti-takeover laws reduce need for managerial ownership.
Managerial labour market	Evaluates and rewards managerial services and reputation		Weak labour market increases need for strong board and other monitoring.
Institutional & other outside block ownership	Overcomes 'free-riding', concentrated voting power to re-shape board, sell decision signals disapproval of management, stock price declines.	Strengthens board independence. Facilitates takeover by sale of large blocks.	Active monitoring reduces need for takeover.
Lenders	Continual monitoring through debt covenants, access to private information, monitoring during renewal of short term credit.	Increased board and shareholder monitoring may be needed to reduce opportunistic coalition between managers and lenders.	Reduces need for other monitoring devices. Anti-takeover laws reduce debt level. High managerial ownership reduces need for high debt. Debt increases firm's value & reduces takeover chances.
Market for corporate control	Mergers, hostile tender offers, proxy contest, block acquisition.	Other devices may reduce anti-takeover defences and increase chances of hostile tender offer success.	Strong monitoring by other devices reduces need for takeover. High debt level reduces takeover threat.

3.1 Large block share transactions

Our review of the role of large shareholders suggests that they can monitor and improve managerial performance. It then follows that large block acquisitions are likely to be treated, by shareholders and investors, as presaging enhanced performance and therefore as positive news.

Holderness & Sheehan (1985) and Barclay & Holderness (1991) find that block share purchases are followed by increases in share value and abnormally high rates of top management turnover. In Mikkelson & Ruback (1985), Schedule 13D filings of block acquisitions, of 5% or more, trigger a positive market reaction. Shome & Singh (1995) report that both share price increase and some improvement in accounting returns follow block share purchases. Bethel, Liebeskind & Opler (1998) document the relation between purchase of large share blocks and corporate performance. They find that activist investors acquiring large share blocks typically target poorly performing diversified firms. Increased divestitures, share repurchases and reduction in mergers and acquisitions follow such purchases. Activist block share purchases are associated with improvements in profitability and shareholder value. They conclude that "the market for partial corporate control identifies and rectifies poor corporate performance."

Sudarsanam (1996), who examines the stock market reaction to large block purchases in a sample of U.K. firms, also reports large wealth gains for target firm shareholders. He finds that a larger block purchase increases the likelihood of a takeover bid for the target firm, although it reduces the chances of a hostile bid. These results are consistent with large shareholders playing an effective corporate governance role.

3.2 Proxy contests

A proxy contest is a mechanism by which shareholders can change the firm's board. Where the incumbent board controls the firm, a successful proxy contest transfers control of the firm to the 'dissidents' (also called 'insurgents'). A proxy contest may instigate change in corporate management when the board has failed to respond to pressure for such a change (Dodd & Warner, 1983). Thus it is a way of correcting board failure to monitor the executive management properly. In the range of possible disciplinary actions, the proxy contest lies somewhere between a board dismissal of management and an outside takeover by another corporation (Dodd & Warner, 1983).

It has been argued that takeover, as a managerial corrective mechanism, has been hindered, in the U.S., by the panoply of state anti-takeover laws, defensive devices such as poison pills, shark repellents and court judgements favouring incumbent management and that proxy contests would become an increasingly important means of monitoring and eliminating inefficient management (Pound, 1992; & Roe, 1993). This suggests that proxy fights are an alternative corporate control device to tender offers and hostile bids. Proxy contests in the U.K. are quite rare.

Several U.S. studies have examined proxy contests and their impact on change in board composition, top management change and subsequent takeover activity. They have also investigated the shareholder wealth impact of proxy contests. Dodd & Warner (1983) and DeAngelo & DeAngelo (1989) report cumulative abnormal returns of 6% to 8%, over the period of announcement to resolution of proxy contest. Borstadt & Zwirlein (1992) and Ikenberry & Lakonishok (1993) examine the contest period and the post-contest period for abnormal returns. In the former study, over 12 post-contest months, the target firms experience abnormal returns of –4.5% whereas, in Ikenberry and Lakonishok, the abnormal returns, over +5 to +24 months after contest resolution, are –17%. These negative returns raise the question whether proxy contests are unequivocally effective corporate control events.

Dodd & Warner (1983) find abnormal returns of about 8%, whether or not the insurgents win seats on the board. Mulherin & Poulsen (1998) also report no significant difference in abnormal returns between these categories of contests. DeAngelo & DeAngelo (1989) partition the returns by whether or not the target is acquired after the proxy contest. They report 15% abnormal returns where the sale of target is linked to dissidents and only 3% otherwise. Mulherin & Poulsen (1998), while confirming a difference in returns of a similar magnitude for the contest period, extend their observation over one year post-contest. Whereas for the targets subsequently acquired the abnormal return is 12%, this falls to –24% for the firms undergoing proxy contests not followed by takeover. The differences in both cases are significant at the 1% level. This result is important since it suggests that a proxy contest may facilitate value enhancing takeover bids and is thus complementary to the latter.

In a further refinement of the previous studies, Mulherin & Poulsen (1998) argue that a real test of whether a proxy contest is an effective monitoring device is its impact on top management change. They find that, whether or not the dissidents win seats on the board, the returns are much higher when top management is changed.

A proxy contest may be a less expensive alternative to a full takeover, although it may not result in majority ownership. Sridharan & Reinganum (1995) investigate to what extent these two are alternatives. They compare 79 hostile tender offers and 38 proxy contests and report that a proxy contest is more likely after poor stock return and accounting performance, whereas a hostile tender offer is triggered by the target's failure to pursue profitable investment opportunities.

Important conclusions follow from these studies of proxy contests. A proxy contest, by itself, is not an adequate manifestation of effective corporate control. Effectiveness needs to be judged by the management change brought about by the proxy contest. Further, a proxy contest may not, by itself, bring about control change, but can facilitate it in the form of a takeover. Thus, the two corporate governance devices are complements rather than substitutes. They may also be employed to correct different kinds managerial failure. Proxy contests, by removing the obstacles to takeover, thus increase their likelihood. Overall, "proxy contests play an active role in monitoring the performance of U.S. corporations, by complementing outright takeover bids and by removing poorly performing managers" (Mulherin & Poulsen, 1998, p305).

3.3 Impediments to takeovers

3.3.1 Statutory and firm-initiated anti-takeover defences in the U.S.
The advent of hostile tender offers in the U.S., in the late 1970s, placed many firms under siege and caused widespread dismay and consternation among corporate managers. In reaction to actual or potential hostile tender offers many U.S. firms, aided by inventive corporate lawyers, devised ever more ingenious anti-takeover defences. Many firms also lobbied their local politicians and state legislatures to pass anti-takeover statutes, thereby strengthening the entrenchment of the incumbent management.

State anti-takeover laws fall into 'first generation' and 'second generation' laws. The first generation laws, which required filing of information on initiation of a takeover bid by firms outside the state passing the laws, were declared unconstitutional and infringed the Federal Williams Act dealing with tender offers, including disclosure requirements. The second generation laws deal with issues of corporate governance and have survived subsequent legal challenges (Gaughan, 1996, ch. 3). These latter laws provide for:

(1) a fair price offer to all target shareholders and restrict coercive two-tier tender offers;
(2) business combination restrictions on agreements between the target firm and the bidder, e.g. for the use of the target's assets to finance leveraged acquisitions;
(3) prior approval of current target shareholders before a bidder is allowed to purchase target shares; and
(4) cash-out, which requires a buyer of a certain percentage of target shares to purchase the remaining shares on the same terms.

The cash-out rule is similar to the mandatory bid rule under the City Takeover Code in the U.K. (Sudarsanam, 1995, ch. 6, see below).

In addition, managers have also succeeded in carrying out charter amendments that would raise the cost of hostile tender offers to prohibitively high levels. Some of the defences could also be executed without the need for shareholder approval. Thus, the overall effect of these statutory and company-specific anti-takeover defences is to present seemingly formidable barriers to hostile takeovers.

All anti-takeover defences are not necessarily against the target firm share-holders' interests. Where these defences are used by the target management to extract the highest bid premium, while allowing the hostile tender offer to go through, such a tactical posture is obviously in the shareholders' interests. However, target managers may often be guided by more selfish motives, of avoiding loss of job, position, power etc., in invoking these anti-takeover defences to defeat hostile bids. Thus, anti-takeover defences may help target managers secure maximum bid premium for their shareholders, a case of managerial alignment with shareholder interests. Managers who entrench themselves to the detriment of shareholder interests could also use them.

Both the range and strength of anti-takeover defences depend on the jurisdiction of the target company, its incorporation laws and charter and the corporate governance structure, as well as institutional structure and corporate practice. In the U.S., anti-takeover defences may be classified as preventive or strategic and post-bid or tactical. Strategic defences include taking advantage of state incorporation laws, by incorporating or re-incorporating in states, such as Delaware, with strong anti-takeover laws. Strategic anti-takeover measures are listed in Table 2. Strategic anti-takeover measures may be divided into those requiring charter amendments and those taken at the discretion of the management, e.g. poison pills. Some defences need to be approved by shareholders e.g. charter amendments.

Poison pills are rights given to shareholders, which allow them to buy shares in the target (flip-in pill) or in the acquirer (flip-over pill) at a heavy discount. The effect of these pills is to increase the number of shares of either the target or the bidder, at a low cost to the shareholders but at a high cost to the acquirer. Poison put enables debt holders to sell their debt back to the issuing target and thereby avoid dilution of its value arising from new debt issued. With a staggered board the directors are not elected all at the same time. This will delay the time until the acquirer can gain full control of the board. Supermajority provision requires the bid to be approved by a big majority, e.g. 75% or 80%, to succeed. Dual capitalisation means the issue of shares with differential voting rights, with the voting rights concentrated in the hands of insiders or those friendly to the management. Exchange offers involve exchange of securities of higher voting rights for those with lesser rights, again leading to concentration of voting rights. Leveraged re-capitalisation means debt for equity swap, with a similar effect.

Tactical defensive measures, deployed during a hostile takeover bid, are listed in Table 3. Some of the actions, such as asset or ownership restructuring, may be done in anticipation of takeover bids in general, as well as following a bid. The tables provide descriptions of the anti-takeover defences and cite the empirical studies, which have investigated their impact on target shareholder wealth. These studies are not individually discussed, for brevity, but the broad conclusions from them are indicated.

3.3.2 Anti-takeover defences in the U.K.

Unlike in the U.S., in the U.K. there are few state laws designed to protect firms against takeovers, although the antitrust rules can prohibit a takeover if it will operate against the public interest. (Sudarsanam, 1995, ch. 5). The self-regulatory City Panel on Takeovers and Mergers (The City Panel) polices takeover bids for public companies, under its stringent City Code. Many takeover defences, such as poison pills, are rarely seen in the U.K. Targeted repurchases and greenmail payments require the target shareholders' approval. The Code also lays down a strict timetable for the conclusion of the bid. The courts in the U.K. have upheld the authority of the Panel and refrained from interfering with its proceedings. Thus, in general, hostile takeover bids have a much more benign regulatory regime in the U.K., than in the U.S.

Sudarsanam (1995, ch. 12) reports on the use of 23 post-bid defences, deployed by targets of hostile bids during 1983–89, and concludes that the most effective strategies are: the entry of the 'white knight', lobbying friendly shareholders, support of the unions and litigation. Holl & Kyriazis (1997) investigate the impact of bid resistance on wealth gains of target firms and the probability of bid success, during 1978–89. They find that, in a multiple regression model, individual defences, except dividend increase, are not significant in adding to target gains, but together they increase target shareholder wealth. While white knight strategy increases chances of a successful bid, other defences lower the probability of success of the hostile bidder. Litigation reduces the chances of a successful hostile bid.

3.4 Takeover as a disciplinary mechanism

The notion that takeovers, especially hostile takeovers, represent a management discipline mechanism invites a scrutiny of its efficacy. A number of studies

Table 2. Strategic (pre-bid) Anti-Takeover Defences

Defence	Description	Relevant studies	Broad conclusions
Poison pills	First and second generation, flip-over and flip-in, back-end plans, poison puts.	Malatesta & Walkling (1988); Ryngaert (1988); Comment & Schwert (1995); Datta & Datta (1996); Cook & Easterwood (1994).	Wealth effect small/ insignificant. Takeovers not deterred. Higher takeover premium for targets. Puts protect creditors & managers. Poor performers adopt poison pills.
Corporate charter amendments	Staggered board, supermajority, dual class capitalisation, anti-greenmail.	Brickley, Lease & Smith (1988; 1994); Bhagat & Brickley (1984); DeAngelo & Rice (1983); Ruback (1987); Linn & McConnell (1983); Jarrell & Poulsen (1987); Pound (1987); Jarrell & Poulsen (1988); McWilliams (1990); Karpoff & Malatesta (1989); Karpoff, Malatesta & Walking (1996); Mahoney & Mahoney (1993). Ambrose & Megginson (1992).	Ineffective as takeover deterrents. Target shareholder wealth effect insignificant especially if amendments subject to shareholder approval.
Re-incorporation	Shift incorporation to a state with favourable anti-takeover regime.	Netter & Poulsen (1989); Wahal (1995); Heron & Lewellen (1998).	Only some firms prefer this anti-takeover protection. Where it aids takeover defence shareholder wealth decreased. Wealth effect ambiguous.
Financial restructuring	Exchange offers, dual-class re-capitalisation, leveraged re-capitalisation, ESOP.	Dann & DeAngelo (1988); Dhillon & Ramirez (1994); Beatty (1995).	ESOPs have negative effect on takeover activity and depress firm value of takeover targets.
Golden parachute (GP)	Compensation to management for loss of office in the event of corporate control change.	Lambert & Larcker (1985); Knoeber (1986); Coffee (1988); Jensen (1988); Berkovich & Khanna (1991); Machlin, Choe & Miles (1993); Mogavero & Toyne (1995).	May cause management alignment or entrenchment. Adoption may signal takeover vulnerability. Excess GP subject to tax. Wealth effect ambiguous

Note: ESOP = employee stock option plan, an incentive scheme involving issue of company shares, with some tax benefits to the company.

Table 3. Tactical (post-bid) Defences

Defence	Description	Relevant studies	Broad conclusions
Greenmail & Standstill agreement	Buy out potential predator at a premium, with agreement not to exceed holding above agreed level	Bradley & Wakeman (1983); Dann & DeAngelo (1983); Mikkelson & Ruback (1991); Bhagat & Jefferis (1994).	Early studies report wealth losses suggesting entrenchment. Recent studies refute entrenchment. Stand-still reinforces entrenchment.
White knight	Arrange friendly rival to hostile bidder	Banerjee & Owers (1992); Niden (1993).	White knight shareholders suffer wealth losses.
White squire	Sell large share block to friendly investor		
Recapitalise	Debt for equity swap, buy back shares, open market and targeted share repurchases.	Kamma, Weintrop & Weir (1988); Dann & DeAngelo (1988).	Ownership changes result in shareholder wealth losses.
Litigation	Challenge bid in court for anti-trust violation, breach of trust etc.	Jarrell (1985)	Evokes competing bids. High premium. if successful. If bid is withdrawn targets suffer wealth losses.
Pac-Man defence	Counter-bid for hostile bidder		Very rarely attempted.
Asset restructuring	Acquisitions, sell-offs	Dann & DeAngelo (1988).	Asset restructuring results in shareholder wealth losses

have examined this proposition. Walsh & Ellwood (1991) investigate the relation between the pre-merger performance of the acquired firm and the post-acquisition top management turnover. They find, for a U.S. sample, turnover is 61% for the acquired firms and 34% for the control sample. Interestingly, there is no link between post-acquisition turnover and the acquired company's pre-acquisition performance, measured by the cumulative abnormal returns. This calls into doubt the hypothesis that top management turnover is due to the disciplinary impact of a takeover.

Franks & Mayer (1996) also find that, for a U.K. sample, the pre-acquisition performance of the acquired firms in hostile takeovers was not significantly different from that of a control sample of firms acquired in friendly takeovers or that of a sample of non-acquired firms. However, they report that firms acquired in hostile takeovers experience a significantly higher level of top management turnover and asset restructuring, in the post-acquisition period. These results, as with those of Walsh & Ellwood above, provide no support to the disciplinary model of takeovers.

Martin & McConnell (1991) classify a takeover as disciplinary if there is top management turnover, in the target firm, in the two years after the takeover. They examine the five-year pre-takeover performance of the targets in terms of cumulative abnormal returns, in both disciplinary and non-disciplinary takeovers. The results are that turnover increases after a takeover. For example, in the fourteen months after takeover, the rate of turnover for the top executive is 42%, whereas the annual turnover in the previous five years is only 10%. Further, targets with high turnover under-perform their industry in the pre-takeover period. However, as Walsh & Ellwood's and Franks & Mayer's studies show, top management turnover in the post-acquisition period is neither a necessary nor a sufficient condition for a takeover to be designated disciplinary.

One needs to examine both pre-acquisition performance and post-acquisition management turnover. Further, a takeover can be disciplinary even though the pre-bid performance may be satisfactory, if the incumbent management had failed to exploit all the available growth opportunities of the target firms. This represents a failure of vision. This is an error of omission rather than commission e.g. bad acquisition or poor strategy or lax financial controls. This interpretation receives some support from Sridharan & Reinganum (1995) (see Section 3.2 above) who find that firms which generate poor returns become targets of proxy fights, whereas firms which fail to exploit investment opportunities become targets of hostile tender offers.

Mikkelson & Partch (1997) compare top management turnover in un-acquired U.S. firms, during active and non-active takeover periods, to assess the disciplinary impact of takeovers. Turnover of CEO, president and chairman in two five-year periods is compared. The study finds that management turnover is significantly higher in active takeover periods. Further, turnover is also more sensitive to poor performance during such periods. This evidence suggests that takeover threat also has a disciplinary effect on poorly performing managers.

Morck, Shleifer & Vishny (1989) examine the functioning of corporate boards and contrast the circumstances in which boards succeed in disciplining top managers with those in which substitute control devices, such as hostile takeovers, come into play. They examine a variety of performance and management characteristics of 454 U.S. corporations, in 1980, and follow the management changes and takeovers they experience in the following five years. Morck et al conclude that boards may bring about management change when their firms under-perform industry peers and not when the whole industry is suffering. Takeovers play a role in replacing managers whom the board is unable or unwilling to discipline, e.g. one-man management teams. This study emphasises the need to specify carefully the circumstances under which hostile takeovers and board monitoring become alternative control devices.

3.5 Acquirer managerial motives and post-acquisition performance

Acquisitions represent major investment decisions for firms and allow them to accomplish their strategic objectives in quicker time than through organic growth. While they may be driven by shareholder value maximisation consideration, there are other motives, such as growth of the firm, size, market share etc. that may not necessarily be consistent with such a goal. Acquirer managers may also be driven by hubris, caused by the narcissistic overestimation of their own ability to create value from an acquisition (Roll, 1986). Jensen's (1986) free cash flow model hypothesises that managers may use cash flows in excess of their positive net present value investment requirements to make non-value increasing acquisitions or similar investments.

Managers who have both their financial and human capital invested in their firm, thus, hold a relatively undiversified portfolio and, thus, carry a high level of risk. To reduce this risk, they may follow risk diversification investments, such as unrelated or conglomerate acquisitions, even though these may not be value enhancing for their shareholders (Lewellen, 1971). May (1995) provides evidence that managers consider personal risk when making decisions that affect firm risk. CEOs with more personal wealth vested in firm equity tend to diversify. Such risk avoidance is a cost associated with equity-based compensation which may align effort incentives, but misalign risk taking incentives, between shareholders and managers.

3.5.1 Shareholder wealth performance of acquirers

Numerous studies have documented the abnormal returns to shareholders of acquiring firms, both in the takeover bid period and in the post-acquisition period extending over two to five years.[2] These studies are summarised in Table 4, with Jensen & Ruback (1983) providing an excellent summary of the pre–1983 US acquisitions. The studies cover both U.K. and U.S. research. Where the studies report the returns to hostile and friendly acquisitions these are included separately in Table 4, since the distinction is important in the context of the market for corporate control as a disciplinary mechanism. Such a disciplinary role is more vividly associated with hostile bids, even though some hostile bids may be disguised as friendly bids.

The broad conclusion from this research is that, in the period surrounding takeover bids, target shareholders in acquisitions make substantial gains, of the order of 20% to 43%. They make more gains in tender offers than in mergers, in the U.S. Tender offers are generally, though not always, hostile. Target shareholders also enjoy larger wealth gains in hostile acquisitions than in friendly ones. In the same period, bidder shareholders lose money, break even or make a small gain. Once again, they do better in tender offers. With an U.K. sample, Sudarsanam, Holl & Salami (1996) report that, in regressions of bidder abnormal returns on various determinants of such returns, bid hostility has a significant impact and adds 3% to shareholder returns, compared to friendly acquisitions. In a similar regression, they also report that hostile acquisitions create more value (9% or more) for target shareholders than friendly acquisitions.

When acquisition performance is assessed over 2 to 5 years the picture is much more muddled and becomes sensitive to the bench mark problem i.e. the way the bench market normal return is estimated. While in some studies acquirers lose considerably, in others they just break even. As Agrawal, Jaffe & Mandelker (1992) note, the results are also sensitive to the sampling period. Nevertheless, the superior performance of tender offers and hostile acquisitions is more consistently revealed. This is particularly so when the combined wealth gains of targets and bidders are considered.

While the superior performance of hostile acquirers may be consistent with the disciplinary model of takeovers, the documented evidence that a large number of acquisitions, including many friendly ones, experience negative wealth gains, suggests that acquirer managers are making value destroying acquisitions through hubris, overpayment of bid premium, inappropriate strategy for competitive advantage etc. It also raises disturbing questions about the efficacy of corporate governance in acquirers. It is plausible that managerial motives drive many of these bad acquisitions. Morck, Shleifer & Vishny (1990), after examining 326 U.S. acquisitions, find that three types of acquisitions have

Table 4. Summary of Abnormal Returns (%) to Acquirer Shareholders in Bid
and Post-Acquisition Periods

Panel A: U.S. Studies

Study	Type of	Abnormal	Bid period	Bid period	Post-acquisition Period	
(year)	offer	return model	Target	Bidder	Bidder	Years
Jensen &	Merger	Various	20	0		
Ruback (1983)	Tender	models	30	4		
Magenheim &	Merger	Market		−0.4	−28	about 3
Mueller (1988)	Tender	model		1.4	9	
Jarrell &	Tender		29	1.0		
Poulsen (1989)	Full sample	Various	28	−1.0	0.1	3
Franks, Harris	Contested	models	39	−1.4	0.0	
& Titman (1991)	Uncontested		25	−0.9	0.3	
Loderer &	Merger	Size adjusted			−0.003	5
Martin (1992)	Tender	CAPM			0.004	
Agrawal, Jaffe &	Merger	Size adjusted			−10.3	5
Mandelker (1992)		CAPM and RATS				
Loughran &	Merger	Size and book			−16.0	5
Vijh (1997)	Tender	to market			43.0	
Rao &	Merger	Size and book			−4.0	3
Vermaelen (1998)	Tender	to market			8.6	

Panel B: U.K. Studies

Study	Abnormal	Bid period	Bid period	Post-acquisition Period	
(year)	return model	Target	Bidder	Bidder	Years
Firth (1980)	Market model	28	−6.3	0.0	3
Franks & Harris (1989)	Market	22	0.0	−12.6	2
Limmack (1991)	Market	31	−0.2	−4.5	2
Sudarsanam et al (1996)	Market	29	−4.0		
Gregory (1997)	Market & size multi-index		−0.5 (full sample)	−8.2 (full) 1.7 (hostile) −10.4 (friendly)	2
Higson & Elliott (1998)	Size adjusted	38 (full sample) 43 (hostile) 37 (friendly)	0.4 (full sample) 0.0 (hostile) 0.0 (friendly)	−1.1 (full) 12.8 (hostile) −3.7 (friendly)	2

Note: In Panel A, for Franks et al (1991) the post-acquisition returns are monthly abnormal returns. In: Agrawal, Jaffe and Mandelker (1992), RATS is regression across time series to allow for variation in risk. CAPM is capital asset pricing model. The bid period varies from a few days to a few months on either side of bid announcement.

systematically lower and predominantly negative announcement period abnormal returns to bidding firms. The returns are lower when the bidding firm diversifies or buys a fast growth target or the bidder managers perform poorly prior to the acquisition. Morck et al. conclude that these bad acquisitions manifest agency problems within the acquirers.

4. CORPORATE GOVERNANCE AND ACQUISITION DECISIONS

In the last Section we have discussed the operation of the market for corporate control as an agency control mechanism. In this section we turn to the question of the interaction between corporate governance and the behaviour of acquirers and targets.

4.1 Managerial ownership

How do the acquirer's corporate governance mechanisms ensure that acquisition decisions are value creating for the shareholders? Lewellen, Loderer & Rosenfeld (1985) test the proposition that managers' personal welfare affects the merger decisions they make and investigate the relation between the stock returns to bidder shareholders in completed mergers and the personal wealth circumstances of the senior executives of the bidders. The authors find that managers who have the largest percentage ownership in their companies' shares have undertaken more successful mergers than other managers, as judged by the stock price performance. Thus managerial ownership seems able to align managerial and shareholder interests and lead to value enhancing acquisition decisions.

4.2 Board monitoring

Since acquisitions represent major and strategic decisions, directors are likely to play an important role in shaping and executing them. In doing so, directors have a fiduciary duty to the corporation and its shareholders. It may, therefore, be expected that an independent and vigilant board will ensure that acquisitions made by their firms increase shareholder value. Byrd & Hickman (1992) put this view to test. They identify outside directors who are independent, for a sample of U.S. bidders, during 1980 to 1987. They find that bidding firms in which independent outside directors hold at least 50% of the seats have significantly higher announcement date abnormal returns than other bidders. This evidence is consistent with effective board monitoring of tender offer decisions. Byrd & Hickman (1992) also report that the relation between bidder returns and the proportion of independent directors is non-linear, with these returns falling at high levels of independent board membership. Thus, there is an optimal level of independence of the board.

Since, as we have seen, mergers add much less value than tender offers, the board monitoring of merger decisions may be less effective than board monitoring of tender offers. While this remains to be empirically tested, a possible reason for a more effective board monitoring of tender offers is that tender offers, generally, evoke much greater public attention and a more transparent flow of information, due to the disclosure requirements under the Williams Act. This reasoning will also hold good for hostile acquisitions, which, compared to friendly bids, are conducted in a richer information environment. The empirical evidence, documented in Table 4, of the superior performance of tender offers and hostile acquisitions, is consistent with this interpretation.

4.3 Board monitoring of targets in acquisitions

Brickley & James (1987) test the hypothesis that board monitoring and the takeover market are substitutes. They compare the level of independence of the board, in the U.S. states with and without laws prohibiting bank acquisitions. In the event of substitution, the proportion and number of outside directors, a proxy for board independence, would be higher in the former states. Brickley & James, however, find that boards are significantly more independent in those states which have no anti-takeover laws. They do not find any significant difference in ownership concentration, between the two groups of states, that could act as a substitute for either the takeover market or strong board monitoring.

Shivdasani (1993) investigates the interaction among board monitoring, ownership structure and hostile takeover. For a sample of completed and abandoned hostile takeover attempts, that occurred during 1980–88, Shivdasani finds that, relative to a control sample of non-targets, outside directors unaffiliated to the management represent a higher proportion of directors, but have a smaller ownership stake in targets. On the other hand, block shareholders own a higher percentage of firm shares in targets, than in non-targets. Hostile takeover likelihood is increased by low outside director ownership, but augmented by unaffiliated block ownership. Shivdasani's results support the hypothesis that board monitoring and hostile takeovers are substitute corporate governance mechanisms, whereas block shareholding and hostile takeovers are complementary mechanisms.

As regards insider ownership, Mikkelson & Partch (1989) show that targets have significantly lower insider shareholdings than non-targets, but that the probability of offer success is directly, but insignificantly, related to officers' and directors' holdings. It is not clear whether this result supports management alignment or entrenchment induced by insider shareholding. Shivdasani (1993) also finds that high CEO share ownership reduces hostile takeover likelihood. Cotter & Zenner (1994) provide evidence that the probability of a successful tender offer is directly related to the shareholding of directors and senior managers in target firms and to the capital gains to the top executive, on his shareholding.

Cotter, Shivdasani & Zenner (1997) examine the role of the target firm's independent directors during tender offers. They find target shareholders gain more with independent boards. Such boards also use the presence of poison pills and target resistance to their shareholders' advantage, to enhance target shareholder wealth.

Sudarsanam (1995a) investigates the role of ownership structure in determining the outcome of hostile takeover bids in the U.K. After controlling for a wide range of defensive strategies adopted by target firms and the methods of payment, he finds that large block shareholding by outsiders facilitates successful bid outcome. This is consistent with the view that these large, institutional, shareholders ensure that the target management does not pursue entrenchment through bid resistance. He does not find that insider ownership helps or hinders hostile bid outcome.

4.4 Other governance variables

The impact of other corporate governance variables, such as the managerial labour market and lender monitoring, remains to be empirically examined. Empirical work on the relation between corporate governance and the market for corporate control, with U.K. data, awaits attention. Since, in the U.K., large acquisitions require shareholder approval (Sudarsanam, 1995, ch. 6), block shareholders and institutional shareholders are likely to have the opportunity to vet the proposed acquisitions, from the shareholder value perspective. If, however, institutional shareholders, choose inertia and acquiescence in the bidder management's plans, then such decisions may not be properly monitored. This is an area that merits further research.

SUMMARY AND CONCLUSIONS

There are a variety of monitoring and control mechanisms to resolve the agency conflict between shareholders and their agents, the managers. Given the centrality of the shareholder wealth maximisation goal in corporate finance, the function of these mechanisms is to ensure that managers pursue that goal. These mechanisms include: an independent board, outside block shareholdings including institutional shareholders, managerial ownership and incentives, lenders, managerial labour market and the market for corporate control. We explore the inter-dependency of these control mechanisms and whether and how they complement, or substitute for, one another. The role of the market for corporate control, including proxy contests and outright takeovers, in resolving agency conflicts, the impediments to takeovers and their effectiveness are reviewed. We seek to explain the well-documented failure of acquirers to create value, in terms of the ineffectiveness of the corporate governance system in acquiring companies.

What emerges from our review is that corporate governance is a complex web of mutually interacting control mechanisms. There are no clear and conclusive results as to the superiority of one mechanism over another. The circumstances under which one mechanism, or a combination of mechanisms, is more effective than another, or another combination, need to be modelled theoretically. The testable hypotheses from these models then need to be put to empirical test. The numerous empirical studies we have reviewed tend to be partial and somewhat ad hoc. While they have doubtless added to our understanding of the phenomenon of corporate control, they need to be extended to cover a richer set of contingent variables that will help us resolve the complementarity versus substitution issue.

Our research, covering a profusion of U.S. studies, highlights the need for similar intensity of research in other jurisdictions such as the U.K., closest to the U.S. in corporate governance framework and other countries, such as Germany, that differ markedly from the U.S. model. With increasing internationalisation of capital and business, corporate governance issues have assumed a multinational focus, but the basic issues raised in this chapter still remain to be resolved.

NOTES

1. Agrawal & Knoeber (1996) split block shareholding into institutional and other block shareholdings. Otherwise their agency monitors and ours are identical.

2. Abnormal return is return to the sample company in excess of a 'normal' return. The benchmark normal return is estimated using a model that is assumed to represent a valid return generating model. These models use the stock market return, return to firms of similar size, return to firms with similar book value of equity to market value of equity etc as the benchmarks.

REFERENCES

Agrawal, A., & Knoeber, C. (1996). Firm performance and mechanisms to control agency problems between managers and shareholders. *Journal of Financial & Quantitative Analysis, 31,* 3, Sept.

Agrawal, A., Jaffe, J., & Mandelker, G. N. (1992). Post-merger performance of acquiring firms: A re-examination of an anomaly. *Journal of Finance, 47,* 1605–1621.

Ambrose, B. W., & Megginson, W. L. (1992). The role of asset structure, ownership structure, and takeover defenses in determining acquisition likelihood. *Journal of Financial & Quantitative Analysis, 27,* 4, December.

Baliga, B. R., Moyer, R. C., & Rao, R. M. (1996). CEO duality and firm performance: What is the fuss? *Strategic Management Journal, 17,* 41–53.

Banerjee, A., & Owers, J. E. (1992). Wealth reduction in White Knight bids. *Financial Management, 21,* 3, Autumn.

Barclay, M. J., & Holderness, C. G. (1991).Negotiated block trades and corporate control. *Journal of Finance,* Sept, 861–878.

Bathala, C. T., & Rao K. P. (1995).The determinants of board composition: An agency theory perspective. *Managerial and Decision Economics, 16,* 59–69.

Baysinger, B., & Hoskisson, R. E. (1990). The composition of boards of directors and strategic control: Effects on corporate strategy. *Academy of Management Review, 15,* 72–87.

Beatty, A. (1995). The cash flow and informational effects of employee stock ownership plans. *Journal of Financial Economics, 38,* 211–240.

Berkovich, E., & Khanna, N. (1991). A theory of acquisition markets: Mergers versus tender offers and golden parachutes. *Review of Financial Studies, 4,* 149–74.

Bethel, J. E., & Liebeskind, J. (1993). The effects of ownership structure on corporate restructuring *Strategic Management Journal, 14,* 15–31.

Bethel, J. E., Liebeskind, J. P., & Opler, T. (1998). Block share purchases and corporate performance. *Journal of Finance, LIII,* 2, April.

Bhagat, S., & Brickley, J. A. (1984). Cumulative voting: The value of minority shareholder rights. *Journal of Law and Economics, 27,* 339–366, October.

Bhagat, S., & Jefferis, R. H. (1994). The causes and consequences of takeover defence: Evidence from greenmail. *Journal of Corporate Finance, 1,* 201–231.

Boeker, & Goodstein (1993). Performance and successor choice: The moderating effects of governance and ownership. *Academy of Management Journal, 36, 1,* 172–186.

Borstadt, L. F., & Zwirlein, T. J. (1992). The efficient monitoring of proxy contests: An empirical analysis of post-contest control changes and firm performance. *Financial Management, 21,* 22–34, Autumn.

Boyle, Carter, & Stover (1998). Extraordinary anti-takeover provisions and insider ownership structure: The case of converting savings and loans. *Journal of Financial & Quantitative Analysis, 33,* 2, June.

Bradley, M., & Wakeman, L. M. (1983). The wealth effects of targeted share re-purchases. *Journal of Financial Economics, 11,* 301–328, April.

Brickley, J., Bhagat, S., & Lease R. (1985). The impact of long range managerial compensation plans on shareholder wealth. *Journal of Accounting & Economics, 7,* 115–129, April.

Brickley, J., Lease, R. & Smith, C. W. (1988). Ownership structure and voting on anti-takeover amendments. *Journal of Financial Economics, 20,* 267–292, Jan/March.

Brickley, J. (1994). Corporate voting: Evidence from corporate charter amendment proposals. *Journal of Corporate Finance, 1,* 5–31.

Brickley, J. A., & James, C. M. (1987). The takeover market, corporate board composition and ownership structure: The case of banking. *Journal of Law and Economics, XXX,* 161–180, April.

Byrd, J. W., & Hickman, K. A. (1992). Do outside directors monitor managers? Evidence from tender offer bids. *Journal of Financial Economics, 32,* 195–222, October.

Cadbury Committee (1992). Report on the Financial Aspects of Corporate Governance, ICAEW, London.

Choi, D. (1991). Toehold acquisitions, shareholder wealth and the marker for corporate control. *Journal of Financial and Quantitative Analysis, 26,* 3, Sept.

Coffee, J. C. (1988). Shareholders versus managers: The strain in the corporate web. In: Coffee, Lowenstein & Ackerman (Eds.), *Knights, Raiders and Targets,* Oxford University Press.

Comment, R., & Schwert, W. (1995). Poison or placebo? Evidence on the deterrence and wealth effects of modern anti-takeover measures. *Journal of Financial Economics, 39* 3–43, September.

Conyon, M., & Clegg, P. (1994). Pay at the top: A study of the sensitivity of top director remuneration to company specific shocks. National Institute of Economic Review, August.

Conyon, M., & Peck, S. (1998). Board control, remuneration committees and top management compensation. *Academy of Management Journal, 41,* 2, 146–157, April.

Cook, D. O., & Easterwood, J. C. (1994). Poison put bonds: An analysis of their economic role. *Journal of Finance, 49,* 1905–1920, December.

Cotter, J. F., & Zenner, M. (1994). How managerial wealth affects the tender offer process. *Journal of Financial Economics, 35,* 63–97.

Cotter, J. F., Shivdasani, A., & Zenner, M. (1997). Do independent directors enhance target shareholder wealth during tender offers? *Journal of Financial Economics, 43,* 195–218.

Dann, L. Y., & DeAngelo (1988). Corporate financial policy and corporate control: A study in defensive adjustments in asset and ownership structure. *Journal of Financial Economics, 20, 1,* 2, 87–128.

Dann, L. Y. (1983). Standstill agreements, privately negotiated stock repurchases and the market for corporate control. *Journal of Financial Economics, 11,* 275–300, April.

Datta, S., & Datta M. I. (1996). Takeover defenses and wealth effects on securityholders: The case of poison pill adoptions. *Journal of Banking and Finance, 20,* 1231–1250.

DeAngelo H., & DeAngelo, L. (1989). The role of proxy contests in the governance of publicly held companies. *Journal of Financial Economics,* 29–60, June.

DeAngelo H., & Rice, E. (1983). Anti-takeover charter amendments and stockholder wealth', *Journal of Financial Economics, 11,* 329–360.

Demsetz, H., & Lehn, K. (1985). The structure of corporate ownership: Causes and consequences. *Journal of Political Economy, 93, 6,* 1155–1177.

Denis, D. J., & Sarin, A. (1999). Ownership and board structures in publicly traded firms. *Journal of Financial Economics, 52,* 2, May, 187–223.

Dhillon, U. S., & Ramirez, G. G. (1994). Employee stock ownership and corporate control: An empirical study. *Journal of Banking and Finance, 18,* 9–26.

Dodd, P. R., & Warner, J. (1983). On corporate governance: A study of proxy contests. *Journal of Financial Economics, 11,* 401–438.

Fama, E., & Jensen, M. (1983). Agency problems and residual claims. *Journal of Law and Economics*, 327–349, June.

Finkelstein, S., & D'Aveni, R. A. (1994). CEO duality as a double-edged sword: How boards of directors balance entrenchment avoidance and unity of command. *Academy of Management Journal, 37*, 5,1079–1108.

Firth, M. (1991). Corporate takeovers, stockholder returns and executive rewards. *Managerial and Decision Economics, 12*, 421–428.

Firth, M. (1980). Takeovers, shareholder returns and the theory of the firm. *Quarterly Journal of Economics, 94*, 235–260.

Franks, J., Mayer, C., & Renneboog, L. (1999). Who disciplines management in poorly performing companies? *London Business School, working paper*.

Franks, J., & Mayer, C. (1996). Hostile takeovers and the correction of managerial failure. *Journal of Financial Economics, 40*, 163–181.

Franks, J., & Harris, R. (1989). Shareholder wealth effects of corporate takeovers: The UK experience 1955–85. *Journal of Financial Economics, 23*, 225–249.

Franks, J., & Titman, S. (1991). The post-merger share price performance of acquiring firms. *Journal of Financial Economics, 29*, 81–96.

Garvey, G. T., & Hanka, G. (1999). Capital structure and corporate control: The effect of anti-takeover statutes on firm leverage. *Journal of Finance, LIV*, 2, April.

Gaughan, P. (1996). Mergers, acquisitions and corporate restructurings. John Wiley.

Gaver, J. F., Gaver K. M., & Battisel, G. P. (1992). The stock market reaction to performance plan adoptions. *Accounting Review, 67*, 172–182, January.

Gregory, A. (1997). An examination of the long-run performance of UK acquiring firms. *Journal of Business Finance and Accounting, 24*, 7 & 8, September.

Hermes, (1997). Statement on corporate governance and voting policy, Hermes Investment Management Ltd, London.

Heron, R. A., & Lewellen, W. G. (1998). An empirical analysis of the re-incorporation decision. *Journal of Financial & Quantitative Analysis, 33*, 4, December.

Higson, C., & Elliott, J. (1998). Post-takeover returns: The UK evidence. *Journal of Empirical Finance, 5*, 27–46.

Hill, C. W. L., & Snell, S. A. (1989). Effects of ownership structure and control on corporate productivity. *Academy of Management Journal, 32*, 1, 25–46.

Holderness, C. G., & Sheehan, D. (1985). Raiders or saviours? The evidence of six controversial investors. *Journal of Financial Economics, 14*, 555–579.

Holl, P., & Kyriazis, D. (1997). Agency, bid resistance and the market for corporate control. *Journal of Business Finance and Accounting, 24*, 7 & 8, September.

Holland, J. (1995). The corporate governance role of financial institutions in their investee companies. *Association of Certified Accountants Research Report* 46.

Hoskisson, R., & Turk, T. A. (1990). Corporate restructuring: Governance and control limits of the internal capital market', *Academy of Management Review, 15*, 3, 459–477.

Ikenberry, D., & Lakonishok, J. (1993).Corporate governance through the proxy contest: Evidence and implications. *Journal of Business, 66*, 405–435, July.

Jarrell, G. A. (1985). Wealth effects of litigating by targets: Do interests diverge in a merger?. *Journal of Law & Economics, 28*, April.

Jarrell, G. A., &. Poulsen, A. (1989). The returns to acquiring firms in tender offers: Evidence from three decades. *Financial Management*, 12–19, Autumn.

Jarrell, G. A. (1988). Dual class re-capitalizations as anti-takeover mechanisms. *Journal of Financial Economics, 20*, 129–152, Jan/March.

Jarrell, G. A. (1987). Shark repellents and stock prices: The effects of anti-takeover amendments since 1980. *Journal of Financial Economics, 19*, 127–168, September.

Jensen, M. (1988). Takeovers: Their causes and consequences. *Journal of Economic Perspectives, 2*, 21–48, Winter.

Jensen, M. (1986). Agency costs of free cash flow, corporate finance and takeovers. *American Economic Review, 76*, 323–329

Jensen, M., & Ruback, R. (1983). The market for corporate control: The scientific evidence. *Journal of Financial Economics, 11*, 5–50.

Jensen, M., & W. Meckling, W. (1976). Theory of the firm: Managerial behaviour, agency costs and ownership structure. *Journal of Financial Economics*, 78–131.

Jensen, M., & Murphy, K. (1990). Performance pay and top management incentives. *Journal of Political Economy, 98*, 225–64, April.

Johnson, R. A., Hoskisson, R., & Hitt, M. A. (1993). Board of director involvement in restructuring: The effects of board versus managerial controls and characteristics. *Strategic Management Journal, 14*, 33–50.

Kamma, S., Weintrop, J., & Weir, P. (1988). Investors' perceptions of the Delaware Supreme Court decision in Unocal v Mesa. *Journal of Financial Economics, 20*, Jan/March, 419–430.

Kaplan, S. N., & Reishus, D. (1990). Outside directorships and corporate performance. *Journal of Financial Economics, 27*, 389–410.

Karpoff, J. M., & Malatesta, P. (1989). The wealth effects of second generation state takeover legislation. *Journal of Financial Economics, 25*, 291–322.

Karpoff, J. M., & Walkling, R. (1996). Corporate governance and shareholder initiatives: Empirical evidence. *Journal of Financial Economics, 42*, 365–395.

Knoeber, C. (1986). Golden parachutes, shark repellents and hostile tender offers. *American Economic Review, 76*, 155–167, March.

Lai, J., & Sudarsanam, P. S. (1997). Corporate restructuring in response to performance decline: Impact of ownership, governance and lenders. *European Finance Review, 1*, 197–233.

Lambert, R. A., & Larcker, D. F. (1985). Golden parachutes, executive decision making and shareholder wealth. *Journal of Accounting & Economics, 7*, 79–203.

Larcker, D. (1983). The association between performance plan adoption and corporate capital investment. *Journal of Accounting & Economics, 5*, 3–30, April.

Lewellen, W., Loderer, C., & Martin, K. (1987). Executive compensation and executive incentive problems: An empirical analysis. *Journal of Accounting & Economics, 9*, 287–310, December.

Lewellen, W. (1971). A pure financial rationale for the conglomerate merger. *Journal of Finance, 26*, 521–537.

Lewellen, W., Loderer, C., & Rosenfeld, A. (1985). Merger decisions and executive stock ownership in acquiring firms. *Journal of Accounting & Economics, 7*, 209–231.

Limmack, R. (1991). Corporate mergers and shareholder wealth effects. *Accounting & Business Research, 21*, 83, 239–51.

Linn, S., & McConnell, (1983). An empirical investigation of the impact of anti-takeover amendments on common stock prices. *Journal of Financial Economics, 11*, 361–399, April.

Loderer, C., & Martin, K. (1992). Post-acquisition performance of acquiring firms. *Financial Management,* Autumn, 69–79.

Loughran, T., & Vijh, A. M. (1997). Do long term shareholders benefit from corporate acquisitions? *Journal of Finance, LII*, 3, December.

Machlin, J H., Choe, H., & Miles, J. (1993). The effects of golden parachutes on takeover activity. *Journal of Law and Economics, 36*, 2, 861–876, October.

Magenheim, E. B., & Mueller, D. C. (1988). Are acquiring firm shareholders better off after an acquisition? In: J. Coffee, L. Lowenstein, & S. Ackerman (Eds.), *Knights, Raiders and Targets*, Oxford University Press.

Mahoney, J. M., & Mahoney, J. T. (1993). An empirical investigation of the effect of corporate charter anti-takeover amendments on stockholder wealth. *Strategic Management Journal, 14*, 17–31.

Malatesta, P., & Walkling, R. (1988). Poison pill securities: Stockholder wealth, profitability and ownership structure. *Journal of Financial Economics, 20*, 347–376, January/March.

Mallett. P., & Fowler, K. L. (1992). Effects of board composition and stock ownership on the adoption of poison pills. *Academy of Management Journal, 35*(5), 1010–1035.

Manne, H. (1965). Mergers and the market for corporate control. *Journal of Political Economy, 73*, 110–120, April.

Martin, K. J., & McConnell, J. J. (1991). Corporate performance, corporate takeovers and management turnover. *Journal of Finance, 46*(2), 671–688.

May, D. O. (1995). Do managerial motives influence firm risk reduction strategies? *Journal of Finance, L*(4), September, 1291–1308.

McConnell, J. J., & Servaes, H. (1990). Additional evidence on equity ownership and corporate value. *Journal of Financial Economics, 27*, 595–612.

McWilliams, V. (1990). Managerial share ownership and the stock price effects of anti-takeover amendment proposals. *Journal of Finance, 45*(3), 1627–1640, December.

Mikkelson, W., & Ruback, R. (1985). An empirical analysis of the inter-firm equity investment process. *Journal of Financial Economics. 14*, 523–553.

Mikkelson, W. (1991). Targeted repurchases and common stock returns. *RAND Journal of Economics, 22*, 544–561, Winter.

Mikkelson, W., & Partch, M. (1997). The decline of takeovers and disciplinary managerial turnover. *Journal of Financial Economics, 44*, 205–228.

Mikkelson, W. (1989). Managers' voting rights and corporate control. *Journal of Financial Economics, 25*, 263–290.

Mogavero, D., & Toyne, M. F. (1995). The impact of golden parachutes on Fortune 500 stock returns: A re-examination of the evidence. Quarterly *Journal of Business and Economics, 34*, 30–38.

Monks, R., & Minow, N. (1995). Corporate Governance, Blackwell.

Morck, R., Shleifer, A., & Vishny, R. (1988). Managerial ownership and market valuation. *Journal of Financial Economics, 20*, 293–315.

Morck, R. (1989). Alternative mechanisms for corporate control. *American Economic Review, 79*, 4, September.

Morck, R. (1990). Do managerial objectives drive bad acquisitions? *Journal of Finance, XLV*(1), March.

Mulherin, J. H., & Poulsen, A. (1998). Proxy contests and corporate change: Implications for shareholder wealth. *Journal of Financial Economics, 47*, 279–313.

Nesbitt, S. L. (1994). Long term rewards from shareholder activism: A study of CalPERS effect. *Journal of Applied Corporate Finance, 6*, 75–80.

Netter, J., & Poulsen, A. (1989). State corporation laws and shareholders: The recent experience. *Financial Management, 18*(3), 29–40.

Niden, C. M. (1993). An empirical examination of White Knight corporate takeovers: Synergy and Overbidding. *Financial Management, 22*(4), 28–45, Winter.

Parkinson, (1993). Corporate Power and Responsibility, Oxford University Press.

Pavlik, E. L., Scott, T. W., & Tiessen, P. (1993). Executive compensation: Issues and research. *Journal of Accounting Literature, 12*, 131–189.

Peasnell, K. V.,. Pope, P., & Young, S. (1999). Managerial equity ownership and the demand for outside directors. *University of Lancaster Working Paper.*

Pound, J. (1992). Beyond takeovers: Politics comes to corporate control. *Harvard Business Review, 70*, 83–93.

Pound, J. (1987). The effect of anti-takeover amendments on takeover activity. *Journal of Law and Economics, 30*, 353–367, October.

Pound, J. (1988). Proxy voting and the efficiency of shareholder oversight. *Journal of Financial Economics, 20*, 237–265.

Rao, R., & Vermaelen, T. (1998). Glamour and the post-acquisition performance of acquiring firms. *Journal of Financial Economics, 49*, 223–253.

Rechner, .P L., & Dalton, D. R. (1989). The impact of CEO as board chairperson on corporate performance: Evidence vs rhetoric. *Academy of Management Executive, 3*, 141–143.

Roe, M. (1993). Takeover politics. In: M. Blair (Ed.), *The Deal Decade: What takeovers and leveraged buyouts mean for corporate governance,* (321–353). Brookings Institution, Washington DC.

Roll, R. (1986). The hubris hypothesis of corporate takeovers. *Journal of Business, 59*(2), 197–216.

Rosenstein, S., & Wyatt, J. (1990). Outside directors, board independence and shareholder wealth. *Journal of Financial Economics, 26*, 175–191.

Ruback, R. (1987). An overview of takeover defenses. In: A. J. Auerbach (Ed.), *Mergers and Acquisitions*, University of Chicago Press, 49–67.

Ryngaert, M. (1988). The effects of poison pill securities on stockholder wealth. *Journal of Financial Economics, 20*, 377–417, January/March.

Shivdasani, A. (1993). Board composition, ownership structure and hostile takeovers. *Journal of Accounting and Economics, 16*, 167–198.

Shleifer, A., & Vishny, R. (1986). Large shareholders and corporate control. *Journal of Political Economy, 94*, 31.

Shleifer, A., & Vishny, R. (1997). A survey of corporate governance, *Journal of Finance, 52*, 2.

Shome, D. K., & Singh, S. (1995). Firm value and external blockholding. *Financial Management, 24*, 3–14.

Smith, M. P. (1996). Shareholder activism by institutional investors: Evidence from CalPERS, *Journal of Finance, LI*(1), March.

Sridharan, U. V., & Reinganum, M. R. (1995). Determinants of the choice of the hostile takeover mechanism: An empirical analysis of tender offers and proxy contests. *Financial Management, 24*, 57–57, Spring.

Sudarsanam, P. S. (1996). Large shareholders, takeovers and target valuation. *Journal of Business Finance and Accounting, 23*, 2, March.

Sudarsanam, P. S., Holl, P., & Salami, A. (1996). Shareholder wealth gains in mergers: Effect of synergy and Ownership structure. *Journal of Business Finance and Accounting, 23*, 5 & 6, July.

Sudarsanam, P. S. (1995). The Essence of Mergers and Acquisitions, Prentice Hall

Sudarsanam, P. S. (1995a). The role of defensive strategies and ownership structure of target firms: Evidence from UK hostile takeover bids. *European Financial Management*, 1(3), 223–240.

Tricker, (1984). *Corporate Governance. Corporate Policy Group*, Oxford, Gower Publishing.

Wahal, S. (1996). Pension fund activism and firm performance. *Journal of Financial and Quantitative Analysis, 31*(1), March.

Wahal, S., Wiles, K., & Zenner, M. (1995). Who opts out of state anti-takeover protection? The case of Pennsylvania's SB 1310. *Financial Management, 24*(3), Autumn, 22–39.

Walsh, J., & Ellwood, J. (1991). Mergers, acquisitions and the pruning of managerial deadwood. *Strategic Management Journal, 12,* 201–217.

Weisbach, M. (1988). Outside directors and CEO turnover. *Journal of Financial Economics, 20,* 431–460.

Zajac, E. J., & Westphal, (1994). The costs and benefits of managerial incentives and monitoring in large US corporations: When is more not better? *Strategic Management Journal, 15,* 121–142.

ACQUISITION STRATEGY AND TARGET RESISTANCE: A THEORY OF COUNTERVAILING EFFECTS OF PRE-MERGER BIDDING AND POST-MERGER INTEGRATION

Jeffrey S. Harrison, Hugh M. O'Neill and Robert E. Hoskisson

ABSTRACT

This chapter examines the interrelationships among pre-merger acquisition strategy, target resistance and post-merger integration and the effects of these interrelationships on post-merger performance. Perspectives from financial and strategic management theory are combined to suggest that an interaction effect of pre-merger and post-merger activities more fully explains merged firm performance, especially in cases in which the acquiring firm is related to the target. Relatedness between acquiring and target firms is more likely to lead to operating synergy, which may increase performance. However, potential positive effects from synergy are likely to be offset by resistance from target firm executives, which may lead to premium-increasing tactics, such as bidder solicitation or holding out for a higher price, or, in the post-merger stage, integration difficulties.

Advances in Mergers and Acquisitions, Volume 1, pages 157–182.
Copyright © 2000 by Elsevier Science Inc.
All rights of reproduction in any form reserved.
ISBN: 0–7623–0683–1

INTRODUCTION

Mergers and acquisitions are a popular corporate strategy. During the 1990s, the number and value of mergers and acquisitions grew steadily each year, beginning in 1993 (Hitt, Ireland & Hoskisson, 1999). The mergers and acquisitions of the 1990s represented the fifth merger wave of the twentieth century and also the largest, based on the number of acquisitions each year and the size of transactions (Hitt, Harrison, Ireland & Best, 1998). These statistics are somewhat surprising in the light of research evidence with regard to the financial performance of mergers and acquisitions. The evidence is mounting that most mergers fail to create value for the shareholders of the acquiring firm (Carper, 1990; Datta, Pinches & Narayanan, 1992; Hogarty, 1970; Holl & Kyriazis, 1997; Loderer & Martin, 1992; Porter, 1987; Ravenscraft & Scherer, 1987; Rau & Vermaelen, 1998). In fact, mergers often destroy value (Lubatkin, Srinivasan & Merchant, 1997) and the effects can be long term. For example, Agarwal, Jaffe & Mandelker (1992) discovered that acquiring firm shareholders suffer a 10% loss over the five-year post-merger period. Also, Porter (1987) offers evidence that many acquiring firms later divest what they buy.

On the other hand, target firm shareholders experience significant positive returns from acquisitions (Datta, et al., 1992; Jensen & Rubak, 1983; Lubatkin, et al., 1997). In spite of the potential for high returns, managers in target firms often resist acquisitions (Baron, 1983; Holl & Kyriazis, 1997; Kosnik, 1987; Walkling & Long, 1984). Explanations of resistance point to entrenched managers, concerned that their interests will not be served well by an acquisition. Indeed, post-merger turnover of target firm managers is unusually high (Cannella & Hambrick, 1993; O'Shaughnessy & Flanagan, 1998; Walsh, 1988; Walsh & Ellwood, 1991). Managerial resistance can take a variety of forms, from complicated legal strategies, such as the adoption of anti-takeover charter amendments, to simply announcing refusal to negotiate with executives of the bidding firm (Baron, 1983; Davis, 1991; Turk, 1992). The antidote for managerial resistance is often thought to be a marriage of the interests of the managers of the target firm and the firm's owners, through the use of agency incentives such as managerial stock ownership (Davis, 1991; Jensen & Meckling, 1976).

However, agency incentives can lose some of their efficacy after a transaction is finalized, as the new management team takes control of acquired firm assets. Surviving target firm managers may resist new policies, procedures, systems, and managerial techniques, especially if the target was highly successful in the pre-merger period or had a strong culture (Nahavandi & Malekzadeh, 1988). Put differently, incentives that join the interests of the acquired firm's management and owners may serve well to the point of sale, but less well after the sale. The market incentives for control, based on fear of lost control, are not pertinent after the acquired management has lost control. Success after the merger requires cooperation and lingering resistance either inhibits the probability of cooperation or increases its cost. In the first instance, the merger fails because of the lack of cooperation. In the second instance, the merger fails because the cost of cooperation exceeds the benefit of efficiencies gained.

While target management resistance can destroy value for the acquiring firm, evidence about the performance of targets in failed tender offers (Chatterjee, 1992) and strategic theories of diversification (Flanagan, 1996; Jemison & Sitkin, 1986; Lubatkin, 1983; Markides & Williamson, 1994) suggest that relatedness, between the acquiring and acquired firms, is a key determinant of value creation. Curiously, though, the empirical evidence, drawn from studies of mergers that exhibit relatedness, is mixed, at best. Shelton (1988) found that related acquisitions create value. Also, Singh & Montgomery (1987) and Flanagan (1996) found higher returns in related mergers. However, the cumulative abnormal returns for those mergers were not significant, in either case. On the contrary, Lubatkin (1983) discovered that unrelated acquisitions rank higher, in value appreciation, than those that are related and Elgers & Clark (1980) discovered that unrelated mergers provided higher returns to stockholders of both acquired and acquiring firms. Finally, Lubatkin, et al. (1997) discovered that fully related mergers (single business or horizontal) actually destroyed value during the 1980s, although they tended to destroy less value than other types of mergers.

Several explanations might be offered for the failure to find consistent relationships between relatedness and acquisition success. One is the choice of a dependent variable. Most studies of acquisitions focus on the stock appreciation of the acquired firm at the time of the acquisition. As Balakrishnan (1988) notes, stock values may appreciate prior to the announcement of a particular event, as investors learn about the intended strategy of the firm engaged in the acquisition. In this information leakage perspective, the market has full knowledge that a synergistic union of some sort will take place. The completion of a transaction with a specific firm, to enact that synergistic union, adds no marginal information to prompt a revaluation of the firm. However, some stock appreciation studies are based on longer event windows, precisely to control for this effect (i.e. Flanagan, 1996; Lubatkin, et al., 1997), and their results still are not supportive of the notion that related acquisitions create value.

An alternative explanation, for the failure to find a relationship between synergy and acquisition success, may be an over-emphasis on the choice perspective, at the expense of the process perspective. Jemison & Sitkin (1986) theorized that impediments in the process of completing acquisitions cause the loss of idealized synergies, especially in related acquisitions. Process impediments are less likely to deter performance in unrelated acquisitions that don't rely on operating synergies between a parent and a subsidiary.

In this chapter, we build on Jemison & Sitkin's process perspective, by describing the acquisition process from the perspective of the management of an acquired entity. An implicit assumption often made in strategic studies is that activities and actions of the acquiring firm are the sole determinants of value. Thus, studies either observe how managers in the acquiring firm search for alternatives (i.e. Ansoff, Avener, Brandenberg, Portner & Radosevich, 1971; Haunschild, 1993) or probe the content of their strategies (i.e. Flanagan, 1996; Lubatkin, et al., 1997; Lubatkin, 1987). Here, we argue that the management and the employees of the purchased firm play a key role in determining the outcome of a merger. They play that role in three ways. First, they erect various takeover defenses. Second, they help define the closing price. Third, they are involved in post-merger integration. As Barnard (1962) suggested, executive management requires the consent of the governed. Such consent is not easily earned in merger contexts. In Parsons' (1960) terms, firms take on institutional properties and managers/key employees pass on those institutional properties to newcomers. If acquired management leaves the firm, as is often the case (Walsh, 1988), or if incumbent management in the acquired firm fails to embrace the implementation effort, then the merger can easily fail because the acquired managers will not pass the institutional properties on to newcomers.

Management of the acquired firm plays a key role in an acquisition's success. Yet, to this point, only a limited number of management studies identify the factors that might contribute to resistance or cooperation, by managers and employers, in the acquired firm. In contrast, studies in financial economics contain a wealth of ideas about ways to make the interests of stockholders and target firm managers congruent. Here, we use that literature as a platform to describe how the interests of the acquiring and acquired firm converge and diverge. Building on the ideas of Jemison & Sitkin (1986), we focus on the processes of resistance/cooperation and apply these ideas across related and unrelated acquisitions. We focus on acquired firm member behaviors both before and after the acquisition. Joining pre-merger and post-merger perspectives helps to explain the contradictions found in the merger performance literature. For example, we argue that the amount and type of target firm resistance (in the pre-merger stage) correlates with the level of relatedness and fosters resistance in the post-merger stage. We then contend that this resistance, an emergent rather than intended strategy, vitiates planned synergistic benefits. Finally, we use a strategy implementation perspective to articulate how methods of implementation might lead to exit from the acquired firm, when voice and loyalty would be preferable responses (Hirschman, 1970).

In sum, we show that related acquisition strategies unleash forces that have both positive and negative consequences for overall performance. These countervailing forces make the probability of merger gains low and thus account for the equivocal results reported in empirical studies of mergers. One purpose of this chapter is to combine elements of the bidding stage of the acquisition process with elements of the post-merger integrative stage, to further explain past research findings and suggest directions for future research. A second purpose of this chapter is to view acquisition as both the interaction of pre-merger and post-merger phenomena and the interaction of intended and emergent strategies.

RESISTANCE AND MERGER PERFORMANCE: AN INTEGRATIVE MODEL

Figure 1 presents a model that helps explain how the pre- and post-merger behavior, of managers and employees in the acquiring and acquired firm, influences value creation or loss. Performance implications, arising from the effects of both pre- and post-merger factors, are assumed to be both short and long term in nature, and are associated with both accounting-based and market-based measures of value creation. The approach taken here resembles the net present value framework often used to evaluate financial investments (Boudreaux & Long, 1977). Some value is gained or lost almost immediately, through changes in equity values, while other gains or losses may take several years to run their full course. A positive change in performance refers to a cumulative performance change covering the effects of both the pre- and post-merger period.

This long term measurement approach has logical appeal and also has support in the financial literature on efficient markets (Fama, 1976; Fama, Fisher, Jensen & Roll, 1969). That is, operating synergies should result in higher accounting returns, which should be reflected in higher market returns. Also, while one could argue that the short-term effects associated with the bidding process should disappear after the first operating cycle, in actuality, many of these effects linger due to increases in debt servicing costs (both from increased leverage and increased bond risk), especially when premiums are large. These influences are likely to be evident regardless of the form of payment (cash vs. stock), since stock financing can have long term effects on market returns, through dilution of earnings. Also, post-merger integration problems, resulting from hostility during the negotiation process, may result in performance implications for many years. In practice, researchers often adopt measures covering short time windows, based on their inability to control extraneous influences on performance over the long term (Lubatkin & Shrieves, 1986). It's worth noting that conclusions based on these short-term perspectives will be misleading, to the extent that

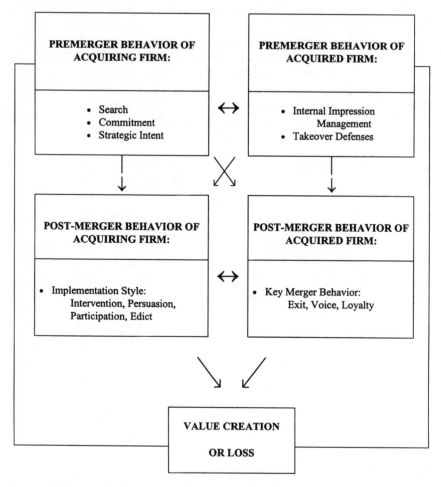

Figure 1.   Resistance and Merger Performance: An Integrative Model.

merger outcomes are based on discontinuous and fractionated processes (Jemison & Sitkin, 1986).

Figure 1 lists four major influences in the creation of long term value: the pre-merger behavior of the acquiring firm and the acquired firm and the post-merger behavior of the acquiring firm and the acquired firm. Most of the strategic research, on both the content and process of acquisitions, has focused on the pre-merger behavior of the acquiring firm, with limited study on post-merger behavior of the acquiring firm and almost no study of the post-merger behavior displayed by members of the acquired firm (Capron, 1999; Chatterjee, Lubatkin, Schweiger & Weber, 1992 and the turnover literature serve as notable exceptions). Furthermore, few studies assess long term impacts. The pre-merger behavior of the acquiring firm includes search (that is, the depth and breadth of search for candidates) and commitment (that is, commitment to a specific target). The pre-merger behavior of the acquiring firm also involves strategic intent, that is, the intent to purchase a related or unrelated target.

Three preliminary points can be made about the pre-merger behavior of the acquiring firm. First, a wide ranging search increases the slate of candidates, while a narrow search decreases the slate of candidates. Second, a narrow search increases the level of commitment to any single candidate, since there will be fewer alternatives available following a narrow search. As Jemison & Sitkin (1986) aptly note, commitment can quickly escalate in a narrow search, with alarming behavioral consequences. Third, a related acquisition strategy triggers a narrow search and simultaneously increases the probability of escalating commitment.

The pre-merger behavior of the acquired firm includes internal impression management and the construction of takeover defenses. Internal impression management refers to management's attempt, in the acquired firm, to position the acquisition as a positive, negative or neutral event. As in other contexts, management attempts to influence the attributions of powerful actors inside and outside the firm (Salancik & Meindl, 1984). Often, impression management is used to justify management's preferred position. Takeover defenses include actions that create more bidders (induce auctions) and reduce the competitive value of the acquired firm.

Two preliminary points can be made about the pre-merger behavior of the acquired firm. First, management of the acquired firm serves as a conduit for interpretations of events throughout the acquired firm. Second, the impressions formed, as management justifies either past performance or current takeover defenses, linger long past the completion of the deal and have a salient effect on post-merger performance. As the poet notes, words are not dead when they are said, but live long after.

The post-merger behavior of the acquiring firm is comprised of the various steps that the acquired firm takes to integrate the purchased subsidiary. Several researchers note that integration success varies with cultural differences (Chatterjee, et al., 1992; Nahavandi & Malekzadeh, 1988; Very, Lubatkin, Calori & Veiga, 1997; Weber, Shenkar & Raveh, 1996) and strategic differences (Jemison & Sitkin, 1986; Pitts, 1976). As with all strategies, activity segmentation

(Jemison & Sitkin, 1986) leads to a separation of responsibility between those who make the deal and those who implement the deal. In implementation, the management of the acquiring firm can choose a variety of implementation styles. Nutt (1987), in a study of organizational innovation, described four styles of implementation: intervention, participation, persuasion, and edict.

The post-merger behavior of the acquired firm is comprised of the various behaviors that managers and other key performers adopt, in the acquired firm, after the merger. Hirschman (1970) described a succinct range of behaviors that might apply in merger contexts: exit, voice and loyalty. In the post-merger period, exit is voluntary or involuntary exit from the firm, voice is internal contribution to support or resist the firm, and loyalty is dedication to the new management.

Regarding the post-merger behavior of both the acquiring firm and the acquired firm, we make four assertions at this point. First, edict is often the style of implementation adopted by the acquiring firm. Second, edict hastens exit, increases resistant voice, decreases supportive voice, and decreases loyalty, among members of the acquired firm. Third, pre-merger resistance, in the acquired firm, increases the probability that the acquiring firm will use edict in the implementation stage. Finally, resistance in both the pre- and post-merger stages is more likely in related, than unrelated, acquisitions (Holl & Kyriazis, 1997). These assertions will be explored in greater depth in the sections that follow.

We now consider the pre-merger stage more fully.

THE COMPETITIVE BIDDING PROCESS

The competitive bidding process, in large part, determines the initial costs that must be recovered for the acquisition to be considered a success. To a great extent, acquisition negotiations occur in asymmetric markets (Hoskisson & Hitt, 1990; Porter, 1980; Rumelt, 1979; Williamson, 1985). In theory, each bidding firm faces a unique set of opportunities. This implies that the value of a particular target is different for each of the bidders. The successful bidder will bid a price, which is less than its expected gain, but marginally higher than the second highest bid. The difference between the expected gain and the bid represents the economic gain, if any. This process of negotiation is described by auction theory (Baron, 1983).

One factor that has been shown to influence outcomes from this competitive bidding process is target firm resistance. For example, Fowler & Schmidt (1989) discovered lower post-acquisition performance for acquirers of firms that resist takeover than for acquirers of friendly targets. Also, Jarrell (1985) observed significant gains for target firms associated with initiating litigation against the acquiring firm. The following section explains how these performance differences are associated with the amount of information that is made public during the negotiation process.

Information Leakage and the Performance of Acquiring Firms

Turk (1992) discovered that auction-inducing resistance leads to higher returns for the target, while competition-reducing resistance has the opposite effect. He explained that these differences are due to varying amounts of information leakage to the public. For example, when a tender offer is made public, information is revealed about the acquiring firm, the target firm, the offer price and, to a limited extent, the post-acquisition plans of the acquirer. When this information is released, other potential bidders have the opportunity to compete, which can result in an auction. For example, competitors may discover that they have the same potential for economies of scope that was sought by the original bidder. Also, if the original bidder would gain a competitive advantage in the industry through a successful takeover, industry competitors may bid to drive up the price, forestalling the original bidder's gain. These forces should result in a transfer of wealth from the shareholders of the successful bidder to the shareholders of the target.

Some types of resistance should result in the release of even more information, which can intensify these competitive forces and further reduce any potential gains for the acquirer. For example, target firm management can use lawsuits, or encourage government antitrust authorities to get involved, to force extra information about the proposed merger to be revealed (Holl & Kyriazis, 1997). Lawsuits also prolong the merger process, which may encourage additional bidders to enter the competition. Also, target firm management may release private information to other companies while seeking a 'white knight'. Finally, public opposition, expressed by target firm management, can enhance the perceived value of outstanding shares and, thus, encourage shareholders to hold out for a higher offer. These tactics, consistent with Turk's (1992) definition, will be referred to as auction-inducing strategies. Consistent with Turk's findings, these strategies are expected to reduce the potential gains to acquiring firms by increasing the premium paid for shares.

> *Proposition 1*: Auction-inducing resistance by the target firm in the pre-merger period reduces the acquiring firm performance.

On the other hand, some target firm defensive tactics can be considered destructive, in that they harm the future competitiveness of the target firm. The potential acquirer would still be expected to pay a premium if the acquisition is completed, but would also face additional post-acquisition costs and integration problems.

For example, some target companies dramatically increase debt to make themselves less attractive to potential acquirers. The proceeds of the debt are often used to buy back stock or pay large dividends (Holl & Kyriazis, 1997). If an acquiring firm completes the acquisition, it will face higher debt servicing obligations and/or risk in the post-merger period. Target firms have also used a variety of poison pills (Malatesta & Walkling, 1988). One of the most popular gives shareholders the right to buy stock, in their own company or any company that acquires them, at a substantial discount, if an acquisition occurs (Davis, 1991). In addition, 'golden parachutes', which give target firm managers attractive severance packages upon acquisition, as well as other types of side payments to target firm executives, can be very costly (Cochran, Wood & Jones, 1985; Singh & Harianto, 1989, 1990). Finally, target firms have been known to sell off the 'crown jewels', assets that are highly valued by potential acquirers. Each of these competitiveness-reducing (called competition-reducing by Turk (1992)) strategies would be expected to decrease the performance of the acquiring firm after merger.

> *Proposition 2*: Acquiring firm performance is lower in acquisitions associated with competitiveness-reducing resistance by the target firm in the pre-merger period. Also, acquisitions associated with competitiveness-reducing resistance will result in lower performance than acquisitions associated with auction-inducing resistance.

Some have claimed that certain defenses, such as golden parachutes, may not actually be competitiveness-reducing. Singh & Harianto (1989, 1990) argue that the presence of golden parachutes allows the top managers of the target firm to be indifferent to target price and therefore accept a lower bid price. In this case, the target would be sold at a discount and post-acquisition performance would be higher than suggested by Proposition 2. Although this may be true for golden parachutes taken alone, Proposition 2 focuses on those mergers where there is a pattern of resistance behavior, not on one issue such as golden parachutes.

In some acquisitions, target resistance is not evident at all during the merger process. For example, target firms may support a proposed merger for competitive or other reasons. In this case, the premium paid should be smaller and post-merger integration should be less costly.

Therefore, the type of resistance initiated by the target firm can have a material impact on both the premium paid by the acquirer and post-acquisition integration and costs. Central to our argument is the notion that the relatedness between acquirer and target will have an impact on the nature and intensity of resistance, as the next section will explain.

RELATEDNESS AND THE COMPETITIVE BIDDING PROCESS: UNLEASHING COUNTERVAILING FORCES

Related acquisitions are defined herein as acquisitions that do not require a change in the 'center of gravity' of the acquiring firm (e.g. the target firm has the same supply chain orientation (Galbraith & Kazanjian, 1986)). These types of acquisitions can lead to economies through managerial skill transference and may also be associated with other types of synergy, such as the use of common marketing channels, research methods, advertising media or suppliers. However, the success of this type of acquisition will also depend on the nature of the competitive bidding process and the impact of the bidding process on post-merger behavior. Thus, even if potential synergy exists, wealth creation dissipates in the presence of bidding or integration problems. Our main contention is that related mergers unleash forces that prompt auction-inducing information leakage, competitiveness-reducing information leakage and post-merger resistance. These ideas will now be more fully developed, starting with a discussion of the concept of center of gravity.

Center of Gravity and Corporate-level Relatedness

Galbraith & Kazanjian (1986) demonstrated that firms that are at the same stages of the supply chain have similar objectives and orientations. Thus, their executives would be expected to have similar dominant logic (Grant, 1988). According to Prahalad & Bettis (1986), the dominant logic of an organization consists of a knowledge structure and a set of management processes that are developed by corporate managers through their experiences in the organizations in which they work. They explain that: "the characteristics of the core business, often the source of top managers in diversified firms, tend to cause managers to define problems in certain ways and develop familiarity with, and facility in the use of, those administrative tools that are particularly useful in accomplishing the critical tasks of the core business" (p. 491). For example, some operating environments require corporate executives to make quick, intuitive decisions, while in other environments these types of decisions are replaced with painstaking management science models and techniques.

According to the model proposed by Galbraith & Kazanjian (1986), firms that engage in raw materials extraction and primary manufacturing differ fundamentally from firms that produce and market finished goods (see also Tregoe & Zimmerman, 1980; Nathanson & Cassano, 1982; Galbraith, 1983). The first group of companies, called upstream companies, seek efficiency through standardization, process innovation and engineering breakthroughs. The products sold by these companies are generic in nature and thus hard to differentiate. Furthermore, these firms generally have unsophisticated technologies. Therefore, efficiency, as opposed to differentiation, is the key factor for success. Raw materials extraction and primary manufacturing require significant investments in plant and equipment. Therefore, these companies are more often highly capital intensive. Few staff departments are necessary because less coordination is required, which results in line, as opposed to staff, driven organizations.

The second group of companies, called downstream companies, emphasizes marketing skills, product innovation and customization. They focus on satisfying a particular customer need. Brand recognition is a key to success in these companies. High advertising budgets and large staff departments result in the need for higher margins than those found in upstream companies. These organizations are people, as opposed to capital, intensive.

The manufacturing supply chain is further subdivided into six major categories: raw materials production, primary manufacturing, fabrication, finished product manufacturing, wholesaling and retailing (Galbraith & Kazanjian, 1986). The first three categories pertain to upstream companies and the last three categories describe downstream companies. Firms start with an emphasis at one stage in their industry and then begin to spread out to other stages. The dominant stage, or 'center of gravity', sets the tone for all other operations. Galbraith & Kazanjian (1986) state that: "changing the center of gravity is probably the most difficult strategic change to make . . . because it involves large-scale change in all of the organizational dimensions. A center of gravity shift requires a dismantling of the current power structure, rejection of parts of the old culture and establishing all new management systems" (p. 65).

Given this reasoning, acquisitions that do not require a change in the center of gravity of the acquiring firm (related mergers) are likely to cause the fewest integration problems and provide the greatest opportunities for skill transference. The concept of dominant logic, closely aligned with the idea of synergy, allows the utilization of not-fully-exploited intangible skills, such as tacit knowledge or managerial know-how, in managing a new acquisition. Therefore, defining relatedness in terms of similar supply chain orientations provides a corporate-level dimension (dominant logic) concerned with understanding what is really important to success in the newly acquired firm. This corporate-level dimension is particularly relevant to our discussion because it is at the corporate level that some of the potential advantages associated with relatedness may be traded off during the bidding process. However, this does not mean that operating-level relatedness dimensions are not also evident, as we will explain in the next section.

Center of Gravity and Operating-level Relatedness

One of the most commonly cited reasons for acquisitions is to achieve operational synergy, by combining activities to gain efficiencies that could not have been gained otherwise (Chatterjee, 1986; Flanagan, 1996; Lauenstein, 1985; Lubatkin, 1983; Porter, 1985; Singh & Montgomery, 1987). The word synergy is often used synonymously with economies of scope, which describes the concept of utilizing resources (e.g. slack) from the production of one product in manufacturing another (Teece, 1980; Panzar & Willig, 1981; Rumelt, 1982).

The concept of economies of scope includes both tangible inter-relationships, such as the sharing of common machinery or marketing channels among divisions, and intangible interrelationships, such as the application of a skill to several of a firm's businesses (Porter, 1985). Among the most frequently mentioned are operational synergistic opportunities: utilization of the same marketing channels to sell multiple products, employing previously unused production capacity, allocating capital more efficiently (economies of scale) and sharing technology. Two firms that are both primarily engaged in the same stage of the supply chain are likely to have opportunities to take advantage of some types of operating synergies, in addition to enjoying the potential corporate-level benefits explained above. Therefore, our definition of relatedness is parsimonious.

Conventional thought holds that related acquisitions are likely to outperform other (unrelated) acquisitions. We now show that the pre-merger competitive bidding process has the potential to reduce or enhance these performance differences. We then demonstrate that the bidding process also contaminates the integration process.

Relatedness and Resistance by Target Firm Managers: Countervailing Force No. 1

One cannot address acquisition strategy without understanding how the processes of negotiation are related to strategic outcomes. For instance, the amount of competitiveness-reducing resistance by the target firm should increase if the target firm's strategy is related to the strategy of the bidding firm. This is, in part, because managers of target firms with processes similar to the bidder (same center of gravity) may contest the takeover in order to escape employment termination. This fear of termination is logical because conventional 'rules' suggest that the first step necessary in integrating a new entity is the replacement of top management (Drucker, 1981; Paine & Power, 1984). Walsh (1988) observed more management exits in related acquisitions. Since two CEOs with similar expertise are unnecessary to run the merged firm, target firm managerial displacement may be necessary in order to achieve economies of scope, in the merged firm. Publicized involuntary exits, following related acquisitions, prove a powerful inducement to resistance. Articles and books (i.e. Hirsch, 1987) detailing such exits are commonplace. Bennett (1986) states that: "mergers and acquisitions are removing scores of CEOs from their jobs" (p. 19). Turnover is not limited to executives. O'Shaughnessy & Flanagan (1998) found that the probability of an announcement of a layoff increased if the companies involved in the acquisition were related.

Many of the arguments brought forth in the foregoing discussion of related acquisitions are even stronger in pure horizontal (i.e. same business) acquisitions. For example, fear of job loss is likely to be extreme among target firm executives, because they realize that the bidding firm could replace them immediately. In fact, such a change in management is highly probable as the acquiring firm attempts to convert employees in the newly acquired firm to their own particular way of doing things (e.g. transform culture and processes).

Fear of job loss should be a less important factor in an unrelated acquisition. Because managers in the bidding firm are not expected to understand the target's business, target firm managers are needed to run the acquired business (Dundas & Richardson, 1982). An unrelated acquirer is often more decentralized and lacks a thorough understanding of the particular business undertaken. Therefore, target firm managers are critical to target firm continuity.

Proposition 3: Auction-inducing and competitiveness-reducing resistance by target firms is more likely in related than in unrelated acquisitions.

Relatedness and Post-Merger Behavior by Target Managers:
Countervailing Force No. 2

Because many of the forces associated with pre- and post-merger processes offset each other, predicting performance on the basis of only one set of processes is difficult. This problem is exacerbated by the fact that relatedness and resistance vary directly. Related targets are more likely to resist takeover in a destructive way, as indicated above. Furthermore, the acquisition process can affect post-merger integration (Jemison & Sitkin, 1986). For example, resistance and other forms of hostility during the bidding process can erode trust and create resentment, which makes cooperation less likely during integration. Also, the post-merger period is the time when the full cost of destructive resistance is felt. This resistance is highest in related firms, where post-merger integration is most important. Because past researchers typically have not accounted for resistance and relatedness simultaneously, inconsistent findings are not surprising. The inconsistent findings support our contentions about the performance impact of the potent interaction effect between pre-merger acquiring firm strategy and post-merger integration processes.

Hostility on the part of target firm management, during the bidding process, leads to difficulties during the integration process (as these managers vent their frustration, leave the organization, or sabotage implementation plans), which blocks any potential synergies from occurring. Also, post-merger integration among related firms creates significantly greater bureaucratic (Jones & Hill, 1988) and information processing (Hill & Hoskisson, 1987) costs than unrelated acquisitions. Together, resistance and the higher costs eliminate any potential gains. The conundrum here is that though the related merger has the highest potential for gains, it also has the highest potential for resistance and the highest administrative costs.

Figure 1 illustrates the specific impact that pre-merger target resistance will have in the post-merger context. The resistance of the target firm fosters escalating commitment in the acquiring firm. In addition, resistance increases the 'stake' that the acquiring firm's management has in the success of the merger, for two reasons. First, resistance makes the merger more visible and, therefore, more important. Second, resistance leads to an increased price for the merger. The increased price, in turn, leads to requirements for increased cash flow to meet targeted investment returns.

Management of the acquired firm faces four implementation options: intervention, participation, persuasion and edict. Following target resistance, edict is the most attractive implementation process, since intervention and participation require long windows of time and high levels of interpersonal attraction. The pressures of increased visibility and the need for higher returns make time pressures more salient, and the history of resistance lessens the probability of interpersonal attraction. Regarding intervention, Nutt (1987) notes that managers rarely use it. Its use is unlikely in a situation that has the tense properties which follow a resisted merger.

Persuasion is an unlikely candidate for implementation, because managers and critical employees in the target firm will discount the credibility of the acquiring firm's managers. This discounting is natural following the impression management that the firm's formerly independent managers might have used to resist the acquisition. By default, then, the implementation strategy that is used is edict. Yet, as Nutt notes, edicts are poor implementation tactics: "this tactic was ineffective, leading to low adoption rates and poor quality ratings. Edicts seem to be quite ineffective." (1987: 12).

Floyd & Wooldridge (1992) described implementation as a long-term learning process. The tasks that middle management are responsible for in implementation include facilitating adaptability, synthesizing information and installing deliberate strategies. Surely, the tasks of facilitating, synthesizing and installing cannot be imposed; rather, they have to be accepted. In Barnard's (1962) classic terms, merger implementation is a process that requires the acceptance of the governed. In a resisted merger, this acceptance is rare. Target firm managers are unlikely to cooperate in organizational learning. Phrased differently, organizational learning, especially on the part of those newly acquired, demands active voice and loyalty. Active voice and loyalty are unlikely responses to edict. In the absence of middle management voice and loyalty, there can't be cooperation. Thus, the related merger is unlikely to work.

On the other hand, if the related target publicly supports a takeover, the acquirer will be likely to pay a modest premium. The acquirer will willingly pay a premium in exchange for support from the target in discouraging competitors from entering the fray. Also, the merger process should be quicker, reducing the amount of information available to other potential bidders. Support during the merger process should also facilitate integration processes, thus promoting synergy. Because the potential for synergy exists and the premium may be smaller than that paid after a bidding contest, gains to the acquiring firm are likely and should be significant. However, because competitiveness-reducing resistance to takeover is probable in related acquisitions, the incidence of this type of friendly acquisition is not expected to be very great.

Furthermore, the acquirer may have to offer side payments to target management, such as guarantees of continued employment, to encourage support of the acquisition. These side payments can reduce the value of the acquisition to the acquiring firm. Most side payments will go to the top managers of the acquired firm, rather than to middle management or key actors. As noted above, the support of middle managers is crucial to the success of the related strategy. Top management of the acquired firm may be viewed as co-opted agents, once they have accepted side payments. As co-opted agents, they will face credibility problems in installing the acquisition strategy, forcing the co-opted management to choose the edict route to implementation. In issuing edicts, the management of the acquired firm then faces the same dilemmas that acquiring managers face in firms that have resisted: edicts don't work.

Proposition 4: Acquiring firm strategy and post-merger integration interact to affect post-merger performance in related acquisitions.

Performance Interactions among Unrelated Acquisitions

As a point of comparison, we note the different expected outcomes in an unrelated acquisition strategy. Target resistance is also likely when the bidder pursues an unrelated acquisition strategy. Although both types of resistance are likely to be present, both pre-merger negotiation tactics and post-merger integration issues are likely to moderate auction behavior. From an information leakage perspective, the target premium will be lower because information revealed about an unrelated acquisition, where the target firm has attributes that are dissimilar to the bidding firm, is less likely to be acted upon by bidder competitors. Bidders will be less attracted to the target because of lack of apparent potential synergy (Harrison, Hitt, Hoskisson & Ireland, 1991). Also, a successful acquisition by the original bidder will not pose a competitive threat to other competitors in the bidder's industry, because no gain in market power would be perceived. Given our definition of related mergers, this would also apply to bidders moving outside their dominant industry but within their same stage of the product market. However, a bid may arouse the attention of the target's direct competitors, who may pursue a bid on their own. The target's competitors, however, would probably not view the bidder with fear, because the bidder is outside the direct industry of the target. Thus, an auction may ensue, but the auction should not be as intense as for a firm that pursues a related strategy.

Although job loss by key executives is possible in any acquisition, it is not perceived to be as likely when the acquiring firm follows an unrelated acquisition strategy. By definition, an unrelated target has managerial expertise needed by the unrelated bidder. Therefore, destructive resistance is unlikely in the unrelated acquisition, because target firm managers should have less fear of job loss. Nonetheless, auction-inducing resistance should result in a premium for target shareholders and reduce the post-merger performance of the acquiring firm. However, because the potential for synergy is low, if the price rises too high, bidding firms should drop out. While resistance on the part of an unrelated target may prolong the bidding process, the information revealed during this process will have less of an impact on the returns to the merger than in the case of a related target. Furthermore, the unrelated bidder is less likely to be compulsively aggressive in pursuing the bid, because the potential for synergy is limited.

On the post-merger side, there is little potential for synergy (by definition) and integration, if attempted, would be difficult (Lorsch & Allen, 1973). Many unrelated acquisitions are handled purely as financial investments; thus, no integration of companies takes place. For example, Datta & Grant (1990) discovered

Table 1.   Countervailing forces across related mergers

	Potential Synergy	Auction Inducing Effects	Competition Reducing Effects	Postmerger Resistance	Summary of Performance Consequences
Related Acquisition	high synergy, positive impact	bidding frenzy, negative impact	highly likely, negative impact	highly likely, negative impact	not significant
Unrelated Acquisition	low synergy, little impact	less likely, low impact	less likely, low impact	less likely, low impact	not significant

that the extent of acquired firm management autonomy is higher in unrelated, compared to related, acquisitions. Overall, the net performance effect in these types of acquisitions is likely to be statistically undetectable.

Summary

Our conceptual assessment, found in Table 1, agrees with previous research, which generally concludes that acquisitions have little impact on merged-firm performance. However, the explanation given here suggests that, in the case of related mergers, this is due to increased target resistance (both competitiveness-reducing and auction-inducing) and increased cost of post-merger integration. Although synergy may create expectations of increases in firm performance through takeover, target resistance and increased integration costs are likely to offset gains to the acquiring firm.

Both types of resistance are less significant in unrelated targets, as explained above. Therefore, acquiring firms are likely to lose less in a pre-merger auction for an unrelated target, relative to a related target. Also, unrelated acquisitions should be less costly from an integration point of view, because they are not integrated. However, such mergers lack synergistic potential. Furthermore, over time, unrelated acquisitions appear to lead to reductions in innovation (Hitt, Hoskisson, Ireland & Harrison, 1991) and stock value (Hoskisson & Hitt, 1988). Therefore, performance effects are likely to be negligible in unrelated mergers.

DISCUSSION

Because many of the forces associated with pre- and post-merger processes offset each other, predicting performance on the basis of only one set of processes is difficult. This problem is magnified by the fact that the two processes are related to each other. Specifically, related targets are more likely to resist takeover. Holl & Kyriazis (1997) were surprised when they found that resistance is more likely in related, than unrelated, acquisitions (Holl & Kyriazis, 1997). They expected the opposite to be true. However, their finding is in harmony with the arguments contained herein. Resistance and other forms of hostility during the bidding process can erode trust and create resentment, which makes cooperation less likely during integration as well. This post-merger period is the time when the full cost of destructive resistance is felt.

Given that past researchers have not accounted for resistance and relatedness simultaneously, inconsistent findings are not surprising. The foregoing analysis demonstrates why it has been so difficult to empirically support the theory of relatedness in acquisitions. In particular, non-findings or negative findings, with regard to the performance of related acquisitions, are not surprising (Elgers & Clark, 1980; Flanagan, 1996; Lubatkin, 1983; Singh & Montgomery, 1987; Lubatkin, et al., 1997).

Chatterjee (1986) argued that collusive synergy in horizontal acquisitions is associated with greater value creation than other types of synergy. However, he did not directly test this hypothesis. In fact, he eliminated horizontal acquisitions from his sample because, he argued, they lead to both operational and collusive synergies. We agree with Chatterjee on these points. Horizontal acquisitions, when they are supported by target firm executives, should have the highest performance of any of the groups. Like Lubatkin (1987), Chatterjee was unable to differentiate among his relatedness groups on the basis of acquiring firm performance. Once again, this lack of a performance effect might be traced to target resistance and post-merger integration costs.

Jones & Hill (1988) proposed that potential synergies from related diversification will be offset by higher bureaucratic costs associated with integration. Where related diversification is implemented through acquisition, bureaucratic costs, as well as potential economic benefits, are expected to increase. Related diversification requires greater amounts of information than unrelated diversification for successful implementation (Hill & Hoskisson, 1987) and target resistance is likely to have a negative impact on information flows within the combined firm. Our analysis concurs with the Jones & Hill thesis, adding resistance and consequent implementation misfits as two of the causes of higher bureaucratic costs.

Our analysis is also consistent with research findings on resistance strategies. For example, Turk (1992) found that auction-inducing resistance led to the highest premiums, relative to competitiveness-reducing resistance and support. The cumulative effects of resistance across relatedness categories should produce similar results for target firm shareholders, because premiums are expected to be moderate to large in the auction-inducing resistance category.

This conceptual analysis suggests that the notion of synergy may have been overemphasized in the strategy literature, except in rare instances. Private synergy (Barney, 1988) would be one setting where resistance would not be likely to spark an auction in a hostile takeover. But private synergy is rare. In fact, since the cumulative effects of the pre- and post-merger factors described in this chapter are expected to lead to an average financial gain approaching zero, the primary reason that some mergers are successful may indeed be luck (Barney, 1988). However, other constraints or incentives may foster merger behavior.

The arguments in this chapter are primarily based on managerial motivations. Of course, strategic outcomes are affected by other variables, such as governance mechanisms, that constrain managers to act rationally and on shareholders' behalf. If firms, either bidder or target, have governance structures that limit management discretion, the proposed relationships would be affected. For instance, concentrated ownership may prevent a bidder from paying a high premium or prevent destructive resistance in a target. Current discussions about governance describe incentives that forge congruent interests between stockholders and the dominant executives in independent firms. Similar governance mechanisms might link the interests of important participants in both the acquiring and acquired firm. Potential mechanisms might include ownership of capital stock, variable compensation arrangements, the inclusion of outside managers and director monitoring (Oviatt, 1988). The use of such governance mechanisms could either increase the propensity of the acquiring firm to use mechanisms other than edict for implementation, or increase the incidence of positive voice and loyalty in the acquired firm.

Furthermore, regulatory events may spark merger behavior. Williams, Paez & Sanders (1988) found that divestitures increased in the late 1970s and early 1980s and suggested that conglomerates were downscoping. Turk & Baysinger (1991) suggested that tax policy changes in 1981, and antitrust enforcement policy changes during the Reagan years, created an environment supporting a shift in corporate merger strategy (see also Davis, 1991). With relaxed antitrust enforcement, horizontal and vertical mergers were more attractive, while tax policy discouraged conglomerate investment. This trend was the opposite of what was found in the 1960s and early 1970s. Therefore, one needs to be careful about general predictions, without examining the governance constraints and environmental incentives, for particular strategic approaches in mergers.

CONCLUSIONS & RECOMMENDATIONS

Our analysis agrees with the conclusion of basic micro-economic theory that, in general, mergers are not likely to create value but, unlike basic micro theory, our discussion assumes that asymmetric information exists between firms and that markets are imperfect. This paper has proposed that target firm resistance strategy tempers the relationship between relatedness and performance, which accounts for the ambiguous findings of past researchers. In particular, because relatedness is expected to lead to greater resistance on the part of target firm executives, the positive effects of synergy are canceled out. One conclusion that can be drawn from this discussion is that the characteristics of the bidding process should be included in future studies of the relationship between relatedness strategy and performance. Also, examinations probing both pre-merger bidding and post-merger integration have the potential to untangle the confusing results on acquiring firm performance.

Three additional research questions emerge readily from this discussion. First, and perhaps foremost, why do mergers persist, even in the presence of compelling evidence that they rarely work? In a world of rational action, we might expect that managers would learn from past results, and not persist in merger behavior. There are competing explanations for why the merger behavior does persist. One explanation is that managers have blind spots and cognitive biases, and don't learn well. Alternatively, managers may seek outcomes other than profits in merger. These outcomes might include growth, increase in firm prestige, salary enhancement, and increases in personal power. If these are the intended outcomes from merger, and the outcomes commonly occur in merger, then the persistence of merger strategies presents no surprise. To date, though, an overwhelming number of research designs assume that financial outcomes (growth in profits; stockholder wealth enhancement) are the only relevant dependent variables.

Second, what factors encourage active support for the merger among managers and employees of the acquired firm? Merger studies in the management field normally adopt the focus of the acquiring firm, ignoring the performance impact of managers and other firm members in the acquired firm. Studies in the finance field often investigate the governance structures that bind the interests of target firm managers to stockholders until the time of the sale, but these studies are silent about other actors in the firm and about forces that encourage congruent interests after the merger. At a minimum, it appears any benefit to target management and employees should be clear and compelling for the interests of the acquired and acquiring firms to exhibit congruence.

Special circumstances can enhance the potential to unlock synergy from relatedness. For example, managers of a target firm with very low performance may actually welcome acquiring firm managers, especially if they believe that skill and capital transfers could lead to improvements in performance. Bruton, Oviatt & White (1994) found evidence that acquisitions of distressed firms in related businesses performed better than a control group of acquiring firms with similar strategies, but in which the target firms were not distressed. Another context that might present an opportunity to test the impact of target management commitment is acquisition by a 'white knight.' In this context, target management chooses the acquiring firm, changing the social-political dynamics of implementation quite dramatically. A final special context may involve the acquisition of highly specialized 'high-tech' firms, where the target's value is embedded in the specific skills of the firm's employees (Ranft & Lord, 1998). In this instance, acquiring firms may pay special attention to programs designed to enhance the cooperation of the target's managers and technologists.

Finally, why do some mergers succeed? The evidence suggests that strategy is not a strong predictor of merger success. Luck is an explanation for the success of some mergers (Barney, 1988). However, we expect that constructs less randomly distributed than luck would predict successful merger outcomes. The foregoing analysis suggests that the discipline to avoid pricing auctions and/or the willingness to use non-conventional styles of implementation would foster successful merger. In turn, the bidding discipline might be fostered by broad search strategies, while implementation skill might grow with experience. Beyond the propositions suggested here, we propose that case research, similar in design to Dundas & Richardson's (1982) study of unrelated diversification, might lead to a grounded theory of merger success.

In conclusion, we call attention to the fact that, regarding acquisitions, the spotlight has focused too narrowly on characteristics of product fit. To understand mergers, we need to re-focus attention to the tenor of the bidding game, the response of the target managers, and the relationships that emerge as the two entities join together. For too long research designs have rested on the specious assumption of synergy. It's time for a richer world of merger research, with a broader domain of concepts and constructs.

ACKNOWLEDGEMENT

We gratefully acknowledge the helpful comments of Michael Lubatkin, Thomas Turk and Caron St. John on an earlier draft of this manuscript.

REFERENCES

Agarwal, A., Jaffe, J. F., & Mandelker, G. N. (1992). The post-merger performance of acquiring firms: A re-examination of an anomaly. *Journal of Finance, 47,* 1605–1621.
Ansoff, H. I., Avener, J., Brandenburg, F. E., Portner, F. E., & Radosevich, R. (1971). Acquisition behavior of U.S. manufacturing firms. Nashville, TN.: Vanderbilt University Press.

Balakrishnan, S. (1988). The prognostics of diversifying acquisitions. *Strategic Management Journal, 9,* 185–196.

Barnard, C. I. (1962). *The functions of the executive.* Cambridge, MA.: Harvard University Press.

Barney, J. (1988). Returns to bidding firms in mergers and acquisitions: Reconsidering the relatedness hypothesis. *Strategic Management Journal, 9,* 71–78.

Baron, D .P. (1983). Tender offers and management resistance. *Journal of Finance, 38,* 331–343.

Bennett, A. (1986). After the merger, more CEOs left in uneasy spot: looking for work. *Wall Street Journal,* August 27, 19.

Boudreaux, K. J., & Long, H. W. (1977). *The basic theory of corporate finance.* Englewood Cliffs, N.J.: Prentice-Hall.

Bruton, G. D., Oviatt, B. M., & White, M. A. (1994). Performance of acquisitions of distressed firms. *Academy of Management Journal, 37,* 972–989.

Cannella, A., & Hambrick, D. (1993). Effects of executive departures on the performance of acquired firms. *Strategic Management Journal, Summer Special Issue, 14.* 137–152.

Capron, L. (1999). The long-term performance of horizontal acquisitions. *Strategic Managementt Journal, 20,* 987–1018.

Carper, W. B. (1990). Corporate acquisitions and shareholder wealth: A review and exploratory analysis. *Journal of Management, 16,* 807–823.

Chatterjee, S. (1986). Types of synergy and economic value: The impact of acquisitions on merging firms. *Strategic Management Journal, 7,* 119–139.

Chatterjee, S. (1992). Sources of value in takeovers: Synergy or restructuring-implications for target and bidder firms. *Strategic Management Journal, 13,* 267–286.

Chatterjee, S., Lubatkin, M. H., Schweiger, D. M., & Weber, Y. (1992). Cultural differences and share holder value in related mergers: Linking equity and human capital. *Strategic Managementt Journal, 13,* 319–334.

Cochran, P. L., Wood, R. A., & Jones, T. B. (1985). The composition of boards of directors and incidence of golden parachutes. *Academy of Management Journal, 28,* 664–671.

Datta, D. K., & Grant, J. H. (1990). Relationships between type of acquisition, the autonomy given to the acquired firm, and acquisition success: An empirical analysis. *Journal of Management, 16,* 29–44.

Datta, D. K., Pinches, G. E., & Narayanan, V. K. (1992). Factors influencing wealth creation from mergers and acquisitions: A meta-analysis. *Strategic Management Journal, 13,* 67–84.

Davis, G. F. (1991). Agents without principles? The spread of the poison pill through the intercorporate network. *Administrative Science Quarterly, 36,* 583–613.

Drucker, P. F. (1981). The five rules of successful acquisition. *Wall Street Journal, 28.* October 15,

Dundas, K. N. M., & Richardson, P. R. (1982). Implementing the unrelated product strategy. *Strategic Management Journal, 3,* 287–301.

Elgers, P. T., & Clark, J. J. (1980). Merger types and shareholder returns: Additional evidence. *Financial Management, 9*(2), 66–72.

Fama, E. F. (1976). Foundations in finance. New York: Basic Books.

Fama, E. F., Fisher, L., Jensen, M. C., & Roll, R. (1969). The adjustment of stock prices to new information. *International Economic Review,* 1–21.

Flanagan, D. J. (1996). Announcements of purely related and purely unrelated mergers and shareholder returns: Reconciling the relatedness paradox. *Journal of Management, 22,* 823–835.

Floyd, S. W., & Wooldridge, B. (1992). Middle management involvement in strategy and its association with strategic type: A research note. *Strategic Management Journal, 13* (Summer), 153–168.

Fowler, K. L., & Schmidt, D. R. (1989.) Determinants of tender offer post-acquisition financial performance. *Strategic Management Journal, 10,* 339–350.

Galbraith, J. R. (1983). Strategy and organization planning. *Human Resource Management*, Spr/Sum, 63–77.

Galbraith, J. R., & Kazanjian, R. K. (1986). *Strategy implementation: Structure, systems and process.* St. Paul: West Publishing Company.

Grant, R. (1988). On 'Dominant Logic', relatedness and the link between diversity and performance. *Strategic Management Journal, 9,* 639–642.

Harrison, J. S., Hitt, M. E., Hoskisson, R. E., & Ireland, R. D. (1991). Synergies and post-acquisition performance: Differences versus similarities in resource allocations. *Journal of Management, 17,* 173–190.

Haunschild, P. R. (1993). Interorganizational imitation: The impact of interlocks on corporate acquisition activity. *Administrative Science Quarterly, 38,* 564–592.

Hill, C. W. L., & Hoskisson, R. E., (1987). Strategy and structure in the multiproduct firm. *Academy of Management Review, 12,* 331–341.

Hirsch, P. (1987). *Pack your own parachute: How to survive mergers, takeovers and other corporate disasters.* Reading, MA. Addison-Wesley Publishing Co.

Hirschman, A. O. (1970). *Exit, voice, and loyalty.* Cambridge, MA.: Harvard University Press.

Hitt, M., Harrison, J., Ireland, R. D. &, Best, A. (1998). Attributes of successful and unsuccessful acquisitions of U.S. firms. *British Journal of Management, 9,* 91–114.

Hitt, M. A., Hoskisson, R. E., Ireland, R. D., & Harrison, J. S. (1991). Effects of acquisitions on R&D inputs and outputs. *Academy of Management Journal, 34,* 693–706.

Hitt, M. A., Ireland, R. D., & Hoskisson, R. E. (1999.) *Strategic Management: Competitiveness and Globalization.* Cincinnatti, OH: SouthWestern Publishing Company.

Hogarty, T. F. (1970). Profits from merger: The evidence of fifty years. *St. John's Law Review, 44* (Special Edition), 378–391.

Holl, P., & Kyriazis, D. (1997). Wealth creation and bid resistance in U.K. takeover bids. *Strategic Management Journal, 18,* 483–498.

Hoskisson, R. E., & Hitt, M. A. (1990). Antecedents and performance outcomes of diversification: A review and critique of theoretical perspectives. *Journal of Management, 16,* 461–509.

Hoskisson, R. E., & Hitt, M. A. (1988). Strategic control systems and relative R&D investment in large multiproduct firms. *Strategic Management Journal, 9.* 605–621.

Jarrell, G. A. (1985). The wealth effects of litigation by targets: Do interests diverge in a merger? *Journal of Law and Economics, 28,* 151–177.

Jemison, D. B., & Sitkin, S. B. (1986). Corporate acquisitions: A process perspective. *Academy of Management Review, 11,* 145–163.

Jensen, M. C., & Meckling, H. (1976). Theory of the firm: Managerial behavior, agency cost and ownership structure. *Journal of Financial Economics, 3,* 305–360.

Jensen, M. C., & Ruback, R. S. (1983.) The market for corporate control: The scientific evidence. *Journal of Financial Economics, 11,* 5–50.

Jones, G. R., & Hill, C. W. L. (1988). Transaction cost analysis of strategy-structure choice. *Strategic Management Journal, 9,* 159–172.

Kosnik, R. D. (1987). Greenmail: A study of board performance in corporate governance. *Administrative Science Quarterly, 32,* 163–185.

Lauenstein, M. C. 1985. Diversification-The hidden explanation of success. *Sloan Management Review, 27*(1), 49–55.

Loderer, C., & Martin, K. (1992). Postacquisition performance of acquiring firms. *Financial Management, 21*(3), 69–77.

Lorsch, J. W., & Allen, S. A. (1973). *Managing diversity and interdependence.* Boston: Division of Research, Harvard University.

Lubatkin, M. (1983). Mergers and the performance of the acquiring firm. *Academy of Management Review, 8,* 218–225.

Lubatkin, M. (1987). Merger strategies and stockholder value. *Strategic Management Journal, 8,* 39–53.

Lubatkin, M., Srinivasan, N., & Merchant, H. (1997). Merger strategies and shareholder value during times of relaxed antitrust enforcement: The case of large mergers during the 1980s. *Journal of Management, 23,* 59–81.

Lubatkin, M., & Shrieves, R. E. (1986). Toward reconciliation of market performance measures to strategic management research. *Academy of Management Review, 11,* 497–512.

Malatesta, P. H., & Walkling, R.A. (1988). Poison pill securities: Stockholder wealth, profitability, and ownership structure. *Journal of Financial Economics, 20,* 347–376.

Markides, C. C., & Williamson, P. J. (1994). Related diversification, core competencies and corporate performance *Strategic Management Journal, 15,* 149–165.

Nahavandi, A., & Malekzadeh, A. R. (1988). Acculturation in mergers and acquisitions. *Academy of Management Review, 13,* 79–90.

Nathanson, D. A., & Cassano, J. S. (1982). Organization, diversity and performance. *Wharton Magazine, 6*(4), 19–26.

Nutt, P. C. (1987). Identifying and appraising how managers install strategy. *Strategic Management Journal, 8*(1), 1–14.

O'Shaughnessy, K. C., & Flanagan, D. J. (1998). Determinants of layoff announcements following M&As: An empirical investigation. *Strategic Management Journal, 19,* 989–999.

Oviatt, B. M. (1988). Agency and transaction costs perspectives on the manager-shareholder relationship: Incentives for congruent interests. *Academy of Management Review, 13,* 214–225.

Paine, F. T., & Power, D. J. (1984). Merger strategy: An examination of Drucker's five rules for successful acquisitions. *Strategic Management Journal, 5,* 99–110.

Panzar, J. C., & Willig, R. D. (1981). Economies of scope. *American Economic Review, 71,* 268–272.

Parsons, T. (1960). *Structure and process in modern societies.* New York: The Free Press.

Pitts, R. A. (1976). Diversification strategies and organizational policies of large diversified firms. *Journal of Economics and Business, 28,* 181–188.

Porter, M. E. (1980). *Competitive strategy: Techniques for analyzing industries and competitors.* New York: The Free Press.

Porter, M. E. (1985). *Competitive advantage: Creating and sustaining superior performance.* New York: The Free Press.

Porter, M. E. (1987). From competitive advantage to corporate strategy. *Harvard Business Review, 56*(3), 28–46.

Prahalad, C. K., & Bettis, R. A. (1986). The dominant logic: A new linkage between diversity and performance. *Strategic Management Journal, 7,* 485–501.

Ranft, A., & Lord, M. (1998). Acquiring knowledge-based resources through the retention of human capital: Evidence from high-tech acquisitions. *Academy of Management Best Paper Proceedings,* compact disk.

Rau, P. R., & Vermaelen, T. (1998). Glamour, value and the post-acquisition performance of acquiring firms. *Journal of Financial Economics, 49,* 223–253.

Ravenscraft, D., & Scherer, F. M. (1987). *Mergers, sell-offs and economic efficiency.* Washington, DC.: Brookings.

Rumelt, R. P. (1982). Diversification strategy and profitability. *Strategic Management Journal, 3,* 359–369.

Rumelt, R. P. (1979). Evaluation of strategy: Theory and models. In: D. Schendel, & C. Hofer, (Eds.), *Strategic Management: A new view of policy and planning:* (pp. 196–212). Boston: Little, Brown.

Salancik, G. R., & Meindl, J. R. (1984). Corporate attributions as strategic illusions of management control. *Administrative Science Quarterly, 29,* 238–255.

Shelton, L. M. (1988). Strategic business fits and corporate acquisitions: Empirical evidence. *Strategic Management Journal, 9,* 279–288.

Singh, H., & Harianto, F. (1990). Top management tenure, corporate ownership structure and the magnitude of golden parachutes. *Strategic Management Journal, 10* (Special Issue), 143–156.

Singh, H., & Harianto, F. (1989). Management-board relationships, takeover risk, and adoption of golden parachutes. *Academy of Management Journal, 32,* 7–24.

Singh, H., & Montgomery, C. A. (1987). Corporate acquisition strategies and economic performance. *Strategic Management Journal, 8,* 377–386.

Song, J. H. (1983). Diversifying acquisitions and financial relationships: Testing 1974–1976 performance. *Strategic Management Journal, 4,* 97–108.

Teece, D. J. (1980). Economies of scope and the scope of the enterprise. *Journal of Economic Behavior and Organization, 1,* 223–247.

Tregoe, B., & Zimmerman, J. (1980). *Top management strategy.* New York: Simon and Schuster.

Turk, T. A. (1992). Takeover resistance, information leakage, and target firm value. *Journal of Management, 18,* 503–522.

Turk, T. A., & Baysinger, B. D. (1991). *Environmental factors affecting corporate strategy: Taxes, antitrust policy, and corporate restructuring.* Working paper, Texas A&M University.

Very, P., Lubatkin, M., Calori, R., & Veiga, J. (1997). Relative standing and the performance of recently acquired European firms. *Strategic Management Journal, 18,* 593–614.

Walkling, R. A., & Long, M. S. (1984). Agency theory, managerial welfare and takeover bid resistance. *Rand Journal of Econmics, 1,* 54–68.

Walsh, J. P. (1988). Top management turnover following mergers and acquisitions. *Strategic Management Journal, 9,* 173–183.

Walsh, J. P., & Ellwood, J. (1991). Mergers, acquisitions and the pruning of managerial deadwood. *Strategic Management Journal, 12,* 201–217.

Weber, Y., Shenkar, O., & Raveh, A. (1996). National and corporate cultural fit in mergers/acquisitions: An exploratory study. *Management Science, 42,* 1215–1227.

Williams, J. R., Paez, B.L., & Sanders, L. (1988). Conglomerates revisited. *Strategic Management Journal, 9,* 403–414.

Williamson, O. E. (1985). *The economic institutions of capitalism: Firms, markets, and relational contracting.* New York: Macmillan Free Press.

MANAGERIAL OWNERSHIP AND RISK-REDUCING ACQUISITIONS

John Doukas and Martin Holmèn

ABSTRACT

In this chapter we examine the relation between managerial ownership and the announcement returns of 93 Swedish risk-reducing acquisitions, completed over the 1980–1995 period. The evidence shows that there are not distinct governance characteristics associated with bidders' risk-reducing acquisitions. Our results indicate that firms engage in diversifying acquisitions at the expense of shareholders' wealth when managers have no equity stakes on the bidder This result is consistent with the view that risk-reducing acquisitions are motivated by managers' need to diversify the risk associated with their human capital. This result suggests that risk-reducing acquisitions occur when managers' firm-specific human capital is at risk. Managers elect corporate risk-reducing activities as a means of reducing the risk of their human capital. Risk-reducing acquisitions, however, by firms where managers hold equity stakes increase firm value. This result suggests that managerial owners make risk-reducing acquisitions when they have identified potential corporate gains from risk-reduction. Simultaneous equation estimations provide additional evidence suggesting that managerial ownership affects bidder's shareholder returns, while there is no evidence of reverse causality.

Advances in Mergers and Acquisitions, Volume 1, pages 183–203.
2000 by Elsevier Science Inc.
ISBN: 0–7623–0683–1

1. INTRODUCTION

Managerial self-interest has been advanced as one of the motivations behind mergers and acquisitions unrelated to the core business of the bidder (i.e. risk-reducing). These two terms are used interchangeably throughout this study. Amihud & Lev (1981), and Jensen (1986) argue that corporate managers invest across industries to make their skills more indispensable to the firm, protect their human capital (i.e. reduce their employment risk) and private benefits. However, this type of acquisition strategies may be to the detriment of share-holders' wealth. Morck, Shleifer, & Vishny (1990), suggest that managers entrench themselves by undertaking industrially diversifying investment decisions that make it costly for shareholders to replace them. For the 1980–1987 period, they report that bidding shareholders experience wealth losses when U.S. firms announce diversifying (risk-reducing) acquisitions.

If corporate risk-reducing investment decisions arise from agency problems between managers and shareholders, the finance literature suggests a number of mechanisms to control managerial self-interest. The most commonly discussed control mechanism is managerial shareholdings (Jensen & Meckling (1976)). It is argued that managers with personal wealth invested in the firm they manage will experience losses if they engage in value reducing investment activities. Denis, Denis & Sarin (1997) provide results consistent with the predictions of the managerial ownership hypothesis. They report that corporate diversification (investing outside the core business of the firm) is inversely related to manage-rial ownership. When bidders engage in diversifying acquisitions, Lewellen, Loderer, & Rosenfelt (1989) document a positive relation between firm value and managers' equity stakes. While managers of bidding firms may initiate takeovers in their own interest, Amihud, Dodd & Weinstein (1986) fail to show that this type of takeover activity is at the expense of shareholders' wealth.

In this chapter, we examine the effects of managerial ownership on acquisition returns for firms conducting risk-reducing investments using a sample of 93 Swedish acquisitions over the 1980–1995 period. The primary objectives of this study are threefold. First, we examine the governance characteristics of firms involved in diversifying acquisitions. Second, we analyze the determinants of the abnormal returns associated with this type of acquisitions. In particular, we examine the relation between announcement returns and bidder's ownership structure. Third, the direction of causality between managerial ownership and firm performance is examined using a simultaneous equation analysis.

While these issues have been examined by relying mostly on U.S. firms, there is little evidence based on non-US data. The institutional setting of Sweden and the unique corporate ownership structure of Swedish companies are expected to shed additional insights on the relation between managerial ownership and corporate risk reduction activities. Sweden has an insider ownership system where several control groups have major stakes in many of the larger firms and, therefore, have little difficulty in monitoring and controlling managerial misconduct. Usually a member of the controlling group is also the CEO of the firm. The advantages of insider ownership, however, may be offset by the Swedish use of dual class shares, pyramid structures, and cross-holdings between firms (Bebchuck, Kraakman & Triantis (1999) and La Porta, Lopez-de-Silanes, Shleifer & Vishny (1998)). Therefore, this study investigates the effects of managerial ownership in the context of a more pronounced insider ownership system in comparison to the ownership structure characteristics of U.S. firms.

U.S. evidence (Loderer & Martin (1997)) suggests, that managerial ownership is endogenously determined and causality runs from returns to ownership that is less likely to be found in the insider-based ownership system of Sweden. We argue that Swedish ownership is likely to be more exogenously determined in comparison to outsider-based ownership systems. Swedish control groups tend to hold long-term controlling blocks, especially voting stock, that appears to be not actively traded based on information about future cash flows. The study of managerial ownership effects on Swedish diversifying investment activities is also interesting because managerial compensation in the form of stocks and stock options is less common in Sweden than in the U.S.

The detailed Swedish ownership data are unique in the sense that they provide information about the composition of managers' total Swedish equity portfolio. It is therefore possible to approximate how diversified their personal portfolios are in order to examine whether managerial self-interest motivates risk-reducing acquisitions. A wealthy manager may hold a substantial block in the firm that he manages but he may also possess other holdings such that his personal portfolio is well diversified. The Swedish data also let us distinguish between managers with personal wealth invested in the firm they manage and managers representing institutional wealth interests. This feature permits to capture the effect of different types of inside ownership.

Finally, risk-reducing acquisitions may be motivated by tax considerations. Lewellen (1971) argues that this type of acquisitions increase the debt capacity of the firm, that in turn, raise the value of tax shield. Since the Swedish corporate tax rate was fairly high (50%) during most of the investigated period, the potential value of corporate risk reduction is likely to be more pronounced relative to the U.S. This suggests that announcements of risk-reducing acquisitions in Sweden are less likely to be associated with negative stock returns, as potential leverage increases and the associated tax advantages are expected to be beneficial to stockholders.

The empirical evidence concerning the relation between managerial owner-ship, a managerial control mechanism, and firm performance is generally mixed. Demsetz & Lehn (1985) find no relation between operating performance and managerial ownership. Morck, Shleifer & Vishny (1988) and McConnell & Servaes (1990) document non-linear ownership-performance relations. These studies show that there is positive relation between managerial ownership and firm performance at low levels of managerial ownership. This relation turns negative at higher levels of managerial ownership. This result suggests that managers with considerable stakes and voting rights in the firm they manage, tend to engage in self-serving activities as internal and external monitoring mechanisms are less likely to be effective. This effect is expected to be pronounced in acquisition activities. A manager with a substantial amount of his wealth tied up in the firm he is managing has strong incentives to undertake risk-reducing acquisitions. The findings of Amihud & Lev (1981) corroborate this view as they find that the firm is more likely to complete a conglomerate merger when managers hold larger stakes, even if share-prices might fall.

Agrawal & Knoeber (1996) investigate alternative control mechanisms and document that they are interdependent (i.e. they are substitutes). They find that the relation between managerial ownership and performance is flat when they account for other control mechanisms as well.

Finally, attention has also been given to the direction of causality between man-agerial ownership and performance. The issue that has been addressed is whether managers make better decisions because of alignment of interest with stock-holders arising from ownership stakes in the firm they manage, or they hold stock in the firm they manage because the firm has better prospects? Loderer & Martin (1997) find that acquisition performance affects the size of managerial owner-ship. However, they find no evidence in support of the view that larger manage-rial ownership leads to better performance. In the Swedish framework, it is possible that managerial stakes may increase when managers know that risk-reducing acquisitions will be used to capture economic gains (e.g., tax benefits).

The empirical results of this study show that when bidding managers do not hold stock, the shareholders of bidding firms engaged in risk-reducing acquisitions experience significant negative returns, while they experience significant positive returns when managers have equity stakes on the bidder. Simultaneous equation system analysis indicates that causality goes from managerial ownership to returns, not vice versa. We also find that managers' total wealth and tenure determine their equity ownership in the firm. Furthermore, managerial ownership shows no significant relation with the potential corporate risk-reduction accomplished by the acquisition. However, poor performance is positively related to risk-reduction activities of the bidder. This suggests that managers try to reduce the risk associated with their human capital by reducing the firm's risk-exposure and avoid bankruptcy when the firm is performing poorly.

The remainder of the chapter is organized as follows. The next Section describes the managerial ownership structure within the Swedish corporate sector. The data and the variables used are presented in Section 3. The governance characteristics of bidding firms as well as other descriptive statistics are presented in Section 4. Section 5 presents the cross-sectional determinants of the announcements returns. The direction of causality between managerial ownership, announcement returns, and estimated corporate risk-reduction is examined using a simultaneous equation analysis in section 6. Section 7 provides a summary and concluding remarks.

2. SWEDISH MANAGERIAL OWNERSHIP CHARACTERISTICS

The ownership on the Stockholm Stock Exchange (StSE) is dominated by several control groups. For instance, the Wallenberg family is by far the largest owner and controlled 38% of the stock market capitalization in 1998. The five largest groups controlled 68% of the stock market capitalization. The groups control the largest companies and therefore a large fraction of the market capitalization. The percentage of firms on the StSE controlled by Wallenbergs is 6% and the five largest groups together controlled 22% of the listed firms.[1] In our sample, the major groups account for 55 (59%) of the acquisitions.[2]

The control groups are structured around a family (e.g. Wallenberg), an individual (e.g. Robert Weil), a bank (e.g. SHB), or an industrial group (e.g. Volvo/ Skanska). If a family or an individual has substantial ownership in a company, a family member or the individual himself is likely to be CEO, chairman or board member. This leads to substantial direct or indirect managerial ownership in many Swedish firms. Indirect ownership means that other companies, owned or controlled by the family, hold substantial stakes of stock in the firm. Almost half of the firms in our sample have total (direct plus indirect) managerial ownership of 10% or more of the equity traded. The average total managerial ownership in our sample is 15.9% of the capital and 22.7% of the votes.

The institutional groups (i.e. banks and industrial groups), have 'professional managers' who act as board members, chairmen, or CEOs in the firms in which they have substantial ownership.[3] These groups usually have large block ownership compared to traditional institutional owners. The average institutional block ownership in our sample is 17.3% of the capital and 20.5% of the votes.

This also leads to substantial total institutional ownership. The average total institutional ownership is 36.6% of the capital and 38.3% of the votes.

3. SOURCES AND SAMPLE CHARACTERISTICS

In Sweden the bidder can force a merger or consolidation, only if it has acquired 90% of the other firm's equity. The acquisition of publicly traded stock is usually accomplished through a public tender offer. Therefore, almost all acquisitions are preceded by a public tender offer (Bergström & Rydqvist (1989)).[4] The tender offers associated with the acquisitions between 1980–1991 in our sample were collected from StSE records and daily newspapers.[5] The 1992–1995 tender offers were collected from the Stockholm Stock Exchange Quarterly Report. Only the successful non-partial takeover bids, where both the target and the bidder were listed at the time of the bid, are included in our sample. The final sample consists of 93 takeover bids.[6] Since these takeovers represent about 70% of the successful takeover bids, where both firms were listed on the StSE at the time of the announcement during this time period, it is a representative sample of the Swedish takeover market during the 1980–1995 period. Many of the missing observations involved small firms for which we could not find all relevant data.

We use stock price data, collected from the Aktiedata Oy tape for 1980–1992 and from the Superchart tape for 1993–1995, to estimate acquisition announcement effects on shareholder wealth. This is accomplished by conventional event study methodology. Cumulative abnormal returns (CARs) are estimated from the market model prediction errors. The market index used is Affärsvärldens General Index, which is a value weighted index representing 95% of the StSE's market capitalization. Consistent with Bradley, Desai, & Kim (1988), among others, the 11-day window interval is used. When the firm has both A and B shares traded, a value weighted portfolio return is calculated. When the A-shares are not traded, the return on the B-shares has been used as a proxy for the return of the A-shares.[7] For the total sample, the average announcement return is 0.54% (with a t-statistic value 1.05), the 25th percentile is –4.37%, Median is –0.32%, and the 75th percentile is 6.42%.

Thus, about half of the acquisition announcements are associated with a negative market reaction. This implies that a fairly large number of acquisitions are motivated by managerial self-interest. The corporate finance literature provides various governance characteristics, which might affect the level of agency problems between managers and shareholders. These characteristics include shareholdings by managers, institutions, and blockholders; the managerial labor market; debt policy; outside directors; and the market for corporate control (Agrawal & Knoeber (1996)). Since almost all Swedish firms have both employees and outsiders (i.e., non-employees) on the board, a measure of outside directorship is not applicable in the data used. Furthermore, the Swedish market for corporate control is too small to construct a relevant measure of how active the corporate control market is in each industry.

For the 1980–1984 period, ownership data were collected from annual reports while for the 1985–1993 and 1994–1995 periods they were obtained from Sundqvist & Sundin and Sundqvist, respectively. The latter two sources report the holdings of the 25 largest shareholders of all publicly traded firms as of January each year. They are based on a public record, which includes all shareholders with more than 500 shares. The sources group the holdings of family members and point out cross ownership and possible partnerships.[8]

CEOs and all directors are defined as managers. The ownership information has been compared with the list of managers to identify managerial ownership within each company. We restrict managerial ownership to CEOs and directors with personal or family wealth invested directly or indirectly in the firm. This is motivated by the need to capture the alignment of interest effect that managerial ownership is claimed to be associated with. Holdings by corporations and institutions with representatives on the board are not defined as managerial ownership since these directors do not represent their own capital.

The effectiveness of institutions as active monitors of managerial misconduct has been debated. Pound (1988) argues that institutional owners might be passive and always vote with management. Jensen (1989) argues that an individual outsider will be a more active monitor. Therefore, our analysis includes outside blockholders as an alternative control mechanism.

It is difficult to measure the combined human capital managers have invested in the firm. Hence, we concentrate on the CEO. The years that s/he has held the position as CEO is used as an approximation of the human capital invested in the firm. This information is collected from annual reports and is also used to inversely reflect the firm's reliance on the external labor market for managers (Agrawal & Knoeber (1996)). When the CEO has held the position over longer periods it is assumed that the firm has been less active in replacing the CEO. The threat of losing the job acts as a control mechanism.

Debt financing is also supposed to control agency problems by the monitoring role of lenders. However, debt financing also motivated by managers' incentives to reduce the firm's cash flow volatility. Thus, the use of debt policy as an external monitoring mechanism of value reducing risk-reduction strategies is ambiguous. Summary statistics of the potential control mechanisms are presented in Table 1.

Table 1.   Summary Statistics for the Potential Control Mechanisms in
Swedish Bidding Firms in Acquisitions 1980–1995

	N	Mean	Std. Dev	Min	Med	Max
Managerial ownership						
equity	89	0.159	0.195	0	0.062	0.709
vote	89	0.227	0.265	0	0.112	0.926
Institutional Block						
equity	89	0.173	0.174	0	0.101	0.848
vote	89	0.205	0.208	0	0.108	0.871
Outside Block						
equity	89	0.052	0.089	0	0.015	0.435
vote	89	0.062	0.111	0	0.017	0.671
CEO tenure	89	6.045	5.797	0	4	30
Debt/ Total Assets	89	0.697	0.161	0.079	0.708	0.973
Firm Size (M SEK)	89	19211	38516	146	4532	238011

The sample used in this study consists of 93 Swedish acquisitions 1980–1995 in which both the bidder and the target were listed on the Stockholm Stock Exchange, the OTC list, or the Unofficial list at the time of the announcement. N = 89 since 4 firms made two acquisitions the same year. Outside block is defined as the largest block held by an individual outsider. Institutional Block is defined as the largest block held by an institution. CEO tenure is defined as the number of years the CEO has held this position.

4. DESCRIPTIVE STATISTICS

The potential risk-reduction accomplished by an acquisition is estimated by the ratio of the bidder's stock market volatility over the estimation period of the market model (day −180 to day −20) divided by the volatility of the implied value weighted portfolio of the bidder and target stock over the same period. Thus, this measure identifies how volatility would have differed if the estimated cash flows of the bidder and the target had been traded as a single entity instead of separate entities.

Managers with firm-specific human capital invested in the firm they manage are exposed to considerable non-diversifiable risk. If the firm goes bankrupt or is taken over due to financial distress, managers will most certainly lose their jobs and incur significant human capital losses. Thus, managers have incentives to reduce the probability of bankruptcy. The probability of bankruptcy is a function of the total corporate risk, not just of the market risk. By comparing the volatility of the bidding firm's stock market volatility and the volatility of the implied value weighted portfolio's stock market returns over the estimation period, it is possible to define whether the investment is more or less risk-reducing.

In Table 2 the sample is divided into quartiles according to the estimated risk-reduction accomplished by the acquisition. The negative value for quartile 1 means that the value weighted portfolio's market returns were more volatile than the bidder's market returns, indicating a negative correlation between the bidder and the target. The announcement returns do not show any significant differences between the risk-reduction quartiles. Thus, the statistics do not indicate that risk-reducing acquisitions were to the detriment of outside shareholders, even if they had been motivated by managerial self-interest.

The ownership measures estimate equity ownership. The results for vote ownership are similar. The vote-to-equity fraction has also been examined without any clear results. Managers with high vote-to-equity ratios might create additional agency problems since they control the firm without holding the majority of cash flow rights. However, a manager may also use this possibility to diversify his personal portfolio without relinquishing control, which would decrease his incentives to engage in value reducing risk-reduction at the firm level. Thus, the effect of dual class shares is ambiguous in determining managers' incentives to reduce corporate risk.

If managers hold diversified personal portfolios they should have less incentive to pursue diversifying acquisition. We approximate their personal portfolios by estimating the total value of their investment on the StSE. This information was obtained from Sundqvist 1985–1993 and Sundin & Sundqvist 1994–1995, respectively. Due to the existence of individual and family dominated power spheres this variable is skewed with a mean of 6.4 billion SEK and a median of 0.1 billion SEK. Several managers have no major shareholdings on the StSE, while some managers have over 50 other substantial holdings. The statistics show an insignificant trend that the managers with little or no investments on the StSE tend to make acquisitions, which potentially reduce risk substantially.

If the control mechanisms reduce agency problems and if risk-reducing investment activities arise from agency problems then: equity stakes by managers, outside blockholders and institutions should be lower for the fourth quartile; CEO tenure should be higher; and debt ratios should be lower. However, the descriptive statistics reported in Table 2 show with the exception of institutional ownership that there are no significant differences between the risk-reduction quartiles. This seems to imply that either these monitoring mechanisms do not work in controlling agency problems or risk-reducing acquisitions can not be attributed to agency problems. Alternatively, one can argue that the use of a

Table 2. Descriptive Statistics Divided by the Estimated Risk-Reduction Accomplished by the Acquisition

| | Quartile 1 (n = 24) | | Quartile 2 (n = 23) | | Quartile 3 (n = 23) | | Quartile 4 (n = 23) | | t-value mean difference | | |
	mean	median	mean	median	mean	median	mean	median	2–1	3–1	4–1
Estimated risk-reduction (%)	−9.7	1.0	13.0	12.4	31.9	31.8	85.3	73.6	3.31***	2.96***	8.16***
Announcement returns (%)	1.52	1.47	0.15	−0.44	0.42	−0.69	0.03	−0.40	−0.83	−0.67	−0.91
Managerial ownership (%)	14.1	8.1	20.6	19.5	18.6	9.8	11.6	0	1.29	0.88	−0.50
% of man. StSE investment	4.5	1.7	7.4	2.6	2.6	2.1	1.9	0	1.04	−0.68	−0.94
Managers' StSE inv. (B SEK)	10.61	0.26	8.52	0.12	4.23	0.21	2.03	0	−0.37	−0.75	−040
Institutional Block (%)	13.6	7.0	13.4	8.3	17.8	12.9	22.8	16.4	−0.05	1.05	2.28**
Outside Block	5.2	0.7	4.7	0.8	6.6	1.6	4.7	1.9	−0.18	0.63	−0.20
CEO tenure	6.6	4	7.4	5	7.3	5	6.5	5	0.52	0.47	−0.67
Debt/ Total Assets	0.73	0.76	0.71	0.69	0.67	0.69	0.68	0.71	−0.63	−1.65*	−1.19
Firm Size (B SEK)	43.7	23.6	14.9	6.7	13.0	4.2	4.0	1.9	−1.77*	−1.91*	−2.45**
Approximate q ratio	1.18	1.09	1.32	1.23	1.38	1.16	1.07	1.06	1.21	1.48	−0.90

The sample used in this study consists of 93 Swedish acquisitions 1980–1995 in which both the bidder and the target were listed on the Stockholm Stock Exchange, the OTC list, or the Unofficial list at the time of the announcement. Risk-reduction is estimated by the ratio of the bidder's stock market volatility over the estimation period (day −180 to day −20) divided by the volatility of the implied value weighted portfolio of bidder and target stock over the estimation period minus 1. Outside block is defined as the largest block held by an individual outsider. Institutional Block is defined as the largest block held by an institution. CEO tenure is defined as the number of years the CEO has held this position. ***, ** and * denote a significant mean difference at the 1%, 5% and 10% levels, respectively.

simultaneous system framework (see Agrawal & Knoeber (1996)) is required, because some of the monitoring mechanisms are simultaneously determined within the firm. The firm size significant differences among the quartiles may be just an arithmetic relation. Since we expect a reduction in volatility when two stocks form a new entity, the impact of the target on bidder's volatility is likely to be more pronounced on a smaller bidder.

Lang & Stulz (1994) and May (1995) document that firms with poor performance tend to engage in risk-reducing activities by undertaking diversifying investments. This implies that the q value, measured as the sum of market value of equity and the book value of debt divided by the book value of total assets, of the bidder should be lower when risk-reducing acquisitions are pursued. The evidence listed in Table 2 does not support the view that corporate risk reduction is motivated by poor performance.

Table 3 reports announcement returns for different risk reduction. and managerial ownership classifications: risk-reduction (above) below the median and by managerial ownership above (below) 10%. Even though managerial ownership does not appear to affect the overall announcement returns, it plays a significant role in risk-reducing acquisitions. The median announcement return for risk-reducing acquisitions is 7.17% when the managers hold more than 10% of equity. It is −1.7% when the managers hold less than 10% equity in the firm. The median difference between the two categories is 8.87% and significant at the 1% level. This difference suggests that managers with considerable equity stakes on the firm pursue risk-reducing acquisitions as a means of increasing firm value. However, managers without equity stakes appear to pursue acquisitions that reduce risk associated with their human capital at the expense of stockholders.

5. CROSS-SECTIONAL REGRESSION ANALYSIS

To examine the influence of ownership on firm value we estimate the relation between announcement returns and the fraction of managerial ownership (OFFDIR). To control for other effects, the method of payment, METPAY, and the size, LSIZE, of the bidding firm are included in the analysis. The METPAY is an indicator variable equal to one if the acquisition is based on a pure cash offer, and zero otherwise. The LSIZE variable is the natural logarithm of bidder's market value of equity.

The results are reported in Table 4.[9] Regression 1 suggests that managerial ownership has no significant effect on the announcement returns even when we control for the method of payment and size effects. Regression 2 tests for the effect of managerial ownership associated with risk-reducing acquisitions, using

Table 3. Means and Medians of Announcement Returns grouped by Risk-
Reduction and Managerial Ownership

Managerial Ownership	Risk-Reduction below median	Risk-Reduction above median	Difference
> 10%	0.0051	0.0380**	–0.0328***
	(–0.0001)	(0.0717)***	(–0.0718)***
	n = 25	n = 20	
< 10%	0.0042	–0.026*	0.0298**
	(0.0058)	(–0.0170)*	(0.0112)
	n = 22	n = 26	
Difference	0.0009	0.0635***	
	(0.0047)	(0.0887)***	

The sample used in this study consists of Swedish Acquisitions 1980–1995 in which both the bidder and the target were listed on the Stockholm Stock Exchange, the OTC list or the Unofficial list at the time of the announcement. Cumulative (CARs) abnormal returns are computed from the market model prediction errors. Average CARs are reported with medians in parenthesis. Risk-reduction is estimated by the ratio of the bidder's stock market volatility over the estimation period (day –180 to day –20) divided by the volatility of the implied value weighted portfolio of bidder and target stock over the estimation period minus 1. ***, ** and * denote a significant mean difference at the 1%, 5% and 10% levels, respectively.

a risk-reduction dummy (RISKRED) along with an interaction term between risk-reduction and managerial ownership (OFFDIRRED). The RISKRED dummy takes the value of one if the estimated risk-reduction accomplished by the acquisition is above the median risk-reduction and zero otherwise. The interaction term reflects how managerial ownership affects the announcement returns of risk-reducing acquisitions. The results suggest that risk-reduction has a significant negative effect on the announcement returns when managers hold no equity in the firm. However, the interactive coefficient suggests that this negative effect significantly decreases with managerial ownership increases. These results are robust to the method of payment and firm size.

Regression 3 tests for the non-linear relationship between managerial ownership and announcement returns. The coefficient of the OFFDIR^{2}RED does not indicate that there is a non-linear relation between managerial ownership and announcement returns. Regression 4 tests how interdependent the different ownership characteristics are by including interaction terms between risk-reduction and institutional ownership, INSTRED, outside block-ownership, BLOCKRED, and CEO tenure, TENRED, as well.[10] The results continue to show that OFFDIRRED is still significantly positive, while interaction terms

Table 4. Cross-Sectional Regressions of 11-day Cumulative Abnormal
Returns

Variables	(1)	(2)	(3)	(4)
INTERCEPT	0.0192	0.0645	0.0600	0.0564
	(0.437)	(1.201)	(1.103)	(1.032)
OFFDIR	0.0518	−0.0610	−0.0596	−0.0583
	(1.306)	(−1.114)	(−1.083)	(−1.069)
RISKRED		−0.0427	−0.0456	0.0133
		(−2.054)**	(−1.083)	(0.719)
OFFDIRRED		0.2156	0.3024	0.1514
		(2.870)***	(1.939)*	(1.784)*
OFFDIR^{2}RED			−0.1647	
			(−0.636)	
INSTRED				−0.0875
				(−1.523)
BLOCKRED				−0.2305
				(−1.583)
TENRED				−0.0087
				(−0.621)
METPAY	0.0215	0.0194	0.0195	0.0203
	(1.404)	(1.311)	(1.313)	(1.374)
LSIZE	−0.0038	−0.0063	−0.0059	−0.0055
	(−0.783)	(−1.166)	(−1.070)	(−1.007)
Adj R^2 (%)	1.3	7.9	7.3	9.0
Inflection point	n.a.	n.a.	0.918	n.a.

The sample used in this study consists of Swedish Acquisitions 1980–1995 in which both the bidder and the target were listed on the Stockholm Stock Exchange, the OTC list or the Unofficial list at the time of the announcement. The 11-day cumulative abnormal returns (CARs) are computed from the market model prediction errors. The t-values are reported in the parenthesis. ***, ** and * denote significance at the 1%, 5% and 10% levels, respectively. N = 93. OFFDIR is the percentage ownership by the CEO and the board of directors. RISKRED is set equal to 1 if estimated risk-reduction accomplished by the acquisition is above the median risk-reduction, and 0 otherwise. OFFDIRRED is OFFDIR times RISKRED. OFFDIR2RED is the fraction of managerial ownership squared times RISKRED. INSTRED is the largest block held by an institution times RISKRED. BLOCKRED is the largest outside block held by an individual times RISKRED. TENRED is the natural logarithm of one plus the years the CEO has held this position times RISKRED. METPAY is set equal to 1 if it is a pure cash offer, and 0 otherwise. LSIZE is the natural logarithm of the bidding firm's market value.

for the other ownership characteristics appear to have insignificant effects on announcement returns.

Thus, managerial ownership is positively related to stock market performance when the firm undertakes risk-reducing acquisitions. The positive relation is present even when we control for other effects. The evidence points out that managers, whose incentives are aligned with outside shareholders through stock ownership, make risk-reducing acquisitions that do not harm shareholders' wealth. Alternatively, risk-reducing acquisitions are beneficial to both managers and outside stockholders when the former have equity stakes on the firm they manage.

6. A SIMULTANEOUS EQUATION ANALYSIS

The evidence thus far suggests that risk-reducing acquisitions increase firm value when managerial ownership stakes align their interests with those of outside shareholders. In this section, however, we examine whether managerial ownership is attributed to the firm's better prospects (Loderer & Martin (1997)). That is, we ask whether managers' equity stakes are motivated by the alignment of interests with the outside shareholders, or because the firms they manage have better prospects? In our context the reversed causality would imply that the managers hold stock in the firm when they know that corporate risk-reduction will be used to increase debt levels and thereby the value of the tax shield. Managers do not hold stock when corporate risk-reduction is used to diversify managerial human capital. Furthermore, managers have incentives to reduce corporate risk when they hold larger equity stakes while risk-reduction motivated by managerial self-interest could have a negative effect on announcement returns. We examine these issues using a simultaneous equation system with announcement returns, managerial ownership, and risk-reduction as dependent variables. To keep the system simple, a minimum set of exogenous variables is included.

The first structural equation determines 11-day cumulative announcement returns, CAR, as a function of managerial ownership, OFFDIR, the potential level of risk-reduction accomplished by the acquisition, RISKRED, method of payment, METPAY, firm size, LSIZE, and the bidder's pre-acquisition performance (measured by the q ratio), Q. Equation 2 determines managerial ownership as a function of announcement returns, CAR, firm size, the CEO tenure, TENURE, and managers' total investment on the StSE, WEALTH. Finally, Equation 3 determines the potential risk reduction accomplished by the acquisition as a function of managerial ownership, firm size, the managers' total investment on the StSE, and the bidder's pre-acquisition performance. The simultaneous equation system is:

$$CAR_i = \gamma_{12} \, OFFDIR_i + \gamma_{13} RISKRED_i + \beta_{11} \, METPAY_i + \beta_{12} \, LSIZE_i + \beta_{13} Q_i + \varepsilon_{1i} \tag{1}$$

$$OFFDIR_i = \gamma_{21} \, CAR_i + \beta_{21} \, LSIZE_i + \beta_{22} \, TENURE_i + \beta_{23} \, WEALTH_i + \varepsilon_{2i} \tag{2}$$

$$RISKRED_i = \gamma_{32} \, OFFDIR_i + \beta_{31} \, LSIZE_i + \beta_{32} \, WEALTH_i + \beta_{33} Q_i + \varepsilon_{3i} \tag{3}$$

In this system several variables are left out. Ultimately, one would aim to include all the control mechanisms and the firm's activities (see Agrawal & Knoeber (1996)). This is beyond the scope of this analysis since our focus is to examine the direction of causality between managerial ownership and the effect on shareholder wealth of the acquisition announcement.

If managerial ownership leads to alignment of interests between managers and shareholders where managers engage in corporate risk-reduction acquisitions to the detriment of shareholders wealth, the coefficient of OFFDIR variable is expected to be positive in equation (1). To control for the method of payment and size effects, METPAY and LSIZE are added. In order to meet the identification condition for equation (2), Tobin's Q is added to equation (1). The Tobin's Q is also included because previous studies (Lang, Stulz & Walkling (1989) and Servaes (1991)) have documented a positive relation between Tobin's Q and the gains from takeovers on U.S. data.

If managers use their private information to trade in the firm's stock, they should accumulate stock when the firm has positive NPV opportunities. If this is the case, the coefficient of CAR should be positive in equation (2). A specific amount of wealth invested in a firm will result in different equity fractions depending on the size of the firm. Thus, it will be more difficult for managers to acquire large blocks of equity when they manage a larger firm. We include an approximation of the total value of the managers' personal wealth invested in other firms traded in the market, WEALTH. If the managers have substantial shareholdings in other firms, it will be less risky for them to hold a large fraction in the firm they manage. Thus, we expect the coefficient of the WEALTH variable to have a positive coefficient. CEO's tenure is also included in the analysis. CEO ownership is expected to be positively related to the number of years the manager has been acting as the firm's CEO (Agrawal & Knoeber (1996)).

Our second equation is somewhat different from that of Loderer & Martin's (1997) equation (2). They define managerial ownership as a function of acquisition performance, firm size, and stock market volatility. They argue that greater stock price volatility creates incentives for outsiders to take over management responsibilities, (i.e., managerial ownership should be positively related to volatility). Demsetz & Lehn (1985) have argued that this relation might be concave and, therefore, Loderer & Martin include the standard deviation and the variance of returns.[11]

If an acquisition is motivated by managerial incentives to reduce the risk of managers' personal portfolio, the potential risk-reduction accomplished by the acquisition should be positively related to the managers' equity fraction in the firm, OFFDIR, in equation (3). However, if the managers have substantial investments in other firms on the StSE, their incentives to reduce corporate risk should be weak. Thus, the coefficient of the WEALTH variable should have a negative sign in equation (3). Lang & Stulz (1994) and May (1995) suggest that managers in firms which are performing badly have incentives to reduce corporate risk. This implies that Q should have a negative coefficient in equation (3). Finally, size is included in the analysis.

Since the necessary conditions for identification are met, the system can be estimated with two-stage least squares (2SLS) regression. With three dependent variables, identification requires at least two omitted predetermined variables from each equation and that the omitted variables do not affect the dependent variable in the equation they are omitted.

The results are presented in Table 5. Regression 1 shows that the managerial ownership, OFFDIRHAT defined as the predictor of managerial ownership from the first stage regression, has an insignificant positive effect on the announcement return. However, the effect is significant at the 10% level at a one-sided test. None of the other variables appear to be significant at any conventional level.

Regression 2 indicates that the abnormal returns, CAR defined as the predictor of abnormal returns obtained from the first stage regression, have virtually zero influence on managerial ownership. This is inconsistent with the findings of Loderer & Martin (1997), implying that Swedish managers do not use their private information to trade in the firm's stock. Alternatively, managerial ownership does not appear to be driven by the better prospering bidders. Because some of the coefficients of the exogenous variables are insignificant, especially in regression (1), coefficient estimates for the endogenous variables may be imprecise. However, alternative model specifications have been estimated and the CAR predictor never gains significance in regression (2). The managerial ownership predictor, however, is always positive with a t-statistic above one in explaining abnormal returns. Thus, if a relation between the profitability of risk-reducing acquisitions and managerial ownership exists in Sweden, it goes from ownership to profitability, not vice versa.

Table 5. Two-Stage Least Squares Regression with Announcement Returns, Managerial Ownership, and Risk-Reduction as Dependent Variables, respectively

Variables	CAR	OFFDIR	RISKRED
INTERCEPT	0.0102	0.1495	1.9748
	(0.046)	(1.604)	(3.669)***
CARHAT		0.0686	
		(0.052)	
OFFDIRHAT	0.0743		–1.8821
	(1.295)		(–1.059)
RISKREDHAT	–0.0198		
	(–0.141)		
METPAY	0.0214		
	(1.111)		
LSIZE	–0.0046	–0.0205	–0.1550
	(–0.278)	(–2.117)**	(–2.954)***
TENURE		0.0314	
		(1.815)*	
WEALTH		0.0321	0.0678
		(6.925)***	(1.168)
Q	0.0149		–0.2641
	(0.362)		(–2.221)**
Adj R^2 (%)	0.3	51.8	13.1

The sample used in this study consists of Swedish Acquisitions 1980–1995 in which both the bidder and the target were listed on the Stockholm Stock Exchange, the OTC list or the Unofficial list at the time of the announcement. CARHAT is the predictor of CAR from first stage regression. OFFDIRHAT is the predictor of managerial ownership from first stage regression. RISKREDHAT is the predictor of risk-reduction from the first stage regression. The t-values are reported in the parenthesis. ***, ** and * denote significance at the 1%, 5% and 10% levels, respectively. N = 93. CAR is Cumulative Abnormal Return over the interval day –5 to day +5, where day 0 is the day of the announcement. OFFDIR is the fraction of the firm's stock held by managers. RISKRED is the ratio of the bidder's stock market volatility over the estimation period (day –180 to day –20) divided by the volatility of the implied value weighted portfolio of bidder and target stock over the estimation period. METPAY is One if the method of payment is 100% cash, and zero otherwise. LSIZE is The natural logarithm of the bidding firm's market value. TENURE is The natural logarithm of one plus the number of years the CEO has held this position. WEALTH is the natural logarithm of one plus the amount in millions the managers have invested on the StSE. Q is the bidder's market value of equity plus book value of debt divided by book value of total assets.

This is not a surprising result since the Swedish ownership structure appears to be more exogenous in comparison to the U.S.'s ownership structure. In Sweden, the controlling blocks are kept by different groups and are not actively traded based on information about future cash flows. Furthermore, in the U.S. managers receive stocks and stock options as part of their compensation packages when they generate satisfying stock returns for the shareholders. Thus, the fraction of managerial ownership increases with the firm's increasing future prospect. In Sweden, stock and option compensation has been much less common. Instead of being determined by the profitability of the acquisition, the fraction of managerial shareholdings are determined by such intuitive factors as total managerial wealth, tenure, and firm size, which all show significant explanatory power in line with our expectations.

Regression 3 determines the potential risk-reduction accomplished by risk-reducing acquisitions. The coefficient of OFFDIRHAT, the predictor of managerial shareholdings from the first stage regression, is negative and insignificant. This suggests that the managers' incentive to reduce corporate risk does not increase with their equity stake in the firm. Neither does the managers' total wealth have a negative effect on their incentives to corporate risk-reducing activities. However, the negative and significant effect of Tobin's Q on risk-reduction implies that managers reduce the risk of their human capital by reducing the firm's risk-exposure and probability of bankruptcy when the firm is performing poorly.

7. CONCLUDING REMARKS

In this paper we examine whether risk-reducing acquisitions by Swedish firms are motivated by managerial self-interest. The evidence shows that firms engage in diversifying acquisitions at the expense of shareholders' wealth when managers have no equity stakes on the bidder This result is consistent with the view that risk-reducing acquisitions are motivated by managers' need to diversify the risk associated with their human capital. Our results also show that risk-reducing acquisitions by firms where managers hold equity stakes increase firm value. This result suggests that managerial owners make risk-reducing acquisitions when they have identified potential corporate gains from risk-reduction.

The simultaneous equation estimations also suggest that, if there is a relation between shareholder wealth and managerial ownership, causality runs from ownership to shareholder wealth, not vice versa. The simultaneous equation analysis also suggests that risk-reduction is negatively related to firm performance. This confirms the view that managers of poorly performing firms, have strong incentives to reduce the risk of their human capital through diversifying acquisitions. Hence, the threat of bankruptcy or hostile acquisition appears to motivate managers to be involved in risk-reducing acquisitions even though this corporate activity harms firm value. Alternatively, the results suggest that corporate diversification activities are designed to reduce the riskiness of managers' firm-specific human capital.

NOTES

1. The high numbers for control of market capitalization are possible by cross ownership and the existence of differentiated voting rights. The A shares carry one share-one vote, while the B shares usually carry one tenth of a vote per share. In a few old companies, the B shares carry 1/1000 of a vote per share. In 1995, 72% of the companies on the StSE had dual class shares.
2. Wallenberg (11), SHB (10), Wall (9), The State (5), Penser (4), Volvo/Skanska (4), Weil (4), Bonnier (2), Douglas (2), Lundberg (2), SEB (2)
3 We do not consider this as managerial ownership since they do not have personal wealth invested in the firm.
4. We know of only two successful non-partial acquisitions without a public tender offer
5. Obtained from Clas Bergström and Kristian Rydqvist.
6. This is after deleting observations where the bidder made two or more bids the same day. Furthermore, one observation (Trygg Hansa SSP- Gota) was deleted since it was motivated by Trygg Hansa SSP being the major owner in Gota and therefore wanting to save Gota from Bankruptcy. Finally, acquisitions of state dominated companies by other state dominated companies have been deleted since they may have been politically motivated.
7. When both types of stock is traded, the abnormal returns on the A-shares are not significantly different from the abnormal return on the B-shares.
8. These grouped ownership figures have been used to measure the different ownership variables.
9. All regression models have been tested for heteroskedasticity using White's (1980) procedure.
10. The debt ratio is not included since its effect at risk-reduction is ambiguous.
11. Results based on specification of Martin & Loderer's system, do not show significant differences with those reported here.

ACKNOWLEDGMENTS

The authors would like to thank Clas Bergström and Kristian Rydqvist for generously providing some of the data used in this study. We are also grateful to Saugata Banerjee, David Denis, participants at the EFMA conference in Lisbon, June 1998, workshop participants at the Stockholm School of Economics and the University of Gothenburg.

REFERENCES

Agrawal, A., & Knoeber, C. (1996). Firm performance and mechanisms to control agency problems between managers and shareholders. *Journal of Financial and Quantitative Analysis*, 377–397.

Amihud, Y., & Lev, B. (1981). Risk reduction as a managerial motive for conglomerate mergers. *Bell Journal of Economics*, 605–617.

Amihud, Y., Dodd, P., & Weinstein, M. (1986). Conglomerate mergers, managerial motives and stockholder wealth. *Journal of Banking and Finance*.

Bebchuck, L. A., Kraakman, R., & Triantis, G. (1999). Stock pyramids, cross-ownership, and dual class equity: The creation and agency costs of separating control from cash flow rights. NBER *Working paper* #6951.

Bergström, C., & Rydqvist, K. (1989). Stock price reactions to tender offers in Sweden. *SNS Occasional Paper* No. 11.

Bradley, M., Desai, A., & Kim, E. (1988). Synergistic gains from corporate acquisitions and their divisions between stockholders of target and acquiring firms. *Journal of Financial Economics*, 3–40.

Demsetz, H., &. Lehn, K (1985). The structure of corporate ownership structure. *Journal of Political Economy*, 1155–1177.

Denis, D. J., Denis, D. K., & Sarin, A. (1997). Agency problems, equity ownership, corporate diversification. *Journal of Finance, 52,* 135–160.

Jensen, M. C. (1986), Agency costs of free cash flow, corporate finance and takeovers. *American Economic Review, 76,* 323–329.

Jensen, M. (1989). Eclipse of the public corporation. *Harvard Business Review*, 61–74.

Jensen, M., & Meckling, W. (1976). Theory of the firm: Managerial behavior, agency costs and ownership structure. *Journal of Financial Economics,* 305–360.

La Porta, R., Lopez-de-Silanes, F., Shleifer, A., & Vishny, R. W. (1998). Law and finance. *Journal of Political Economy*.

Lang, L., & and Stulz, R. (1994). Tobin's q, corporate diversification, and firm performance *Journal of Political Economy*, 1248–1280.

Lang, L. H. P., Stulz, R. M., & Walking, R. A. (1989). Managerial performance, Tobin's q, and the gains from successful tender offers. *Journal of Financial Economics, 24,* 137–154.

Lewellen, W. (1971). A pure financial rationale for the conglomerate merger. *Journal of Finance*, 521–537.

Lewellen, W., Loderer, C., & Rosenfeld, A. (1989). Mergers, executive risk reduction, and stockholder wealth, *Journal of Financial and Quantitative Analysis,* 459–472.

Loderer, C., & Martin, K. (1997). Executive stock ownership and performance: Tracking faint traces. *Journal of Financial Economics, 45,* 223–255.

May, D., (1995). Do managerial motives influence firm risk reduction strategies? *Journal of Finance,* 1291–1308.

McConnell, J., & Servaes, H. (1990). Additional evidence on equity ownership and corporate control *Journal of Financial Economics, 27,* 595–612.

Morck, R., Shleifer, A., & Vishny, R. (1988). Management ownership and market valuation. *Journal of Financial Economics, 20,* 293–315.

Morck, R., Shleifer, A., & Vishny, R. (1988). Do managerial objectives drive bad acquisitions? *Journal of Finance,* 31–48.

Pound, G. (1988). Proxy contests and the efficiency of shareholder oversight. *Journal of Financial Economics, 20,* 237–265.

Servaes, H. (1991). Tobin's q and the gains from takeovers. *Journal of Finance,* 409–419.

Sundqvist, S. I. (1985–1993). Owners and power in Sweden's listed companies. Dagens Nyheter's Publishing Company.

Sundin, A., & Sundqvist, S. I. (1994–1995). Owners and power in Sweden's listed companies. Dagens Nyheter's Publishing Company.

White, H. (1980). A heteroskedasticity-consistent covariance matrix and a direct test for heteroskedasticity. *Econometrica,* 721–746.

MERGERS BETWEEN PROFESSIONAL SERVICES FIRMS: EXPLORING AN UNDIRECTED PROCESS OF INTEGRATION

Laura Empson

ABSTRACT

Research on mergers and acquisitions focuses almost exclusively on manufacturing and retail services firms. Professional services firms (PSFs) have been largely ignored, yet they present a distinctive managerial challenge. In PSFs, the key value-creating resources (technical knowledge and client relationships) are often proprietary to individuals, who may enjoy considerable operational autonomy within their firm. The challenge for senior managers is to persuade professional staff to remain with the firm and to share these resources with their merger partner colleagues. This chapter reports the results of a series of inductive, in-depth, longitudinal case studies of both mergers and acquisitions in the context of PSFs. It identifies an undirected model of organizational integration, termed the High School Dance model, where managerial action is highly constrained and where the pace and extent of integration is determined by professional staff throughout the combining firms. The study questions some of the fundamental assumptions within the mergers and acquisitions literature concerning the role of managers and the response of employees.

Advances in Mergers and Acquisitions, Volume 1, pages 205–237
2000 by Elsevier Science Inc.
ISBN: 0-7623-0683-1

It demonstrates that, in both mergers and acquisitions, the pace and extent of integration is determined by professional staff throughout both of the combining PSFs. In this context, managerial action is highly constrained, regardless of the formal authority structure, as ultimate power resides with those who embody the key intangible resources.

INTRODUCTION

Research on mergers and acquisitions focuses almost exclusively on manufacturing and retail services firms. Mergers[1] between professional[2] services firms, such as accounting and consulting firms, have been largely ignored, though preliminary studies by Greenwood, Hinings & Brown (1994) and Ashkanasky & Holmes (1995) have highlighted the length and complexity of the integration process in this context.

Professional services firm mergers present a distinctive managerial challenge. In theory, they are a rapid means of gaining access to new sources of technical knowledge and client relationships, which are the key value-creating resources of a professional services firm (Lowendahl, 1997). In practice, however, these resources are often proprietary to individuals, who may enjoy considerable operational autonomy within their firm. The challenge for senior managers is to persuade professional staff to remain with the firm and to share their technical knowledge and client relationships with their merger partner colleagues.

Mergers and acquisitions remain a popular strategic choice for professional services firms, in spite of the significant managerial challenge they represent (Mergers and Acquisitions Journal, 1999). During the 1980s and 1990s, clients have demonstrated a preference for multi-service providers that operate in a range of international markets (Brock, Powell & Hinings, 1999). Consulting, accounting and law firms have responded to this pressure by building extensive global multi-business networks through alliances, mergers and acquisitions (Jones, Hesterly, Fladmoe-Lindquist & Borgatti, 1998).

Given the ongoing importance of mergers and acquisitions to professional services firms and the distinctive managerial challenges they present, it is somewhat surprising that they have been largely neglected by management researchers. This paper reports the results of a series of inductive, in-depth, longitudinal case studies of both mergers and acquisitions in the context of professional services firms. Fieldwork took place over a three year period in four consulting and two accounting firms (see Empson, 1998, for a full report on the study).

The research identifies an undirected model of organizational integration, termed the High School Dance model. The study demonstrates that, in mergers and acquisitions between professional services firms, the pace of integration is determined by professional staff throughout the combining firms. In this context, managerial action is highly constrained, regardless of the formal authority structure, as ultimate power lies with those who embody the key intangible resources. The study questions some of the fundamental assumptions within the mergers and acquisitions literature: in particular, (1) that managers can and should direct the integration process; (2) that staff are passive targets of managerial action; and (3) that mergers are managed via consensus, while acquisitions are controlled by the acquirer.

THEORETICAL CONTEXT

The lack of previous research into this subject necessitated an inductive, theory-building approach. Nevertheless, the study was informed and guided by the extensive literatures on mergers and acquisitions, knowledge management, professionals and professional services firms.

A Resource-Based Perspective on the Merger Process

Within the resource-based literature, mergers and acquisitions are viewed as a means of gaining access to new resources. The firm is defined as a bundle of productive resources (Barney, 1991; Wernerfelt, 1984). The priority, for senior managers, is to develop existing resources and to create new resources in response to changing market conditions. Sustainable competitive advantage derives from possessing resources that are simultaneously valuable, rare and inimitable (Barney, 1996). By definition, inimitable resources are impossible to develop organically within the organization. Mergers and acquisitions, therefore, offer firms the opportunity to achieve competitive advantage by gaining access to key value-creating resources (Haspeslagh & Jemison, 1991; Walter & Barney, 1990).

It is not enough to gain access to these new resources. While a firm may 'acquire' the assets of another firm, it cannot really be said to 'own' its knowledge (with the exception of patentable intellectual property). Ownership rights cannot be asserted over knowledge that resides within individuals; codified knowledge is liable to be copied by competitors. Value creation can only occur when these resources are transferred between the merging firms and are combined and enhanced, in order to create new resources (Haspeslagh & Jemison, 1991). However, the act of transferring resources can destroy them, either because the resources are embedded in individuals who leave the firm (Coff, 1997) or because they are located in a specific organizational context that changes during the process of integration (Nahavandi & Malekzadeh, 1988;

Ranft, 1997). The management of the integration process is, therefore, a key determinant of the performance of the merger or acquisition (Haspeslagh & Jemison, 1991; Kitching, 1967).

Knowledge Transfer Within Professional Services Firms

Within the resource-based literature, tacit knowledge is identified as the most valuable and most fragile organizational resource (Grant & Spender, 1996). Tacit knowledge is difficult to articulate and is often proprietary to individuals within the firm (Nonaka & Takeuchi, 1995; Polyani, 1967). The challenge for managers is to develop processes for disseminating that tacit knowledge throughout the organization so that it can be more widely exploited, without converting it into such an easily communicable form that it can be easily copied by competitors (Hansen, Nohria & Tierney, 1999). Davenport & Prusak (1998) have emphasised that trust between colleagues is an essential condition for the efficient functioning of an internal market for knowledge.

Mergers and acquisitions provide an opportunity for firms to gain access to new sources of tacit knowledge. The managerial challenge is to persuade individuals to demonstrate and articulate their knowledge to their merger partner colleagues. This process depends upon individuals choosing to remain with the firm and engage in the extensive inter-personal interactions required to bring about resource exchange. However, the post-closure[3] environment is not conducive to knowledge transfer. The essential condition, trust, is not present between merger partner colleagues at the start of the merger process. At the same time, individuals may experience high levels of merger-related stress as they anticipate disruptive organizational change, as discussed below.

Employees' Responses to Mergers and Acquisitions

The extensive literature on the 'human side' of mergers and acquisitions has demonstrated the extent to which they can provoke extreme negative emotional and behavioural responses among staff. While much of the research has focused on the reactions of staff in the context of hostile take-overs (Hambrick & Cannella, 1993; Schneider & Dunbar, 1992), mergers can also generate high levels of stress (Cartwright & Cooper, 1992; Somers & Bird, 1990). Individuals may fear anticipated changes, such as shifts in power balances, loss of employment and the abandonment of established norms (Hunt, Lees, Grumbar & Vivian, 1987; Schweiger & Denisi, 1991). They may experience anger directed towards their previous bosses, as well as their new bosses, and may also grieve over the death of their old firm and idealise its memory (Buono & Bowditch, 1989; Levinson,

1970). Individuals may engage in defensive self-centred behaviour and political activity as they focus on their personal objectives and fight to defend or improve their position within the firm (Buono & Bowditch, 1989; Mirvis & Marks, 1992). Individuals may also resist change more subtly, by withdrawing and reducing their commitment to the organization (Newman & Kryzstofiak, 1993). Staff turnover may increase sharply, as employees choose to leave rather than make a commitment to the new firm (Cartwright & Cooper, 1990; Hambrick & Cannella, 1993; Walsh, 1988). Staff turnover presents a particular threat in the context of professional services firms (Coff, 1997), as discussed below.

Key Resources in Professional Services Firms

A professional services firm applies specialist technical knowledge to the creation of customised solutions to clients' problems (Alvesson, 1995; Mills, Hall, Leidecker & Marguillies, 1983). Its primary value-creating resources are, therefore, technical knowledge and client relationships (Sveiby, 1997; Winch & Schneider, 1993). While professional services firms may possess an extensive body of technical knowledge, which is both codified and collective, competitive advantage is more likely to derive from the tacit technical knowledge which resides within each individual, resulting from his or her unique combination of skills and experiences (Alvesson, 1993). This distinctive tacit knowledge enables each professional to judge how best to apply formalised, codified knowledge to the creation of customised client services.

While the resource-based perspective has highlighted the importance of tacit knowledge in all organizations, in professional services firms the nature of the professional task means that client relationships are an equally valuable resource. Clients approach professional services firms to deal with issues of great uncertainty and importance to them (Johnson, 1972; Wilensky, 1964). As they cannot sample the product prior to purchase, clients must base their purchase decision largely on the reputation of the professional services firm and the relationship they develop with the individual professional during the course of the sales process (Darby & Karni, 1973). Over the course of several engagements, clients may develop close relationships with individual professionals, as the process of customising the service-offering requires professionals and clients to work together (Mills et al., 1983). As a result, when professionals leave the firm, they may take their client relationships with them (Maister, 1993).

The two most valuable resources of a professional services firm can, therefore, be proprietary to individuals within the firm, rather than to the firm as a whole. In an attempt to increase economic efficiency and reduce vulnerability to staff departures, senior managers may seek to codify and disseminate individuals' tacit knowledge throughout the firm and to share specific client relationships among a broader group of individuals (Morris & Empson, 1998). However, individuals may be unwilling to share their proprietary knowledge and client relationships with their colleagues because these represent a source of power for them within the firm. Senior managers will have very little scope to compel their professional colleagues to co-operate (Mintzberg & Quinn, 1991).

Managerial Authority Within Professional Services Firms

Senior managers of professional services firms, typically, have relatively limited formal power and tend to exercise authority indirectly, through a consensus-based management style (Dirsmith, Heian & Covalski, 1997; Tolbert & Stern, 1991). A diffuse authority structure is legally enshrined within the partnership form of governance, which has been traditionally associated with professional services firms (Greenwood, Hinings & Brown, 1990). Even when formal authority is concentrated, and the firm is incorporated as a limited company, the power of senior managers is constrained by the extensive operational autonomy often enjoyed by individual professionals (Bailyn, 1985; Raelin, 1984). While junior professionals may be closely supervised by their seniors through the apprenticeship process (Gilson & Mnookin, 1990), they tend to have greater operational autonomy than their equivalents within conventional hierarchical structures (Hinings, Brown & Greenwood, 1991), as the process of client interaction and service customisation requires a relatively high degree of independent action. Greenwood et al. (1990) argue that diffuse authority, coupled with the professional staff's inclination to resist autocratic actions, militates against personalised directive leadership. "Strategic management and leadership is a matter of guiding, nudging and persuading" (p. 748).

Mergers Between Professional Services Firms: Distincitve Characteristics of the Integration Process

While an inductive approach was adopted for the study as a whole, various preliminary propositions can be developed from the literature that emphasise the distinctive characteristics of the integration process in the context of professional services firms. The merger process literature (e.g. Haspeslagh & Jemison, 1991; Pablo, 1994; Ranft, 1997) does not contain an explicit model of organizational change. Its implicit model is consistent with linear and rational models of strategy (Chaffee, 1985) where top managers analyse available data, establish targets and deadlines, and manage the process of strategic change. As

Haspeslagh & Jemison state, "a clear view of how to start, how fast to proceed, and how to get there is critical to successful integration" (p. 50). The implicit assumption is that managers can and should direct the change process.

However, in professional services firms, managerial action is highly constrained. Whilst authority may rest with senior managers, power resides with the key resource-holders throughout the firm, who may possess valuable technical knowledge and control the lucrative client relationships. In addition, the partnership form of governance juxtaposes individual autonomy over day-to-day activities with collegial group-based policy decision-making, which militates against directive managerial action. Change cannot be imposed 'top down' in this context, for two reasons. First, the 'top' is ill-defined, consisting as it does of a loose association of owner-managers. Second, dissatisfied key resource-holders may simply resign, rather than agree to adapt to change. The following inference can, therefore, be drawn.

In mergers between professional services firms, senior managers do not take an active role in directing the integration process (*Proposition 1*).

To achieve effective knowledge transfer between merging firms, the individuals and groups who embody the most valuable knowledge within the firm must remain with the firm and co-operate with knowledge sharing initiatives. However, as already discussed, the extensive literature on the 'human side' of acquisitions has demonstrated how, in resenting and fearing changes to their established work norms, individuals may actively or passively resist initiatives for encouraging co-operation with their merger partner colleagues.

In the context of professional services firm mergers, the process of knowledge transfer is likely to be particularly problematic. Professional services firms exemplify the maxim that 'knowledge is power'. Professionals' value to their organization derives from their specialist technical expertise and knowledge of clients, together with their ability to manage the sales process successfully and to maintain effective client relationships thereafter (Greenwood et al., 1990; Mintzberg, 1983). In this context, asking individuals to share their proprietary knowledge with their merger partner colleagues is like asking them to relinquish their source of power within the firm, at a time when they are likely to be feeling insecure and concerned about their position in the merged firm. As a result, even under stable conditions, individuals may be reluctant to share their technical knowledge and knowledge of clients with their colleagues in the merger partner firm. Cultural norms and implicit contracts must be developed gradually, over time, to facilitate knowledge sharing within the firm (Morris & Empson, 1998).

Under these conditions, senior managers cannot force professional staff to share their proprietary technical knowledge and client relationships with their new merger partner colleagues. Following Davenport and Prusak (1998), it can be inferred that individuals will be willing to co-operate with their merger partner colleagues under only two conditions: (1) they believe that they will receive reciprocal benefits and, (2) they believe their reputation will be enhanced. Trust cannot exist between organizations, but only between individuals. It cannot be imposed on employees by senior managers, but has to develop gradually, through a series of interactions between individuals. The following inference can, therefore be drawn.

> In mergers between professional services firms, the integration process evolves through a series of ad hoc co-operative initiatives between merger partner colleagues throughout the firm (*Proposition 2*).

Propositions 1 and 2 refer specifically to *mergers* between professional services firms. What can be inferred from the literature on *acquisitions*? Greenwood et al. (1994) find that consensus-building is a primary objective for managers of merging professional services firms, but suggest that this will not be the case in acquisitions. As the authority structure in acquisitions differs fundamentally from that of mergers, consensus-building will not be a primary objective for acquiring managers. Certainly, the general literature on mergers and acquisitions would support this suggestion. While the two terms are often used interchangeably, they describe fundamentally different legal structures, with direct implications for power relationships between the firms. In a merger, the legal structure suggests that both sets of senior managers have an equal right to control the integration process, though the balance of power may shift over time. In an acquisition, the senior managers of the acquiring firm have, in effect, paid for the right to control the resources of the acquired firm, including its senior management.

However, Propositions 1 and 2 suggest that in professional services firms the power of senior management to control the integration process is highly constrained by the fact that the key value-creating resources are proprietary to individuals. This impediment applies regardless of the underlying legal structure of the transaction. The following inference can therefore be drawn:

> In professional services firms, propositions 1 and 2 will hold in the context of *both* mergers and acquisitions (*Proposition 3*).

RESEARCH DESIGN AND PROCESS

A multi-site, multi-phase, multi-source case-based methodology was adopted because this design satisfied the following conditions. First, it enabled the researcher to develop an in-depth understanding of the complexities of the merger process in a specific organizational context (Glaser & Strauss, 1967). Second, it made it possible to gather longitudinal data from a multi-phase field-work programme as the integration process evolved (Pettigrew, 1990). Third, it enabled the researcher to triangulate data obtained from a range of sources (Eisenhardt, 1989). Finally, it made it possible to combine multiple levels of analysis within the firms (Yin, 1984). The details of this multi-site, multi-phase, multi-source case-based research design are discussed below.

Multi-Site

Having reviewed the literature and developed a preliminary set of research guidelines, the researcher identified four criteria for case selection. The objective was to enhance theoretical generalisability by increasing the probability of generating contrasting results (Eisenhardt, 1989).

(1) Transaction – As previously discussed, the mergers and acquisitions literature suggests that the integration process in mergers will differ fundamentally from that of acquisitions. Consequently both mergers and acquisitions were included in the sample, to establish the relevance of this assertion in the context of professional services firms.

(2) Governance – According to Greenwood et al. (1990) the partnership form of governance constrains the ability of managers to impose strategic change. The study sought to examine whether similar constraints applied within non-partnership forms of professional services firms. Consequently, both limited companies and partnerships were included in the sample.

(3) Size – The extensive literature on the impact of organizational size asserts that, as an organization grows, it will develop bureaucratic characteristics in the form of hierarchical control structures, centralised administrative systems and standardised working practices. The study sought to examine the effect of formalised control structures on the integration process by including both large and small professional services firms in the sample.

(4) Profession – Unlike established professions (such as accountancy) emergent professions (such as management consulting) do not possess an industry-wide codified body of examinable knowledge (Montagna, 1968). It can be inferred, therefore, that it will be easier to transfer knowledge

within the established professions than within the emergent professions because of their conventions for codifying and disseminating codified knowledge. The study sought to examine this assertion by including firms from both the consulting and the accounting sector in the sample.

Through archival analysis, the researcher identified twenty potential cases that appeared to conform to the above criteria. She approached senior managers in these firms and, ultimately, received approval to conduct research in six firms, on condition that their anonymity was protected by disguising all names and the dates on which the mergers and acquisitions took place. Details of the six firms selected are given in Table 1. The firms selected varied in size from 18 to 4200 professional staff in the U.K. They included two accounting firms and four consulting firms, three partnerships and three incorporated companies, one merger and two acquisitions.

Multi-Phase

Fieldwork began after closure (consistent with the study's focus on the post-closure integration process rather than during the negotiation process), though retrospective data was gathered on the pre-closure process. Previous studies have suggested that, although the majority of post-merger change occurs within two years of closure (Buono & Bowditch, 1989; Ashkanasky & Holmes, 1995), the integration process may continue for several years afterwards (Walter, 1985; Levinson, 1970). In order to develop a detailed understanding of the early stages of the integration process, in the context of a higher level longer term perspective, a bifurcated research design was adopted, combining longitudinal and retrospective studies (Leonard-Barton, 1990). Details are given in Table 2. In the longitudinal studies, data collection began during the first year following closure and concluded during the third year following closure. In the retrospective study, data collection occurred primarily during the fourth year, but continued into the sixth year post closure.

Multi-Source

Three methods of data collection were employed: interviews, archives, and observation. The researcher conducted 177 interviews, consulted 162 archival sources, and observed eight meetings (see Table 2 for further details). Archival and observation data were collected to provide an independent validation of the interviewees' comments, which formed the basis of the study. Archival material included: internal memos relating to negotiations and integration planning, legal

Table 1. Details of Case Studies

Selection Criteria	Case A: Sea/Land		Case B: Hill/Valley		Case C: Sun/Moon	
	Sea	Land	Hill	Valley	Sun	Moon
Type of Profession	Strategy Consulting	Operations Consulting	Human Resource Consulting	Change Management Consulting	Accounting	Accounting
Type of Transaction	Merger. Both firms acquired and then merged by parent company.		Acquisition. Hill acquired Valley.		Acquisition. Sun acquired Moon.	
Type of Governance	Partnership	Incorporated	Incorporated	Incorporated	Partnership	Partnership
Type of Study	Retrospective		Longitudinal		Longitudinal	
Size of Firms						
UK Staff	83 total 55 profs.	92 total 79 profs.	75 total 50 profs.	27 total 18 profs.	4,200 profs.	1,400 profs.
UK Fee Income	UK £10m.	UK £15m.	UK £7.5m.	UK £3.9m.	UK £430m.	UK £70m.
UK Offices	1	1	1	1	10	7

Table 2. Scale and Timetable of Fieldwork

	Total	Case A: Sea/Land		Case B: Hill/Valley		Case C: Sun/Moon	
		Sea	Land	Hill	Valley	Sun	Moon
Scale of Fieldwork							
Professionals in Offices Studied		55	79	50	18	4200	1400
Interviews Conducted	177	9	9	33	28	50	48
Interviewees	92	7	8	15	13	23	26
Archives Consulted	162	30		79		53	
Meetings Observed	8	Not applicable		5			3
Timetable for Fieldwork							
Commenced		4 years post closure		During first year post closure		During first year post closure	
Completed		6 years post closure		3 years post closure		3 years post closure	

documents relating to merger agreements, presentations to staff, press releases, press articles and marketing brochures. Key meetings included: staff communications sessions, integration planning meetings and annual general meetings. Meaningful financial data was not available. Higson (1991) has highlighted the problems associated with using financial data for evaluating the performance in a post-merger environment, specifically the difficulties of distinguishing between market effects and integration effects, in the context of a recently consolidated set of management and financial accounts. This reason, coupled with the traditions of financial secrecy within the case study firms (all of which were privately owned), meant that financial analysis was not performed as part of this study.

Research Process

The researcher developed a within-case sampling frame (Miles & Huberman, 1994), which was designed to provide a broad cross section of opinions across the firm, according to the following criteria: (1) hierarchical level, (2) equity holding, (3) area of business, (4) functional responsibility and (5) length of tenure. Key informants identified potential interviewees whom they perceived to be most positive and most negative about the merger, in order to obtain a range of contrasting perspectives. In the longitudinal studies very few staff had resigned at the start of the data collection period. Those interviewees who did resign during the course of the study were interviewed immediately prior to their departure.

Interviews lasted 90 minutes, on average, and interview notes ranged from three to seven pages of single spaced typing. On completion of each round of interviews in each firm, the researcher developed coding frames to reflect the emerging themes of the study as a whole, as well as firm-specific issues. QSR NUD.IST software was used to code the text of the interviews according to these coding frames. Interview data were analysed in conjunction with the data gathered from the archives and observation, with a view to identifying key themes and inconsistencies. Once preliminary analysis was completed, the findings were reported to key informants, to test the validity of the analysis, and key themes were identified, to be explored in subsequent stages of the research. Where individuals were interviewed more than once, the researcher began all subsequent interviews by summarising the key points that they had made in the previous interviews and asking them to confirm whether the summary accurately expressed their attitudes at the time of the previous interview. On completion of data collection, the researcher wrote six in-depth analytical case studies, describing the organizational context and the integration process and outcome (as reported by the interviewees from each of the six firms in the study) and detailing the researcher's insights during the research process. After many iterations between data and emerging propositions, the researcher returned to the literature to sharpen insights (Eisenhardt, 1989).

In view of the fact that the cases were selected with a view to generating contrasting results, the findings were remarkably similar across all of the firms. The integration process in all three cases is discussed below.

THE HIGH SCHOOL DANCE MODEL: AN UNDIRECTED INTEGRATION PROCESS

The study identified a model of undirected organizational change that can be described through the metaphor of the high school dance. At traditional high school dances, boys and girls line up on either side of the gymnasium, under the watchful eye of their teachers. They are unwilling to make the first approach and may conceal their anxiety by making disparaging comments to their friends about the girls or boys across the dance floor. Eventually, a few of the bolder individuals cross the floor to find a dance partner. Encouraged by their success, more and more students seek out dancing partners. Those who remain solitary leave the gymnasium. By the end of the evening 'integration' has been successfully achieved.

In professional services firms, integration follows a similar process, as illustrated in Figure 1 (where each X and O represents an individual in the merging firms). At the point of closure (Figure 1a), only the merger instigators have established contact. For one to two years following closure (the acclimatisation phase as shown in Figure 1b) the majority of individuals avoid contact with their merger partner colleagues. Senior managers adopt an essentially passive role during this process, but entrepreneurial individuals advance the integration process by seeking out like-minded and potentially useful colleagues in the merger partner firm, to explore opportunities for co-operation. The second and third years post-closure are periods of transition (Figure 1c), as the more recalcitrant individuals recognise the benefits of greater co-operation and the most adamant change-resisters resign. From the third year onwards, integration begins to occur (Figure 1d), as the perceived boundaries of the firm become blurred and individuals' organizational affiliations start to change. The following section explains how this process evolves, in the context of the firms in the current study.

YEARS ONE TO TWO: ACCLIMATISATION

In all three cases, very little integration occurred for one to two years following closure. Existing brand names, management structures and administrative

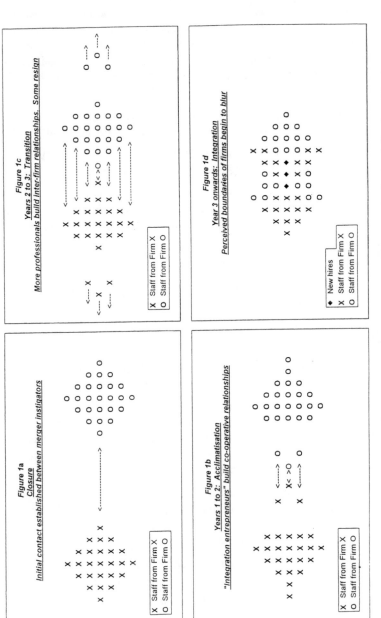

Figure 1. High School Dance Model of Integration in Mergers Between Professional Services Firms.

systems were retained and all firms continued to occupy separate offices. Interviewees describe this period as 'stalemate', 'ring fencing' and 'phoney war'. During this phase, senior managers in all cases adopted an essentially passive role, focusing primarily on managing day-to-day operational issues. They did not develop detailed implementation plans and did not seek to advance the process of integration.

Case A: "Sea and Land had no specific merger plans. The idea was 'Let's just get on with it and see how it works'." (Vice president, Land)

Case B: "The senior managers within Hill UK . . . had no idea how the merger would be implemented." (Senior manager, Hill Corporate)

Case C: "I am not the kind of person who writes things down ... I had a simple and clear objective, to retain the clients of both firms, and I used that to screen any decision about integration." (Managing partner, Sun)

Rather than take an active role in advancing integration, senior managers allowed professional staff and clients to determine the pace of change.

Case A: "There was no apparent architecting at the top. It was a case of 'Thou shalt go out and work together'." (Manager, Sea)

Case B: "We have not formally guided change from the top. We have just said, 'Go to it'." (Managing director, Valley)

Case C: "We said to the Moon corporate tax people, 'Your future is in your hands. We are empowering you'." (Tax partner, Sun)

There are various possible reasons why senior managers did not develop detailed implementation plans and chose instead to adopt a laissez-faire approach to integration. In part it reflected the difficulty of evaluating intangible assets prior to a merger or acquisition. Time was needed for managers to familiarise themselves with their merger partner firm.

Case A: "We thought a lot about integration issues prior to the merger but it was difficult because we did not have access to so much crucial information. There were a whole set of issues that were not strictly analysable, the culture, the values, how we did business." (Vice president, Sea)

Case B: "Hill had a tremendous naiveté about our operation. What they bought in Valley is not what they thought." (Consultant, Valley)

Case C: "There were various hidden jewels in Moon, such as their personal tax practice, which we only really became aware of once the deal was completed." (Audit partner, Sun)

Managers' laissez-faire approach might also reflect their preference for an 'emergent' style of strategy formation and their ability to tolerate high levels of ambiguity.

Case A: "We were not big companies. We were lean. We were used to winging it. People reacted negatively to too much detailed planning." (Vice president, Land)

Case B: "No one is taking a strategic view of how we integrate Valley. Our managing director does not have a vision of the future." (Consultant, Hill)

Case C: "We approached integration as follows. Stay loose. Take time to learn about them. Don't impose your initial vision on them. Don't move faster than the market demands. Be prepared to operate with a degree of chaos." (Director of Human Resources, Sun)

The study suggests that, above all, managers adopted a laissez-faire approach to integration because they did not want to lose their key income-generating assets by imposing unwelcome change on their staff and clients. While existing research into mergers and acquisitions focuses on the risk of staff turnover, the current study demonstrates that client turnover is also a serious risk. In the case of professional services firms, competitors move quickly to exploit instability in client relationships following a merger. For example, a newspaper article in the Sun/Moon case stated that competitors declared 'open season' on Moon's client base following the announcement that Moon and Sun were in negotiations. Just as the psychological contract between an employee and his or her organization may be broken following a merger (Mirvis & Marks, 1992), the current study demonstrates that the psychological contract between a professional and his or her client may also be threatened.

In recognition of this threat, in all three cases in the current study, senior managers promised clients that they would continue to receive the same level of service they had enjoyed in the past, but would have access to enhanced services if they wished. At the same time, while assuring professional staff that change would not be forced upon them, senior managers also encouraged staff to pursue opportunities for co-operation with their merger partner colleagues. Senior managers sought to convey a complex message, to clients and staff, of stability and opportunity (i.e. 'Your job or the service you receive will not change unless you want it to' and 'The merger enables us to serve our clients even better than we did before'). During the first year post-closure, therefore, professionals had ample opportunity to adjust gradually to the new organizational context.

As already discussed, previous research into professionals has highlighted the difficulties of persuading them to share their knowledge and client relationships with their colleagues. The current study suggests that the reluctance will increase following a merger or acquisition. In the Sun/Moon case, the accounting firms, individuals were willing to share the highly codified collective knowledge contained within their audit manuals and tax product databases. Some professionals in the acquired firm, however, were reluctant to share their proprietary technical knowledge with their merger partner colleagues, because they feared that they would make themselves vulnerable to redundancy. The reluctance to co-operate was also evident in the consulting cases, where there was no threat of redundancy.

Case A: "Resistance among Sea consultants reached fever pitch. There was a genuine fear that we, as individuals, would lose our personal and political capital, which we had spent so many years building within the firm." (Manager, Sea)

Case A: "Some Sea people were almost hysterical. They were saying, 'Who are these hairy-arsed guys? Is my reputation as an elite strategy consultant going to be sullied by contact with these labourers?'." (Manager, Sea).

Case B: "We have grossly misunderstood the difficulties that arise from attempting to collaborate when there is an unwillingness to compromise ... It is important that we try to understand how threatened the Valley people must feel, having been taken over by a big US firm." (Principal, Hill)

Case B: "I think the consulting work they do is awful and their people are just awful. We (have) an extremely classy, sexy reputation . . . I feel tainted by having anything to do with them. In theory there are lots of synergies from knowledge sharing but, in practice, I am ashamed to work with them." (Consultant, Valley)

The reasons for this resistance are complex and subtle and are discussed at length elsewhere (Empson, Forthcoming). In summary, the resistance can be attributed to a fear of 'exploitation' and a fear of 'contamination'. The fear of exploitation describes the phenomenon whereby individuals refuse to share their proprietary technical knowledge with their merger partner colleagues because they do not believe that they will receive knowledge of equal or greater value in return. The study finds that professionals do not value the technical knowledge of their merger partner colleagues if its prevailing form differs fundamentally from their own. In particular, professionals will not recognise the legitimacy of the technical knowledge of their merger partner colleagues when their firm's knowledge base is predominantly tacit and the knowledge base of the merger partner firm is predominantly codified. Equally, professionals from a firm with a predominantly codified knowledge base will not recognise the legitimacy of the tacit knowledge of their merger partner colleagues. The second fear, the fear of contamination, arises when professionals perceive themselves as having a more 'upmarket' image than their merger partner colleagues. The personal image of an individual consultant and the brand name of his or her firm play a vital role in the sales process (Alvesson, 1995). A high quality image and an 'upmarket' reputation will help to build trust between client and professional and make it easier for the professional to charge higher fees (Maister, 1993). Professionals may, therefore, fear that the value embodied in their personal image and their organisation's brand will be diminished through association with their merger partner colleagues.

However, not all professional staff resisted integration; some recognised the opportunity it presented. In the current study, these 'integration entrepreneurs' played a vital role in advancing the integration process by seeking out like-minded colleagues in the merger partner firm, to explore opportunities for co-operation. This phenomenon was observed in all three cases.

Case A: "During the first year there was very little communication going on between the two firms. I started talking to Joe about how to sell work jointly. We decided I should move my desk into his office and just get on with it." (Vice President, Land)

Case B: "You find people you like and just start working with them. I like Jane at Hill because she's smart and quick and laughs a lot. It's stuff like that which drives integration, not grand thought." (Consultant, Valley)

Case C: "I have formed a good relationship with one of the Sun partners, David. I approached him initially and he tested me out with a few bits of work. When I passed the test, he gave me more ... David and I have similar interests. It's a personal thing. We are the same kind of people." (Personal tax manager, Moon)

The integration entrepreneurs identified in these cases vary considerably in terms of age, seniority and relative standing within their firm, but appear to share three personal characteristics: confidence in their abilities, an enthusiastic approach towards change in general and an extrovert personality. This observation is consistent with Cartwright & Cooper's (1992) argument that vulnerability to merger-related stress may be mediated by individual characteristics, such as tolerance for ambiguity and self esteem. Interviewees' comments (cited earlier) suggest that, though the initial impetus for co-operation between the integration entrepreneurs might have been the desire to make money, in the process of establishing inter-firm links, the integration entrepreneurs also made friends. One interviewee described these personal relationships as 'bridges for transferring skills between firms'. The following comment from a Hill consultant is a detailed description of the informal and ad hoc process by which this skills transfer occurs.

Case B: "Before I go into a meeting with a client to discuss competency profiling, Stuart Sinclair (name changed) of Valley says to me, 'What are we going to say? How should we respond if they ask so and so?' So I tell him some more stuff about competencies. Then we get into the meeting and I hear him telling the client everything I just said, in a really convincing way. I tell him my anecdotes and I hear him repeating them to the client as though they happened to him, and with real enthusiasm. I don't resent this at all. I have received a lot of recognition for my expertise in the area of competencies and I would like to pass that knowledge on to someone else, so that I don't get stuck doing competency work for the rest of my life. And Stuart really trusts me with his clients. I have nothing to lose from it." (Consultant, Hill)

YEARS TWO TO THREE: TRANSITION

Previous studies (Hunt et al. 1987; Mirvis & Marks, 1992) have shown that, following a merger or acquisition, staff may demonise the partner firm while idealising their own firm. This phenomenon was clearly evident in the current study.

Case A: "We were worried because we had heard that, in the US, Land Consulting had simply rolled over Sea." (Vice president, Sea UK)

Case B: "Tony Bromsgrove (name changed) personified the demon of Hill for me." (Consultant, Valley)

Case C: "We were frightened that Sun would behave like an aggressive animal and tear everything apart." (Manager, Moon)

In the short term at least, the perceived external 'threat' increased internal cohesion. In effect, staff could be said to have reified both firms, as they lost sight of the fact that both firms were made up of individuals. However, the entrepreneurial individuals helped to forestall the demonisation of the merger partner firm by establishing personal relationships with their merger partner colleagues. This development helped to encourage their more recalcitrant colleagues to participate in the integration process. Some individuals responded to positive stories from the integration entrepreneurs about their experience of working with the other firm. Others were concerned that they were losing out in the internal competition for promotion, as their more entrepreneurial colleagues generated higher levels of fee income, by exploiting the anticipated benefits of integration. As the recalcitrant professionals had more contact with their new colleagues, they ceased to demonise the merger partner firm and began to identify individuals with whom they were willing to co-operate. The following comments are representative of widely held views in all of the firms.

Case A: "Gradually the vice presidents started to co-operate. We worked out who were the good guys and who were the bad guys in Land. We started to realise that, behind the gung ho facade, the Land vice president group was just as fragmented and political as we were." (Vice president, Sea)

Case B: "In the last year I have had contact with a lot of individuals from Hill and have worked with a few people I like very much. A whole set of small personal experiences has helped to change the way I feel about Hill." (Consultant, Valley)

Case C: "We had this idea when Sun joined us that they would be superhuman and we would be lost ... But we have built some strong links at an individual level. Some Moon people now feel that they have more in common with Sun people than they do with other Moon people." (Junior, Sun)

In all three cases in the current study, the pressure for change increased as a growing number of professional staff began to co-operate with the integration process, during the second year post-closure. Many staff became increasingly frustrated by the ongoing uncertainty and concerned about the lack of progress towards integration. Staff who were keen to work more closely with their merger partner colleagues became frustrated by the remaining structural impediments to integration, such as the maintenance of separate locations, brand names, reward structures and accounting systems. Staff who were less receptive to merger-related change found it difficult to tolerate prolonged uncertainty about their future. These contrasting perspectives are reflected in the following comments from interviewees in the Sun/Moon case.

Case C: "By the start of the second year, there was a mounting frustration from many of the line partners in Moon, the relatively younger ones and the relatively successful ones, that nothing was changing. We knew that the status quo was not sustainable and we wanted to start to exploit the benefits of the relationship with Sun." (Partner, Moon)

Case C: "One partner came to me recently to say that he was thinking of buying a house and asked me if I thought it was safe for him to do so. This uncer-

tainty has been going on for three years. We're finding it hard to live with."
(Audit partner, Moon)

Having recognised the drawbacks of the 'business as usual' approach, professionals began to complain that their senior managers were failing to provide effective leadership and put pressure on them to accelerate the pace of integration. The following comments are representative of a widespread frustration with the leadership in all three cases.

Case A: "One evening, after I'd had a few drinks, I told our managing director that the company needed more leadership. I told him, 'We are fed up with all this involving of everyone in the integration decisions. We just want someone to stand up and say – This is what is going to happen'." (Manager, Land)

Case B: "I would love our managing director to take people by the balls and push change through." (Consultant, Hill)

Case C: "There was no leadership or overt direction. We became a festering mass of uncertainty." (Audit partner, Sun)

As the majority of staff came to advocate greater integration, the remaining change-resisters recognised that change was inevitable and that passive resistance was no longer sustainable. They responded by resigning. In all three cases the level of staff turnover, which had not increased substantially during the initial Acclimatisation phase, began to increase during the second year, though never to the extent that gave senior managers cause for concern. As the closure dates of the three cases varied by several years, this increase in turnover cannot be attributed simply to changing economic circumstances.

However, not all of the most adamant change-resisters resigned. During the course of the second year, some individuals underwent a 'conversion' whereby they came to recognise the benefits of integration. The change management consultant quoted earlier in this paper who felt 'tainted' by contact with his merger partner colleagues, described his new attitude as follows.

Case B: "A year ago my counterpart at Hill seemed like the devil incarnate. But in the last year he has sold some big projects, which I have not been able to do in this tough market. I respect him for that and I realise that his work may provide me with a route back into certain clients." (Consultant, Valley)

This kind of change in attitudes helped to prepare the way for full scale integration.

YEAR THREE ONWARDS: INTEGRATION

In all three cases, substantial progress towards integration occurred during the third year post closure. In the Sea/Land case, the single brand name 'Planet Consulting' was launched eighteen months after closure, to persuade clients that they were purchasing the services of a new and integrated consulting company. However, it was not until the third year that the external image of the firm started to become a reality inside the organization, as large and lucrative integrated projects were sold and delivered to clients. The remaining managerial and logistical boundaries between the firms were removed by the creation of a matrix organizational structure, the standardisation of administrative structures and the move into a single new office.

In the Hill/Valley case, the beginning of the third year saw the creation of the combined organizational structure, following the appointment of Valley's chief executive as the overall new managing director. The senior manager of the acquired firm brought about what was, in effect, a reverse take-over. The new organizational structure contained numerous client-facing integrating roles, intended to facilitate the marketing of the full range of human resource and change management consulting services and the development of firm-wide client relationships. One interviewee described the consequences as follows:

Case B: "We are doing some work in (client name). The brand is Valley, the relationship manager is Valley. But Hill provided the technical skills and the rest of the team. We sold a Hill product with something wrapped around it from Valley." (Consultant, Valley)

In the Sun/Moon case, two alternative forms of integration developed within the audit and tax practices. For example, the personal tax practices of Sun and Moon were fully integrated into each other, whereas Moon's audit practice remained distinct from Sun's, under the management of a Sun partner. Those Moon practices that retained their separate external identity serviced a fundamentally different set of clients from their counterparts in Sun. During the third year, staff in the tax practices began to generate increased fee income by offering Sun products to clients and by utilising the Sun brand. In the audit practice, access to the substantial marketing resources and support infrastructure of Sun helped Moon staff to develop profitable new lines of business.

In the course of these changes, staff's perceptions of the boundaries of the firms began to blur and the organizational affiliations of many individuals started to change.

Case A: "The new office proved once and for all that Sea and Land were dead and that there was no point in looking back anymore. In a way, I feel as though I joined a new firm the day I moved to the new building." (Manager, Sea)

Case B: "I would love to move to Valley. My colleague who has moved over has said, 'It is wonderful. How soon can you come'?" (Consultant, Hill)

Case C: "I don't mind whether I am called Sun or Moon. I have two sets of business cards and I use whichever is most likely to work in each situation. I would say that I was a Sun person if I wanted to impress someone, though I still don't feel like a Sun person." (Personal tax manager, Moon)

By the end of the third year post-closure, the senior managers in all three cases perceived the mergers to have been successful.

Case A: "We have succeeded beyond all my wildest expectations. What we have managed to create is immeasurably more powerful than we had anticipated." (Vice president, Land)

Case B: "By and large, things have gone wonderfully well. Every expectation I had has materialised." (European managing director, Hill)

Case C: "This transaction is considered to be the best managed acquisition that Sun has ever made world wide. We have ring fenced Moon very tightly and have delivered every one of the commitments we made to the board." (Managing partner, Sun)

Given the tendency towards retrospective bias and self-justification (Golden, 1992), it might be suspected that the merger instigators would inevitably report positive outcomes. No such tendency was, however, evident in Hunt et al.'s study (1987), which found that almost 50% of the acquisition instigators were disappointed with the outcome of their transaction. A more recent study by KPMG (1999) identified a similar willingness, among acquisitions instigators, to criticise the outcome of their transactions. Given the frequently poor performance of mergers and acquisitions in general (Agrawal, Jaffee & Mandelker, 1992; Higson, 1991; Ravenscraft & Scherer, 1987; Roll, 1986) and the specific problems that mergers between professional services firms are likely to encounter, it is all the more remarkable that all three cases in the current study have been judged to be successful by the merger instigators.

DISCUSSION AND CONCLUSIONS

This chapter identifies an undirected model of evolving organizational integration, termed the High School Dance model, where managerial action is highly constrained and where the pace and extent of integration is determined by professional staff throughout the combining firms. It, therefore, questions some of the fundamental assumptions within the merger literature concerning the source and use of power during the integration process.·

The inductive nature of the research design, and the limited number of case studies, means that attempts to develop generalisable conclusions are inevitably tentative. Nevertheless, the study has produced several important findings that are worthy of future research. The study finds evidence to support all three propositions introduced earlier in the chapter, as discussed below.

Undirected Integration

Proposition 1 stated that, in mergers between professional services firms, senior managers do not take an active role in directing the integration process. The High School Dance metaphor of post-merger integration is, in effect, a model of undirected organizational change. The school teachers may organise the dance but they cannot determine which students will dance with each other and whether or not they will enjoy it. Similarly, the senior managers in the current study helped to create the context for integration, but they could not control the process by which it evolved. Specifically, they could not determine which professional staff would form productive working relationships with their merger partner colleagues.

Ad Hoc Integration Initiatives

Proposition 2 stated that, in mergers between professional services firms, the integration process evolves through a series of ad hoc co-operative initiatives between merger partner colleagues throughout the firm. In the current study, senior managers generated the expectation of change, but they did not drive the change process. Instead, the integration process evolved in an undirected manner in response to numerous loosely connected ad hoc activities on the part of individuals at all levels within the firms. The pace and scale of integration were determined by the professional staff in general, rather than the senior managers in particular. The key value-creating resources (tacit knowledge and client relationships) reside within individuals. These individuals cannot be compelled to share these resources with their merger partner colleagues. Instead, the process of resource transfer depends upon individuals choosing to establish close working relationships with their merger partner colleagues.

Mergers Versus Acquisitions

Proposition 3 stated that Propositions 1 and 2 will hold in the context of both mergers and acquisitions. In other words, senior managers in professional services firms have relatively little scope to direct the integration process, regardless of the underlying legal structure of the transaction. The current study examined both mergers and acquisitions and found no substantial difference in the integration processes. Although notional power lay with the senior managers of the acquiring firms, they had very little ability to deploy this power, because of the constraints under which they were obliged to operate. Real power lay with the key resource holders in both organizations. The current study, therefore, suggests that, when the key value-creating resources are proprietary to individuals, within both of the combining firms, there will be relatively little distinction between the integration process in mergers or acquisitions.

Variations Between Cases

The six firms in the current study differed from each other, not just in terms of the legal structures of the transactions, but in terms of their governance structure, professional sector, and size. In view of this it is notable that the three propositions were supported across all of the cases.

Governance and size – Within professional partnerships, senior managers have very little formal power and must manage by consensus within a diffuse authority structure. The current study suggests that, in incorporated professional services firms, similar managerial constraints apply because power lies with the key resource-holders, who are not necessarily the owners or the managers of the firm. Similarly, the study finds that the absolute size of the firms does not appear to influence the integration process strongly. This suggests that, although the larger firms may have possessed more extensive administrative systems and hierarchical structures than the smaller firms, senior managers chose not to use their formal authority in order to force the pace of integration.

Profession – The study found that, in the accounting firms, knowledge transfer was not particularly problematic, but did not provide much opportunity for value-creation either, as much of the technical knowledge was relatively standardised across the industry as a whole. By contrast, in the consulting firms knowledge transfer was perceived as an important source of value creation, but the process proved highly problematic. Differences in the prevailing form of the knowledge base, in particular the extent to which it was predominantly tacit or codified, represented a significant obstacle to knowledge transfer, as individuals refused to accept the legitimacy of the knowledge base of their merger partner colleagues.

Managerial Implications

The fact that all of the firms in the current study underwent an undirected process of post-merger integration does not necessarily mean that this was the best or indeed the only option available. There are many high profile examples of more rapid and less consensual models of integration within the professional services firm sector (for example Coopers & Lybrand/Deloitte, Haskins & Sells, or Ernst & Whinney/Arthur Young). There has been no systematic empirical research into the performance of these mergers, but there is considerable anecdotal evidence to suggest that staff and client turnover increased considerably during the integration process. In the current study, the overriding objective of the senior managers was to retain staff and clients. It can be argued, therefore, that this gradual and consensual model of integration was the only available option for these firms. It is reasonable to ask, however, whether it could have been managed more effectively. As suggested below, the managers in the current study need not have adopted such a laissez-faire approach.

In mergers between professional services firms, managers cannot control the process of integration but they can influence it. Smircich & Morgan (1982) argue that the 'management of meaning' is one of the key responsibilities of senior managers, specifically helping staff to interpret their organization and construct an organizational identity. The current study suggests that, in mergers and acquisitions, the management of meaning is a particularly important task for senior managers. They can challenge their staff's tendency to demonise the partner firm and can attempt to interpret the actions of the members of the merger partner firm from a positively-biased perspective. Managers can also help staff to reflect upon their own organization, by discouraging idealisation and emphasising the opportunity which the merger or acquisition represents to resolve the more negative aspects of their organization. Managers can encourage the development of boundary-spanning relationships, by identifying potential integration entrepreneurs and introducing them to like-minded individuals in the merger partner firm. Above all, managers must recognise when the prevailing attitude within the organization is changing and be ready to act swiftly to remove the structural impediments to integration.

The current study does not imply that managers should do nothing, but it does suggest that they should be careful not to do too much. Senior managers should focus their attention of identifying and removing the key impediments to integration as the process unfolds, rather than attempting to drive the pace of change.

Theoretical Implications

As previously discussed, it is a fundamental tenet of the merger process literature that managers can and should direct the integration process. The current study challenges this assumption. The merger process literature does not contain an implicit model of organizational change, but its implicit model is consistent with linear, rational models of strategy, where top managers analyse available data, establish targets, and manage the process of strategic change. Indeed the terminology of integration styles, which Haspeslagh & Jemison develop (Preservation, Absorption, and Symbiosis), reflects their implicit expectation that senior managers from the acquiring firm can select the appropriate form of integration and impose it upon the acquired firm. The current study adopts less directive terminology (Acclimatisation, Transition and Integration), which emphasises the evolving process of change and the relatively equitable balance of power between the firms. Whereas Preservation is something that senior managers of the acquiring firm 'do' to the acquired firm, Acclimatisation is a process in which all individuals can participate. If we accept that integration in professional services firms is advanced by individuals establishing boundary-spanning interpersonal relationships and constructing alternative interpretations of organizational identity, then we need to incorporate a more subtle and sophisticated understanding of the change process, as it is experienced at the individual level, into our firm-wide models of strategic change.

As previously discussed, the merger literature and the writings on strategic change, in general, contain the implicit assumption that employees are passive victims of managerial action, who represent an obstacle to change. The current study challenges this assumption, also. All of the studies that identify the human toll of mergers and acquisitions have been based on manufacturing and retail services firms. In this context, the opportunity for value creation often lies in sharing operational resources. Given the threat of rationalisation and redundancy programmes, it is not surprising that employees experience high levels of stress. However, the current study suggests that, in professional services firms, value creation is more likely to result from making more effective use of existing resources, than from cost-cutting redundancy programmes. In this context, professionals at all levels in the combining firms were not passive victims of managerial action, but instead played important roles in restraining and in advancing the integration process.

The integration process in this context was made possible because of the great variation in the responses of staff at all levels within the firms. It was the tension between the integration entrepreneurs and their more recalcitrant colleagues that held back the pace of integration in the early stages. It was the resolution of these tensions that led to the eventual breakthrough. In this context, managerial action is not then constrained by middle-management inertia or employee resistance, as much of the literature on organizational change would suggest (e.g. Nandler & Tushman, 1980; Tichy & Devanna, 1986), but by the fact that power resides with the key resource-holders. As long as some of these individuals are willing to explore the potential benefits of integration, then the process of change can begin to evolve.

NOTES

1. In this chapter, the single term 'merger' is used to represent both mergers and acquisitions in general, consistent with the practice in professional services firms and in the research literature. When seeking to distinguish between these two forms of transaction, both terms are used.

2. The definition of the term 'professional' is notoriously ambiguous (Freidson, 1986). In this paper, the term encompasses narrow definitions, which emphasise membership of an exclusive professional association and completion of an externally accredited training programme (Wilensky, 1964), and more inclusive definitions (Maister, 1993), encompassing activities such as consulting, which emphasise the application of specialist technical knowledge to the creation of customised solutions to clients' problems. This definition of the professional services firm recognises that technical knowledge and client relationships are not always proprietary to individuals (Morris & Empson, 1998) and, under certain conditions, individual authority is highly constrained (Gilson & Mnookin, 1990).

3. The term 'closure' refers to the moment at which the legal agreement is signed, either transferring ownership, in the case of an acquisition, or changing the legal identity of the firm, in the case of a merger.

ACKNOWLEDGEMENTS

I would like to thank John Hunt, of London Business School, and Philippe Haspeslagh, of INSEAD, for their insightful comments during the course of my research and numerous others who have commented on earlier drafts of this chapter.

REFERENCES

Agrawal, A., Jaffee, J. F., & Mandelker, G. N. (1992). The post-merger performance of acquiring firms: A re-examination of an anomaly. *Journal of Finance, XLVII* (September), 1605–1621.

Alvesson, M. (1993). Organizations as rhetoric: Knowledge-intensive firms and the struggle with ambiguity. *Journal of Management Studies, 30*(6), November, 997–1015.

Alvesson, M. (1995). *Management of knowledge-intensive companies.* Berlin: Walter de Gruyter.

Ashkanasky, N. M., & Holmes, S. (1995). Perceptions of organisational ideology following a merger: A longitudinal study of merging accounting firms. *Accounting, Organization and Society, 20*(1), 19–34.

Bailyn, L. (1985). Autonomy in the industrial R&D lab. *Human Resource Management Journal, 24*(2), Summer, 129–146.

Barney, J. B. (1991). Firm resources and sustained competitive advantage, *Journal of Management, 17*(1), 99–120.

Barney, J. B. (1996). Organizational culture: Can it be a source of sustained competitive advantage?, *Academy of Management Review, 11*(3), 656–665.

Brock, D., Powell, M., & Hinings, C. R. (1999). *Restructuring the professional organization: Accounting, health care and law.* London: Routledge.

Buono, A. F., & Bowditch, J. L. (1989). *The human side of mergers and acquisitions.* San Franciso: Jossey Bass.

Cartwright, S., & Cooper, C. L. (1990). The impact of mergers and acquisitions on people at work: Existing research and issues. *British Journal of Management, 1*, 65–76.

Cartwright, S., & Cooper, C. L. (1992). *Mergers and acquisitions: The human factor.* Oxford: Butterworth Heinemann.

Chaffee, E. E. (1985). Three models of strategy. *Academy of Management Review, 10*(1), 89–95.

Coff, R. W. (1997). Human assets and management dilemmas: Coping with hazards on the road to resource-based theory. *Academy of Management Review, 22*(2), 374–403.

Darby, M. R., & Karni, E. (1973). Free competition and the optimal amount of fraud. *Journal of Law and Economics, 16* (April), 67–86.

Davenport, T. H., & Prusak, L. (1998). *Working knowledge: How organizations manage what they know.* Boston: Harvard Business School Press.

Dirsmith, M. W., Heian, J. B., & Covalski, M. A. (1997). Structure and agency in an institutionalised setting: The application and social transformation of control in the Big Six. *Accounting, Organizations and Society, 22*(1), 1–27.

Eisenhardt, K. M. (1989). Building theory from case study research. *Academy of Management Review, 14*(4), 532–550.

Empson, L. (1998). *Mergers between professional services firms: How the distinctive organizational characteristics influence the process of value creation.* Unpublished PhD Thesis, London Business School, University of London.

Empson, L. (Forthcoming). Fear of exploitation and fear of contamination: Impediments to knowledge transfer in mergers between professional services firms. To appear in: L. Empson (Ed.), *Special issue of Human Relations: Knowledge management in professional services firms.*

Gilson, R. J., & Mnookin, R. H. (1990). The implicit contract for corporate law firm associates: ex post opportunism and ex ante bonding. In M. Aoki, B. Gustafsson, & O. Williamson *The Firm as a Nexus of Treaties,* London: Sage.

Glaser, B. G., & Strauss, A. L. (1967). *The discovery of grounded theory: strategies for qualitative research.* London: Weidenfeld and Nicholson.

Golden, B. R. (1992). The past is the past, or is it? The use of retrospective accounts as indicators of past strategy. *Academy of Management Journal, 35,* 848—860.

Grant, R. M., & Spender, J. C. (1996). Knowledge and the firm. *Strategic Management Journal, 17* (Winter), 5–11.

Greenwood, R., Hinings, C. R., & Brown, J. (1990). The P2 form of strategic management: Corporate practices in professional partnerships. *Academy of Management Journal, 33*(4), 725–755.

Greenwood, R., Hinings, C. R., & Brown, J. (1994). Merging professional service firms. *Organisation Science, 5*(2), 239–257.

Hambrick, D. C., & Cannella, A. (1993). Relative standing: A framework for understanding departures of acquired executives. *Academy of Management Journal, 36*(4), 733–762.

Hansen, M., Nohria, N., & Tierney, T. (1999). What's your strategy for managing knowledge? *Harvard Business Review,* March-April: 106–116.

Haspeslagh, P., & Jemison, D. B. (1991). *Managing acquisitions: creating value through corporate renewal,* New York: The Free Press.

Higson, C. (1991). The use of accounting information in the analysis of takeovers and mergers: A review. In: *The future shape of financial reports: Research studies,* Institute of Chartered Accountants.

Hinings, C. R., Brown, J. L., & Greenwood, R. (1991). Change in an autonomous professional organization. *Journal of Management Studies, 28*(4), 375–393.

Hunt, J. W., Lees, S., Grumbar, J. J., & Vivian, P. D. (1987). *Acquisitions: The human factor.* Egon Zehnder International.

Johnson, T. (1972). Professions and power. London: Macmillan.

Jones, C., Hesterly, W. S., Fladmoe-Lindquist, K., & Borgatti, S. P. (1998). Professional service constellations: How strategies and capabilities influence collaborative stability and change. *Organization Science, 9*(3), 396–410.

Kitching, J. (1967). Why do mergers miscarry?. *Harvard Business Review*, November-December: 84–101.

KPMG. (1999). *Mergers and acquisitions: A global research report.* KPMG.

Leonard-Barton, D. (1990). A dual methodology for case studies: Synergistic use of longitudinal single site with replicated multiple sites. *Organization Science, 1*(3), 248–266.

Levinson, H. (1970). A psychologist diagnoses merger failure. *Harvard Business Review,* March-April: 139–147.

Lowendahl, B. R. (1997). *Strategic management of professional service firms.* Copenhagen: Handelsshojskolens Forlag.

Maister, D. (1993). *Managing the professional services firm.* New York: The Free Press.

Mergers and Acquisitions Journal. (1999). Mergers and acquisitions scoreboard. 33(4), 57–68.

Miles, M. B., & Huberman, A. M. (1994). *Qualitative data analysis: an expanded sourcebook.* Thousand Oaks, CA: Sage.

Mills, P. K., Hall, J. L., Leidecker, J. K., & Marguillies, N. (1983). Flexiform: a model for professional service organizations. *Academy of Management Review, 8*(1), 118–131.

Mintzberg, H. (1983). *Structure in fives: Designing effective organizations.* Englewood Cliffs, NJ: Prentice Hall.

Mintzberg, H., & Quinn, J. B. (1991). *The strategy process.* Englewood Cliffs, NJ: Prentice Hall.

Mirvis, P. H., & Marks, M. L. (1992). *Managing the merger: Making it work.* Englewood Cliffs, NJ: Prentice Hall.

Montagna, P. D. (1968). Professionalisation and bureaucratisation in large organizations. American *Journal of Sociology, 74,* 138–145.

Morris, T., & Empson, L. (1998). Organization and expertise: An exploration of knowledge bases and the management of accounting and consulting firms. *Accounting, Organizations and Society, 23*(5/6), 609–624.

Nahavandi, A., & Malekzadeh, A. R. (1988). Acculturation in mergers and acquisitions. *Academy of Management Review, 13*(1), 79–90.

Nandler, D., & Tushman, M. L. (1980). A congruence model for diagnosing organizations'. *Organizational Dynamics*, Winter.

Newman, J. M., & Krzystofiak, F. J. (1993). Changes in employee attitudes after an acquisition: A longitudinal analysis. *Group and Organization Management, 18*(4) December: 390–410.

Nonaka, I., & Takeuchi, H. (1995). *The knowledge creating company*. Oxford: The Oxford University Press.

Pablo, A. L. (1994). Determinants of acquisition integration level: A decision -making perspective. *Academy of Management Journal. 37*(4), 803–836.

Pettigrew, A. W. (1990). Longitudinal field research on change: Theory and practice. *Organizational Studies, 1*(3), 267–292.

Polanyi, M. (1967). *The tacit dimension*. London: Routledge and Keegan Paul.

Raelin, J. A. (1984). An examination of deviant/adaptive behaviours in the organizational career of professionals. *Academy of Management Review, 9*(3), 413–427.

Ranft, A. L. (1997). *Preserving and transferring knowledge-based resources during post-acquisition implementation*. Unpublished Ph.D. thesis: University of North Carolina.

Ravenscraft, D., & Scherer, F. M. (1987). *Mergers, selloffs, and economic efficiency*. Washington DC: The Brookings Institute.

Roll, R. (1986). The hubris hypothesis of corporate takeovers. *Journal of Business, 59*(2)1, 197–216.

Schneider, S. C., & Dunbar, R. L. M. (1992). A psychoanalytic reading of hostile take-over events. *Academy of Management Review, 17*(3), 537–567.

Schweiger, D. M., & Denisi, A. S. (1991). Communication with employees following a merger: a longitudinal field experiment. *Academy of Management Journal, 34*(1), 110–135.

Smircich, L., & Morgan, G. (1982). Leadership: The management of meaning. *Journal of Applied Behavioural Science, 18*, 257–273.

Somers, M. J., & Bird, K. (1990). Managing the transition phase of mergers. *Journal of Managerial Psychology, 5*(4), 38–42.

Sveiby, K. E. (1997). *The new organizational wealth: Managing and measuring knowledge-based assets*. San Francisco: Berrett-Koehler.

Tichy, N. M., & Devanna, M. A. (1986). *The transformational leader*. New York: John Wiley & Sons.

Tolbert, P. S., & Stern, R. N. (1991). Organizations of professionals: Governance structures in large law firms. In: P. S. Tolbert, & S. B. Bacharach (Eds.), *Research in the sociology of organizations: organizations and professions*. Greenwich, CT: JAI Press.

Walsh, J. P. (1988). Top management turnover following mergers and acquisitions. *Strategic Management Journal, 9*, 173–183.

Walter, G. A. (1985). Culture collisions in mergers and acquisitions. In: P. J. Frost, L. F. Moore, M. R. Louis, C. C. Lundberg, & J. Martin (Eds.), *Organisational culture*, Newbury Park, CA: Sage.

Walter, G. A., & Barney, J. B. (1990). Managerial objectives in mergers and acquisitions. *Strategic Management Journal, 11*, 79–86.

Wernerfelt, B. (1984). A resource-based view of the firm. *Strategic Management Journal, 5*, 171–180.

Wilensky, H. L. (1964). The professionalisation of everyone? *The American Journal of Sociology, September, LXX*(2), 137–158.

Winch, G., & Schneider, E. (1993). Managing the knowledge-based organization: The case of archi-
tectural practice. *Journal of Management Studies, 30*(6), November: 923–938.
Yin, R. K. (1984). *Case study research: Design and methods.* Thousand Oaks, CA: Sage.

TALES OF TRIAL AND TRIUMPH A NARRATOLOGICAL PERSPECTIVE ON INTERNATIONAL ACQUISITION

Martine Cardel Gertsen and Anne-Marie Søderberg

BOUGHT BY THE BRITISH

A SHOP STEWARD'S NARRATIVE ABOUT AN INTERNATIONAL ACQUISITION

I started working here at Fonodan[1] [a telecommunications company in Denmark] in 1987 as a cleaner. I worked as a cleaner for three years and then, when the company expanded, I applied for a job in production. I've been in production ever since, and we've had our ups and downs. That's the way it is in electronics, anyhow. It goes very fast, sometimes up, sometimes down.

Previously, there were often difficulties with the delivery of components – we didn't get them in time. So it was not unusual or frowned upon for us girls in production to do crosswords or knit, if there wasn't anything to do during working hours. Also, we had a bonus system with bonuses paid out to each section. This meant that there was a kind of barricade between the sections – people wouldn't go to another section to help out, even if they didn't have anything to do. We knew that Fonodan wasn't going well, but we were hoping that somebody would invest in the company.

But in August 1993, we got a big shock. Everybody was summoned to a meeting in our canteen. There, a lawyer briefly told us that the company had no money

Advances in Mergers and Acquisitions, Volume 1, pages 239–272
Copyright © 2000 by Elsevier Science Inc.
All rights of reproduction in any form reserved.
ISBN: 0–7623–0683–1

left and had to send us home. Afterwards, we were sort of stunned – we didn't know what to do. Some went home right away, but a lot of us stayed on and talked for hours. Some even cried. What happened after the suspension of payments was just terrible. Fonodan was a big company in a small community. Everybody was out of work, shops in the village closed, and so on.

We were all excited when we learnt from the papers and TV that Electra [a British consumer electronics company] was getting involved. As for me, I began looking in the papers to see if I could find anything about British management and working conditions in British companies. There were some horrible rumours, but they turned out to be totally wrong. I was expecting that we'd really have to toe the line, that it would be much stricter. But it was all just a lot of prejudice.

Anyway, after Electra had taken over, I contacted the new Fonodan Telecom and asked if there were any jobs. I felt lucky to get a job again. A lot of us were employed again and many of the middle managers, too. The two former shop stewards from our union were not re-employed, though. I know that one of them wasn't interested and didn't apply, but I'm not sure about the other one. She wrote something in our local newspaper about being left out in the cold, but I don't think she's being fair to the company. Still, I don't know exactly what happened. And I know that the shop stewards from the other unions have been re-employed. Anyway, the girls elected me as shop steward right after I started working here again.

The greatest difference I experienced was that Electra had cut down on cleaning, and there was no longer free coffee. Well, and then we are also paid less than before. Actually, now we get less than workers in other companies in this area. But the pay system is better now, because everyone is paid in the same way, by the hour. We have no bonus system now, and there are no barricades between the sections. The girls say that it is better now, though they get less money, but they are more satisfied because they help each other more and feel welcome in other sections. They understand more about what's going on in this way. Now, some girls are laid off if there isn't anything to do in the production. But we are content with that – it's unsatisfactory to sit around and do nothing. And it was also too expensive for the company. We realise that the electronics industry is extremely competitive, and if the company does well financially, we can feel more secure in our jobs. Before, we may have been a bit spoiled – we also had more benefits, in connection with illness, for instance. Still, we are satisfied and, during our local negotiations, we got many of our benefits back. We were not clever enough to get all of them back, though. But we will try again next year. Otherwise, things go well and we can talk openly about most things just like before.

We started a smoking policy from April 1st. Some people felt that the new human resource manager had made a bad decision and that it was just terrible.

Everything new is somewhat difficult. But they say that visiting customers don't like smoking, so we'll have to accept it. If we don't have any customers, we have no jobs either.

I am now a member of the co-operation board. Danny [the British expatriate CEO] is so open and frank. He has put his cards on the table. And the way I see it, he saved us, didn't he? If Electra hadn't bought Fonodan, we'd still be out of work. I think he ought to learn Danish now that he works in Denmark, though, but he is not interested in that. So the board meetings are in English, but it's no problem, really, though my English is not that good. Danny's secretary translates; if there is anything we don't understand, I just have to say, "stop, stop, I don't get it".

INTRODUCTION: WHY A NARRATOLOGICAL PERSPECTIVE ON INTERNATIONAL ACQUISITIONS?

What you have just read is the narrative of an international acquisition, but of course just one version among many others. This narrative was told to the authors by a shop steward in March 1995. The HRM manager, the British expatriate CEO, the development engineers and everyone else involved all had their own accounts of what had happened. Different in some ways, similar in others, but all told in individual voices and representing events as seen from various positions and points of view.

Often, when you read studies of mergers and acquisitions, you wonder whose voices are heard in accounts about success and failure. It is probably safe to say that most studies have a managerial tilt and that managers' narratives and the public story-telling of what has happened in an organisation (e.g. press releases, annual reports, web-sites) may well conflict with and marginalise some voices while privileging others. We find that one of the benefits of a narratological approach on acquisitions is that it is well suited to giving voice to a wide range of organisational actors and to show in which ways their interpretations of organisational reality may correspond and differ. It enables the researcher to see the organisation in an integration perspective, in a differentiation perspective, and in a fragmentation perspective (cf. Martin, 1992) at the same time. In other words: to see that which is agreed upon by all members, that which is shared within certain groups only, and that which is fragmented and ambiguous.

We believe that a narratological perspective, especially when combined with a longitudinal approach, is able to clarify changing patterns of identification, justification and causation that often prove crucial to the outcome of post-acquisition integration processes. This approach is also useful when it comes to assessing to what extent members of an organisation share a certain under-standing of what is going on in the post-acquisition integration processes.

In the following, we intend to focus on a telecommunications company in Denmark. This company was first acquired by a British concern and then, after four years, by a German concern. We have followed these developments closely and have collected a considerable number of narratives about the organisation and the organisational changes that took place. These stories have been related to us in interviews with numerous organisational actors at different hierarchical levels and at different points in time over a period of 6 years. Some are told in an emotional voice, others in a more distant tone, but all have plots, motives and characters. Before we revert to the company we have studied, we would like to elaborate on our theoretical point of departure.

THEORETICAL PERSPECTIVE

What is a narrative?

Narrating is a fundamental human activity, a mode of thinking and being, so to speak. We constantly tell and interpret narratives (cf. Currie, 1998). We organise our experience and our memory of what has happened to us mainly in the form of narrative – stories, excuses, myths, reasons for doing and not doing. We tell narratives in order to understand our own lives, as well as those of other people (cf. Polkinghorne, 1988). Still, individuals are not the only authors of the narratives they tell. The telling of narratives is a social act, and thus involves some degree of negotiation with the interlocutors about positions and meanings. This is also true for the stories that we have been told, as inter-viewers studying international acquisitions. Narratives should not be seen as representing reality, but rather as constituting the narrator's reality.

In this chapter, we will use the terms 'narrative', 'story' and 'tale' inter-changeably, but in the theoretical literature the term 'narrative' is usually preferred. In our working definition of a narrative we have chosen to focus on four essential characteristics (cf. Bruner, 1991):

1. A narrative is an account of events occurring over time.
2. Narratives are retrospective interpretations of sequential events.
3. Narratives focus on human action – the action of the narrator and others.
4. Narrating is part of identity construction.

Re 1. A narrative is an account of events occurring over time
Any narrative has a chronological dimension which shows that it is made up of events along a line of time. Events can be defined as "the transition from

one state to another, caused or experienced by actors" (Bal, 1985, p. 13). An event is a process, an alteration. In a study of narratives of individual lives, Horsdal (1999) describes their temporal aspect in this way: "We create meaning in the movement of life by experiencing it as a series of events, a narrative. We interfere with the course of time, with beginnings and endings which enclose and demarcate a sequence, so that we can ascribe meaning to it" (p. 27, our translation). Narratologists often distinguish between 'discourse time', the time it takes to hear or read a narrative, and 'story time', which is more like 'real time' or 'clock time' and refers to the actual duration of the sequence of events narrated. The relationship between 'discourse time' and 'story time' is important when we interpret narratives. Crucial events are typically narrated in more detail: as a scene instead of just a summary. Thus, 'discourse time' approaches 'story time' in the narratives' focal points (cf. Chatman, 1978; Genette, 1980).

Re 2. Narratives are retrospective interpretations of sequential events
A narrative is composed of a sequence of particular events that are given meaning by a plot. This is the basic means by which events are connected into a meaningful whole. The author/narrator imposes the plot on the events when he/she selects, prioritises and orders the events from a certain point of view and, in a particular context, determines the delineation and demarcation of the course of events. Plot involves a temporal ordering of these events and suggests a connection between them. This connection may be a causal relationship. When a narrator tells of an event, he/she relates the event to a project and thereby integrates it into the plot. Thus he/she reflexively makes sense of the course of events.

Re 3. Narratives focus on human action – the action of the narrator and others
Narratives are about people acting in a setting, and their actions must be relevant to their intentional states – their beliefs, desires, theories, values, etc. Thus, what happens is typically explained by the conscious intentions of actors. We might say that their actions are emplotted and thereby become events in the narrative. In the narratives we will analyse in the following, the narrators themselves (our interviewees) are also actors – they are simultaneously embedded in their account and displaying an awareness of their own role in it, while telling it to us. In addition to the general term 'actor', some narratologists also use the more specific term 'character' and the two are not quite interchangeable (cf. Bal, 1985). Whereas the term 'actor' normally emphasises a structural position in the plot (what is done? – Which actions are carried out?), the term 'character' denotes a more complex semantic unit. A character resembles a human being more, so to speak. It is described by deriving a collection of more

or less coherent traits from the narrative (what is he/she like? – How can we characterise him/her?).

Re 4. Narrating is part of identity construction
The narrator's adopted identity has a central influence on the narrative being told, and in turn, the narrative helps the narrator in constructing, reinforcing, or changing this identity. It is not something we do alone; we share our stories with others and adjust them to their reactions. Throughout our lives, we continually develop, tell, and sometimes even write, our autobiographies (cf. Horsdal, 1999; Lieblich, Tuval-Mashiach & Zilber, 1998 for examples of research in individual life narratives). The identities we create in this are manifold: It may be a professional identity as an engineer, an organisational identity (we are from Fonodan . . .), a regional identity (we are from Northern Jutland . . .), a national identity (we are Danes . . .) or a gender identity (as women at the production line, we . . .). This is close to Weick's argument that sensemaking is grounded in ongoing identity constructions (cf. Weick, 1995).

We use narratives to create or support identities in various manners. Individuals speak of their experiences by converting them into coherent accounts, stories centred around a self acting more or less purposefully in a social world. Families sometimes create a corpus of connected and shared tales. Nation states may invent traditions, based on narratives of certain happenings, and then endow them with privileged status (cf. Hobsbawm & Ranger, 1983).

At the intermediate level, companies and other organisations may also turn past events and future plans into stories and thus endow actions which take place in the organisation with meaning. In this way, they engage in a quest for sensemaking similar to individuals' quests for meaning in their lives (cf. Czarniawska, 1997). Like humans, organisations need a narrative of themselves that is, at least to some extent, coherent. This need for organisational narrating is probably felt more strongly in times of turbulence, for instance in connection with a merger or an acquisition.

What is narratology?

Narratology is the theory and systematic study of narrative (cf. Currie, 1998). It began as a science of narrative form and structure in literature studies, and has been developed throughout the twentieth century (cf. Martin, 1986; Rimmon-Kenan, 1983). The Russian scholar Bakhtin studied, in the 1920s, different voices in Dostojevskij's novels and created the concept of "polyphony" to describe this (cf. Bakhtin, 1981). Another Russian scholar, Vladimir Propp, studied the morphology of folktales (cf. Propp, 1968). And the French scholar

Greimas developed Propp's concepts into the actantial model which we will come back to later.

Later on, the discipline diversified into several other fields. In the 1980s, narratology underwent a transition from the – almost exclusively literary – formalist and structuralist approaches into a complex theory, applicable to narratives wherever they can be found, not only in literature. The scope of narratology was massively expanded into the newborn discipline of cultural studies, and narratologists began analysing, for instance, films, advertisements or jokes (cf. Currie, 1998).

There has also been an increasing recognition that narratives are central to our representations and constructions of identity. Narratives in personal memory and self-representation have been studied by, for instance, Jerome Bruner (1990) in his Acts of Meaning, a seminal work within cognitive psychology. The importance of narratives in studies of collective identity has been stressed in work on how the identity of regions, nations, race, and gender are being constructed and constantly negotiated and changed.

There has also been widespread interest in narrative in history: the best known work here is probably Hayden White's (1973) Metahistory. The Historical Imagination in Nineteenth Century Europe. This work emphasises the discursivity of history, i.e. how our oral and written historical accounts are made up of different discourses, representing certain interests and narrating from certain points of view (cf. also White, 1987).

In business-related disciplines, narratological perspectives are found as well. In marketing, researchers sometimes speak of narratives connected to products or company images, for instance (cf. Olins, 1995). But in this context, we are, of course, particularly interested in organisational studies, where the interest in narrative has grown over the last 10–15 years (cf. Grant, Keenoy & Oswick, 1998; Czarniawska, 1998). One of the best known researchers in this area is Barbara Czarniawska, who has, among other things, done a study of tales from different organisations in the Swedish public sector (Narrating the Organisation. Dramas of Institutional Identity, 1997).

Czarniawska (1997) distinguishes between three types of narratological approach to organisation studies:

1. Narrating organisations, referring to research written in a story-like way. This is typically cases, "tales from the field," where chronology is the main ordering device (e.g. Gertsen & Søderberg, 1998a; 1999a, b).
2. Collecting organisational stories. In the 1980s, organisation studies that treated stories as artefacts predominated (e.g. Martin, 1982). More recently, the trend has moved towards an interest in the process of story-telling as a never-ending construction of meaning (e.g. Boje, 1991).

3. Organising as narration. This refers to interpretative research that concep-
    tualises organisational life as story making (e.g. Czarniawska, 1997). Here,
    story-telling is seen as a form of organisational communication. The
    approach involves story-telling interviews which are interpreted by the
    researcher. These interpretations result in an array of alternative or compet-
    itive stories that may be used to broaden our understanding of organisational
    processes and, possibly, to engage in a continued dialogue with the field.

In this chapter, we take the last approach and view organising as narration.
Although we have so far only had limited opportunity to bring our interpretations back to the interviewees in the field, we hope that our interpretations will
enable us to come up with an enlightening range of stories. For practical reasons,
we are not able to print the stories here in their full length, but hopefully the
exemplary narrative told by the shop steward gives some idea of what they
may look like.

EMPIRICAL MATERIAL AND METHODOLOGY

The company, which was originally called Fonodan, is situated in a small
community in the region of Northern Jutland, where it develops and produces
mobile phones. It was founded by a small group of Danish engineers in 1980
and expanded from 44 employees in 1981 to 870 employees in 1990.
Management of the growing company was characterised by an R&D-focused
entrepreneurial spirit and a consensus-oriented decision-making style.

From the very beginning, the majority of Fonodan's products were sold in
export markets. When the management learned that a new pan-European
telecommunication standard, the GSM system, was to be established in 1992,
they decided to develop a GSM phone together with Northcom, another local
producer of mobile phones. This joint development project was technologically
successful, but it proved extremely costly.

In 1993, after several years with severe financial difficulties, the company
had to suspend its payments. As soon as this was announced, Fonodan's 30
R&D engineers met and discussed the fact that there were only 3 or 4 GSM
R&D groups like them in Europe. This obviously made them attractive as a
team, and they decided to stay together for a month to investigate their
possibilities, even though most of them had already been offered jobs in other
companies. During this month, they contacted several potential purchasers. One
of them was the British consumer electronics company Electra, whose owner
wanted to diversify and had for some time been planning to enter the expanding
telecommunications market.

Electra almost immediately decided to buy Fonodan, and sent a British managing director and a couple of other managers from their headquarters to Denmark. Marketing and sales were relatively weak points in the company, and the new management made great efforts both to improve the company's commercial strategy and to enter into long-term contracts with telecommunication network operators on the European market. Electra was able to purchase components for Fonodan at lower costs, and also invested in new machines for semi-automatic production. Extensive plans were made for mass production and the building of a new factory, but it turned out to be harder than expected to make profits, and the plans were postponed.

In 1997, after almost four years under British ownership, the German multinational industrial group Gerhard Strohm GmbH. bought the company. Today, the managing director and most of the other managers are Danish, but there are a few German managers as well. A new production plant, aimed at mass production, has been built and in addition, Strohm Telecom has invested considerable amounts in research and development. Since the German acquisition, the number of employees in the Danish business unit of Strohm Telecom has increased from 750 to about 1500. The company is, at the moment, the biggest in the region of Northern Jutland.

When we started our empirical investigations, we decided to interview not only the top management, but also a large number of employees on different levels: e.g. unskilled workers, shop foremen, secretaries, R&D engineers, accountants, human resource managers, sales people, and many others. We also interviewed representatives of trade unions and local trade councils, as well as the director of the regional science-park, to get an impression of the company's interaction with the local environment, both before and after the international acquisitions. Our perspective is mainly that of the acquired company. However, we also had the opportunity to interview expatriate managers sent to Denmark by their head office (cf. Gertsen & Søderberg, 1998a, b; 1999a, b; Gertsen, Søderberg & Torp, 1998 for more results from our research on international acquisitions in the Danish electronics industry).

We carried out fieldwork every year in 1994–1999. In this way, we had the chance to follow developments and shifting interpretations in the company over a long period, even though, of course, we only got 'snapshots' of a long course of events. Most of our interviews were narrative in nature; i.e. we encouraged our interviewees to describe their situation in their own words, with as few interruptions from the interviewer as possible. We also collected what was written about the company in the Danish newspapers and had access to other written material: annual accounts, web-sites and the like.

As you can imagine, our case company has gone through quite a lot of crises and changes. Changes are always part of daily life in organisations, but they tend to be especially comprehensive, sudden, and sometimes dramatic in international acquisitions. In our interviews, we have observed that in challenging situations, most organisational actors, but in particular the managers, feel a special need to account for their past, present and future actions. They want to justify the actions to themselves and others, to control the situation (at least in their minds), and to plan ahead. These accounts are often communicated in a narrative mode, as the actors try to make sense of what they do and what is happening to them and the organisation.

We do not interpret these organisational narratives as accurate reports of actual events. We rather tend to see them as tales about various actions and events which are given a certain meaning by our respondents, as part of the plots they are continually constructing and revising. Still, a narratological approach does not mean that the phenomena studied are seen as entirely fictitious. The narratives studied have a basis in material reality, even if we have no unmediated access to this reality; i.e. we can only form an idea of what has happened in the organisation through the narratives we hear.

NARRATIVES OF A TELECOMMUNICATIONS COMPANY IN DENMARK

THE BRITISH ACQUISITION – THE ELECTRA ERA (1993–1997)

As a point of departure for our analyses of selected narratives, we have chosen to use a narratological model from structuralist literary criticism.

A. J. Greimas developed his actantial model (on the basis of Propp's analyses of folk tales) in *Sémantique Structurale* (1966). An actant is a structural unit or a function, not necessarily represented by a person (a character). The actant may also be an abstraction or an institution (e.g. success, the banking system).

Greimas posits 6 actants, in three pairs of binary opposition, which describe fundamental patterns in narratives:

subject/object: desire, search or aim
power/receiver: transport, communication
helper/opponent: auxiliary support or hindrance

The subject-actant is following an aim, aspiring towards a goal (e.g. a prince fighting a dragon to win the princess; a manager working hard for his company's survival). The object-actant is not necessarily a human being (though it may be, e.g. a princess in a fairy tale), it can also consist of reaching a certain state (wisdom, profitability, an increase in salary). The power-actant (sometimes called the sender, but this term suggests an active participation and this does not always apply). The power may be a person (e.g. the king, the chairman of the board), but is often an abstraction (e.g. fate, cleverness, society). The receiver-actant is often the same person as the subject-actant and, in the case of empirical narrative, frequently identical with the narrator. The helper-actant and the opponent-actant may, similarly, be either persons or abstractions, benevolent or malevolent in the quest for the desired object (i.e. the helper may be hard work, a fairy godmother, a creative accountant. The opponent may be laziness, a vicious dragon or a strong competitor).

Greimas' actantial model is structural: it describes the relations between different kinds of phenomena, not, primarily, the phenomena themselves. Its assumption is that fixed relations between classes of phenomena form the basis of the narrative.

Actantial model (applied to a typical fairy tale of a prince who fights evil to free a princess and receives her hand in marriage from her father, the king):

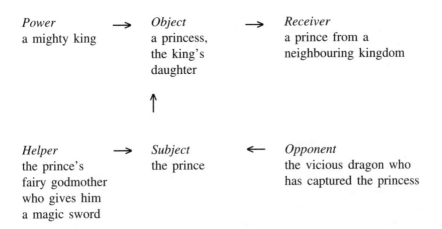

Power	→	*Object*	→	*Receiver*
a mighty king		a princess, the king's daughter		a prince from a neighbouring kingdom

↑

Helper	→	*Subject*	←	*Opponent*
the prince's fairy godmother who gives him a magic sword		the prince		the vicious dragon who has captured the princess

The actantial model was developed to understand the structures underlying literary fiction. Though naturally, the narratives studied here do not demonstrate the premeditated complexity or depth found in much fiction, there is no structural difference between fictional and empirical narratives. Therefore, we believe that the actantial model can also elucidate how employees and managers understand the organisational change processes that they are involved in after an acquisition and throw light on changing interpretations of their own role, as well as of the challenges that the organisation meets.

In the following, we will attempt to apply this model to some of the stories of Fonodan. First, the narrative told by the shop steward in the beginning of this chapter.

The shop steward's first narrative – March 1995

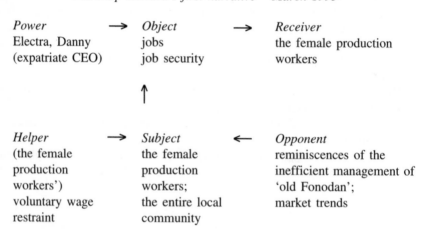

The shop steward, Jonna Jensen, a woman in her 40s, organises her narrative in a series of events and selects certain happenings as crises or transitions that are important from her point of view. These events are described in greater detail, for example the meeting where all employees are gathered in the canteen to be informed about the suspension of payments. At such a stage in the narra- tive, discourse time expands and the narrative becomes more scenic. In situations of threat, trial and transition, the stop steward tells more about her own and the other workers' feelings and thus appeals to the listener's sympathy.

The shop steward speaks on behalf of all the female production workers; they are the subjects of her narrative. She does not draw special attention to her own actions and tends to use the personal pronoun 'we' rather than 'I' ("We knew that Fonodan wasn't going well," "we got a big shock," etc.) In her narrative, the workers all desire the same thing: jobs and as much job secu- rity as possible. She clearly identifies with the group of female workers she represents, though this does not mean that she is in opposition to the British managers, on the contrary.

To some extent, she even includes the entire local community in the subject. Fonodan's suspension of all payments was a traumatic event, which had a massive impact on the small community, since hundreds of employees lost their jobs overnight. Therefore the object, secure jobs, is not just desired by the workers, but by all who depend directly or indirectly on their income.

The receiver is identical with the subject, and the power providing the desired object is clearly the British acquiring company, Electra. The British CEO represents this power – he is the hero and the saviour in Jonna Jensen's story. The shop steward does not seem to distinguish clearly between Danny Allen and the acquiring company Electra, where the decision to buy Fonodan was made: "And the way I see it, he saved us, didn't he? If Electra hadn't bought Fonodan, we'd still be out of work."

The former management is pointed out as the culprit: it was, at least partly, because of inefficient leadership that the workers lost their jobs. The helpers are indicated rather vaguely, but we note that the workers' own voluntary wage restraint is mentioned as something that might make their jobs more secure. Still, it is not emphasised as a crucial fact and could not by itself have brought about the desired object. The central agent in the narrative is obviously Electra.

In the shop steward's story, the workers are rather powerless themselves. She only sees herself and the other workers as agents to a very limited extent. They do not make things happen, things happen to them. Her world-view is, more-over, fatalistic: the workers are not responsible: "That's the way it is – in electronics, anyhow. It goes very fast, sometimes up, sometimes down." Generally, she tends to accept the situation as it is: "Everything new is some-what difficult" is her soothing remark about the smoking policy which has provoked some resistance from other workers. Obvious difficulties such as board meetings in English and partly unsuccessful negotiations are met with comments such as: "it's no problem, really," "Otherwise, things go well" and "we can talk openly about most things."

Even though she is not only shop steward, but also a member of the regional executive committee of the Female Workers' Union, we do not hear the voice of a trade union representative very clearly. Cuts in wages and benefits are met with an almost self-effacing attitude: "Before, we may have been a bit spoilt" and "we were not clever enough to get all of them back." Here, she takes a very (self-)critical perspective on the workers and their actions. She actually describes it as the workers' own fault that they did not get a better result during the negotiation, between union representatives and employers. She might, instead, have blamed the British employers for being unfair and unwilling to see that the workers' demands are reasonable and in line with working condi-tions in other Danish companies, for instance. By adding that the workers used to be "spoilt" (i.e. the incompetent former management spent too much money on them), she even – on behalf the group – accepts part of the blame for the suspension of payments. These examples show that she shares interpretations of some events in the former Fonodan with the human resource manager; in fact her counterpart in the local bargaining.

We also note that the shop steward tells her tale with some pathos and in an emotional voice. She explains how she and the other workers felt at various points in time: they "got a big shock," "cried," felt "excited," "satisfied," etc. She focuses more on feelings than on attempting to explain what has happened in terms of causal relationships. This is hardly just a question of narrative style. It also indicates that from her point of view, certain causal relationships concerning the company's successes and failures may not be visible at all.

The human resource manager's first narrative – March 1995

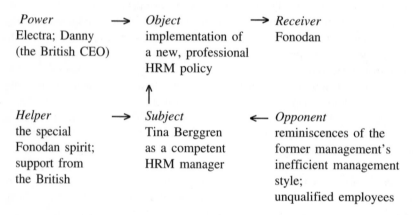

Tina Berggren is a woman in her early 30s. Her first narrative is told in a very energetic and optimistic voice. She has been with the company for several years, but has only recently been promoted by the British CEO from a relatively modest administrative position to her present job as a human resource manager. She is enthusiastic about Fonodan, which has "always been known as a great place to work; there is a special spirit here – zest and openness."

She does not hesitate to place the responsibility for Fonodan's suspension of payments with the former management's lack of financial control: "They were very spendthrift . . . their cash box was always open, so to speak." But she is confident that the new management is in the process of getting finances under control. She also tells us that "Electra realises that Fonodan's relationship with its employees is crucial. Therefore, Danny asked me to work out a new personnel policy for our company, by myself, and I'm now busy implementing it." In fact, the successful implementation of this policy is her object.

She feels that the lack of professional HRM has been a problem and that more emphasis must be placed on the employees' personal and professional development. She tries "to make it clear to them that it is their own responsibility to stay qualified, for instance by attending various types of courses." Most are interested in doing so, but a few seem unwilling to learn, and want things to stay the same. Still, although there is a lot of work ahead, Tina Berggren believes that she, with the good company spirit and with the experienced and charismatic CEO Danny Allen as helpers, will be able to move the company in the right direction.

It is clear that in this narrative, the human resource manager identifies strongly with Fonodan, with the new British owners and the British expatriate CEO (Danny). She expresses admiration for the CEO and appreciates the career opportunity he has given her. But she also feels that she, with her university background and her longer experience in Fonodan, can be of considerable assistance to him. She emphasises that she is theoretically up-to-date and familiar with the newest ideas in HRM.

She distances herself from the former Danish management and from employees who are not sufficiently qualified or not willing to learn and develop, personally or professionally. As she sees it, this is absolutely necessary in order to work in a professional high-tech company in a highly competitive industry, and those that do not realise it are opponents to her project.

The British CEO's first narrative – March 1995

Next, we will look at the first story told by the British managing director, Danny Allen, who was sent to Denmark by the British Electra from late 1993 to 1997. He is a self-made man, in his mid–50s, with a long career in sales and management in Electra, including some international experience.

Danny Allen has, as a CEO, a well-defined object: to make Fonodan number 4 in the global market. And he is confident that he can attain it: "We have the right product and I know from my experience that this product is ripe." He believes in his own abilities as a businessman, manager, and salesman. He is also pleased with the commitment he sees among his employees, a commitment which is expressed in the workers' wage restraint and the generally high level of cost consciousness after the shock produced by the suspension of payments. With these things to help him, he is convinced that he can reach his goal.

The British managing director sees himself as a decisive agent when things go well. He describes himself as an experienced and dynamic international businessman, and he adds: "I have a strong personality and I tend to get my way due to force and arrogance." This is unlike the Danish managers who are described as likeable, but need to be taught quick decision-making and need to develop a stronger market-orientation.

Danny Allen sees the Danish middle managers' slow decision-making, and the engineers' focus on technology instead of market needs, as opponents. He interprets these attitudes as reminiscences of the former management's inefficiency. He is also somewhat critical of the considerable power the Danish unions have, but he admits that they have been quite co-operative so far. He has made plans to reorganise the management team and to delegate some decisions: "But I will still put my fingers in the pie. It is not my style to sit back and watch the world go by. Tina Berggren will participate in all the management meetings and report back to me as a sort of spy." He looks upon the young human resource manager as his helper and ally, but he openly admits that he intends to use her in the somewhat problematic role as a spy among the other managers.

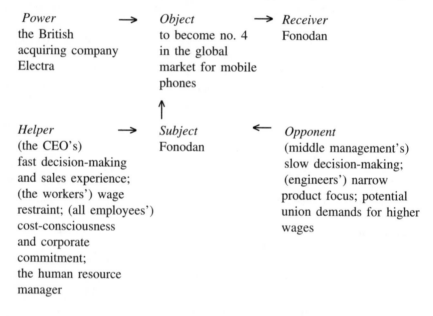

Power → *Object* → *Receiver*
the British   to become no. 4   Fonodan
acquiring company in the global
Electra   market for mobile
                  phones

Helper → *Subject* ← *Opponent*
(the CEO's)   Fonodan   (middle management's)
fast decision-making   slow decision-making;
and sales experience;   (engineers') narrow
(the workers') wage   product focus; potential
restraint; (all employees')   union demands for higher
cost-consciousness   wages
and corporate
commitment;
the human resource
manager

The project manager's story – April 96

Let us now turn to one of the stories told at the middle management level, a year later. The narrator is an engineer in his early 30s. Frede Sonne is employed as a project manager in the research and development department.

Basically, the project manager's story is about his endeavours to establish a well-functioning research team which carries out technologically interesting projects in a successful manner. This is his object. He is confident that he will succeed in this – helped, among others, by the British production manager, who has a good technological understanding and is an intelligent engineer. Still, the narrator does meet some obstacles along the way, often because of the British CEO who, as the narrator sees it, sometimes makes the wrong decisions because his understanding of the complicated GSM technology is insufficient and, in addition, he is unwilling to listen to the engineers' expert advice. Also, the CEO does not understand that it is necessary to invest a lot of money in R&D.

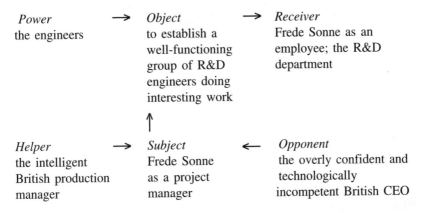

Power	→	*Object*	→	*Receiver*
the engineers		to establish a well-functioning group of R&D engineers doing interesting work		Frede Sonne as an employee; the R&D department

Helper	→	*Subject*	←	*Opponent*
the intelligent British production manager		Frede Sonne as a project manager		the overly confident and technologically incompetent British CEO

Intertwined with the main story are a couple of other success stories about the engineers' triumphs as a group and about Frede Sonne's individual achievements seen in a more personal career perspective. One story is about the pioneering development of the first GSM-phone, another is about the engineers' initiative to find a new owner when Fonodan had to suspend its payments. As already mentioned, this group actually made the first contacts with Electra, without involving the management.

The project manager identifies with the group of R&D engineers as a team of experts (in contrast to the management) and often uses the pronoun "we" (e.g. "we were well aware of the company's problems)." Except for top management, he does not refer to people or departments outside R&D. His world is primarily that of the engineers. At the same time, he is also an individualist who sees his job as a free choice: "it must be fun and technologically challenging." He knows that as a competent engineer, he has a number of other alternatives in the job market and displays no emotional attachment to the company as such. He appreciates his colleagues in the R&D department ("we work well together as a team)," but what really matters is the R&D content of the projects to which he is assigned.

Frede Sonne speaks in a rational voice. He emphasises causal relationships and, in contrast to the shop steward, Jonna Jensen, does not describe his own feelings or those of others. Technology plays a decisive role in his story: 'It won't be worthwhile to move the factory to a developing country because of cheaper labour. In a couple of years, most production processes will be auto-mated and we will need very few people, probably no unskilled workers at all."

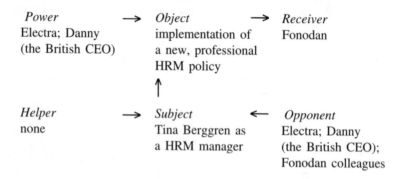

Power	→	Object	→	Receiver
Electra; Danny		implementation of		Fonodan
(the British CEO)		a new, professional		
		HRM policy		

Helper	→	Subject	←	Opponent
none		Tina Berggren as		Electra; Danny
		a HRM manager		(the British CEO);
				Fonodan colleagues

The human resource manager's second narrative – April 1996

The human resource manager starts her second narrative in this way: "People ask 'but isn't your job just exciting?' and yes, it is, but most of all it's hard work and very stressful." It has been much more difficult than she expected to reach the object of implementing a new HRM policy. She feels that she has been let down by Electra and by the British CEO. She has not received the necessary support, and they do not understand or appreciate her ideas. The British are now her opponents, but they are still the decisive power in her story, and this makes her position difficult.

The British are unwilling to spend money on HRM: "Richard (Electra's owner) and Danny do not understand that we must invest in training and development. They think that you're born with certain qualifications, and that's it. They think that you don't need any more training when you leave university as an engineer, for instance. They don't understand that people can learn and develop continu-ally." She is now very critical of Electra in general: "we had expected more pro-fessional competence from them."

She admits that it has been a tough year for her at the psychological level, too. She feels that no one helps her, and that she "cannot have a natural and relaxed relationship with colleagues anymore." But though she sees herself as being in a difficult position, isolated in the company, outside the community of Fonodan employees, she is still fighting for what she believes is right in terms of professional HRM.

Still, though she does not say it so directly, we get the impression that she sometimes feels that the price she pays is too high. She expresses some identification with people who have resigned from Fonodan when she says: "A few people have left the company. But I think it is a positive thing if they have thought about the sort of life they want to have and have decided they want to do something else. Some of them have worked very hard, ever since they graduated from university, and there has been a lot of pressure here."

The British CEO's second story – April 1996

We also had the opportunity to interview the British CEO again one year later, and now Danny Allen tells a story of trials rather than of expected triumphs.

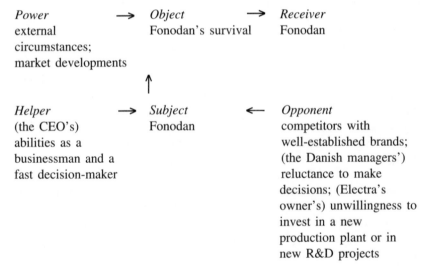

| *Power* | → | *Object* | → | *Receiver* |
| external circumstances; market developments | | Fonodan's survival | | Fonodan |

↑

| *Helper* | → | *Subject* | ← | *Opponent* |
| (the CEO's) abilities as a businessman and a fast decision-maker | | Fonodan | | competitors with well-established brands; (the Danish managers') reluctance to make decisions; (Electra's owner's) unwillingness to invest in a new production plant or in new R&D projects |

The British CEO has not succeeded in making Fonodan no. 4 in the global market, but he explains it by factors outside his control. Most importantly, the market is difficult and the company is up against strong competitors with well-established brands. Now, his object is less ambitious: Fonodan's survival. Furthermore, the Danish managers are still too indecisive to be efficient and due to the poor results, the owner of Electra has refused to invest in a new high volume production plant which has been planned at Fonodan for some time. Danny Allen hopes that he can make the company survive because of his abilities as an experienced businessman, but he does not seem very confident.

His shifting identifications from the first to the second interview are remarkable: In the first interview, the British managing director identifies with the task of making Fonodan successful and making the Danish managers efficient and professional. At the same time, he identifies against the former Danish management. A shared tale in top management is that the former management was indecisive, too little cost-conscious and too consensus-oriented. As he sees it, this is why the middle management is still too slow in their decision-making.

In the second interview, the managing director identifies with the task of making Fonodan profitable to the investors/Electra. He identifies against the present Danish management, whom he experiences as increasingly indecisive. He seems to be somewhat split between a certain identification with the Fonodan engineers' enthusiastic development of innovative products for the future and his old identification with Electra's short-term perspective of profit-making. Now he actually tries to support the engineers in their attempts to get more money for R&D from the British owners. He still sees himself as a competent international businessman. But through no fault of his own, he is now up against very tough competition in the market, with no help from anyone else in Fonodan.

Ten days after this interview takes place, the British expatriate CEO is asked to resign from his position and to return to Electra's headquarters in London. Electra instead turns the management of Fonodan over to the Danish operations director Erik Nielsen. At the same time, 115 workers in the manufacturing unit are laid off. Fonodan again faces serious financial problems. Even though the turnover is 910 million DKK in 1996, the net result of Electra's investment is negative: minus 84 million DKK.

However, the R&D department is still successful in technological terms and, because of its new product developments, Fonodan is attractive to investors. Three multinational electronics companies, one Japanese and two German industrial groups, go into negotiations and start a due diligence process. In April 1997, the large German industrial group Gerhard Strohm GmbH. acquires Fonodan (henceforth Strohm Telecom DK) and another integration process begins.

THE GERMAN ACQUISITION – THE STROHM-ERA (1997–)

THE DANISH CEO'S FIRST NARRATIVE – JUNE 1997

As soon as it is publicly announced that the German multinational company Strohm GmbH. has acquired the Danish company Fonodan in May 1997, the Danish CEO, Erik Nielsen, a man in his early 50s, is interviewed. In a triumphant voice he says that business consultants with 25 years experience in the M & A field, had informed him that only around 10% of all CEOs survive a foreign take-over: "So I was prepared for the worst when the company was acquired. You can either take a chance or just start looking for another job. But I was 100% involved in the daily problems – with employees we had to dismiss, product quality, etc. I was working hard to make this company survive in a period full of trials. We were really about to turn the key and close down, but at the same time I was preparing, in deep secrecy, the sale of the company together with these business consultants. So, mentally, I simply couldn't manage to look around for another job at the same time. Therefore I decided that I'd try to get the company sold in a proper manner so that all the good people here could continue their work with a new owner. And I thought that it might also look nice on my CV ... It is not too bad to leave the position as a CEO when it happens in connection with a take-over."

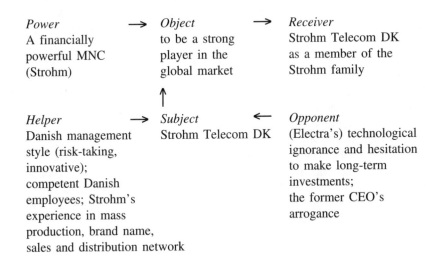

Power	→	*Object*	→	*Receiver*
A financially powerful MNC (Strohm)		to be a strong player in the global market		Strohm Telecom DK as a member of the Strohm family
		↑		
Helper	→	*Subject*	←	*Opponent*
Danish management style (risk-taking, innovative); competent Danish employees; Strohm's experience in mass production, brand name, sales and distribution network		Strohm Telecom DK		(Electra's) technological ignorance and hesitation to make long-term investments; the former CEO's arrogance

An analysis of the Danish CEO's statements shows that his ambition, on behalf of the Danish company, is to make Strohm Telecom DK a stronger player in the turbulent global telecommunications market. As a very important helper in relation to this project, he points to the acquiring company: Strohm has experience with mass production, a world-wide sales and distribution network and a well-established brand name, which is generally associated with high technological competence. However, according to the Danish CEO, the Danish managers and employees also have something to offer. They are well educated and highly motivated, and the R&D department has a good reputation due to the engineers' outstanding know-how in GSM technology. Finally, the Danish management style that the CEO himself represents is described as innovative and risk-taking. Erik Nielsen is very enthusiastic: his former opponents, represented by the owner of British Electra and the British expatriate CEO, are now out of sight. He can finally permit himself to blame them for their technological ignorance and their arrogance towards the well-educated and competent Danish managers and employees.

"Danny (the former British CEO) was the right man to build up the company. He was the inspirator and succeeded in reorganising it. But when the company was reconstructed, he was not a success any longer. He was not able to handle the managerial operations at a high level, he was not capable of managing crises . . . Moreover, Danny was arrogant and had a very big ego; he displayed the attitude that he knew better than everybody else. Fonodan was still a relatively small company at that moment, and Danny was involved in everything. But when things became more complex, his management model was useless. That was why he failed. In the end he simply lost control of everything in Fonodan. People with such a big ego are extremely dangerous as managers. They don't listen to other people, they cannot accept good advice, they only focus on their own ideas and are convinced of their own superior competencies. . . . Eventually, Richard (Electra's owner) asked him to leave Fonodan immediately, and I had to take over the position, as CEO of a company on the brink of disaster."

On this background, the Danish CEO is relieved that a serious and competent German industrial group has now replaced British Electra. Whereas Electra hesitated to make long-term investments and implement the plans for a new high volume plant, the financially strong Strohm is perceived as fully committed to the project of making the Danish company a centre of excellence within GSM technology. Thus, the company has got a new chance to become a strong player in the global telecommunications market.

The research and development manager's first narrative – May 1998

A year later, in May 1998, we interviewed the research and development manager Frede Sonne, one of the former project managers in the company's Electra-era.

Like the Danish CEO, Frede Sonne also makes explicit comparisons between the former British owner and the new German acquiring company. The R&D manager also points to the British Electra as an opponent to his project: to get financial support for new ambitious R&D projects. The R&D manager points to difficulties in negotiations and decision-making: neither Electra's owner nor the British expatriate CEO had any technological insight.

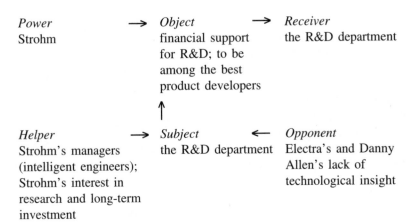

Power   →   *Object*   →   *Receiver*
Strohm   financial support   the R&D department
                           for R&D; to be
                           among the best
                           product developers

                                ↑

Helper   →   *Subject*   ←   *Opponent*
Strohm's managers   the R&D department   Electra's and Danny
(intelligent engineers);   Allen's lack of
Strohm's interest in   technological insight
research and long-term
investment

He explicitly distances himself from Electra and identifies with the new acquiring company. He perceives the German managers as more intelligent than the British, and as engineers, they belong to the same professional culture as he himself and his Danish colleagues in the R&D department. It explains to him why Strohm, rightly, puts emphasis on intensive and stable relations with researchers and students at the universities. Research projects and Ph.D. scholarships are now sponsored, and graduate students are allowed to work on projects in the company, whereas these important company-university relations were to a large extent neglected in Fonodan's Electra-era.

The general manager responsible for finances, logistics and IT – May 1998

An interview was also conducted with the general manager responsible for finances, logistics and IT. Jesper Winther is juxtaposed with the Danish CEO at the top of the Danish management of the company and refers directly to the top management of the Strohm Telecom division. He was headhunted in March 1997, and spent his first month selling the Danish company to Strohm GmbH. He speaks in very rational terms about his considerations when he was offered the job: "I made some preliminary strategic analyses and immediately realised that Fonodan would have to be sold. I also saw some very exciting strategic challenges and possibilities in the future. This is really high technology production and IT is crucial. But logistics, production and supply management are also very important functions."

Jesper Winther shares the other Danish managers' positive identification with the German acquiring company, but only to a certain extent. He foregrounds the German way of planning and structuring work processes as something that the Danish managers and employees can learn from. But he is also well aware that Strohm's managerial style and communication style may have a negative impact on the integration process.

Still, he believes that Strohm wishes to show the Danish company respect: "Strohm has experienced some disastrous take-overs. Total disasters where they just rolled in, took over, and let the blood flow. Afterwards, to their surprise, all the rest of the managers left, too, and they wondered why ... Strohm is now very conscious of the signals they send out to us, as an acquired company, and they try to show that they respect our competencies and culture. They have no know-how in telecommunications, and they realise that they must make people stay here."

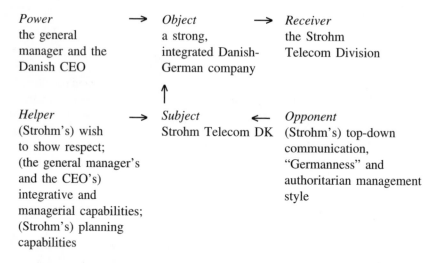

He describes his project as the successful integration of the Danish and the German companies: "I feel it as my responsibility to make the communication run smoothly ... Product synergies, etc. are not enough. And when it does not work, whom do they send out to solve the problems? A trouble-shooter who makes John Wayne look like a Sunday school boy! They really need integrators, and that's how I see myself."

Helpers in relation to the integration project are his own educational background (MBA) and his managerial experience, also from jobs in Germany. In contrast to most of the other Danish managers who speak English with their German counterparts, Jesper Winther speaks German fluently, and he is familiar with German communication style and manners. He thus stresses his own managerial competencies compared to those of the other Danish top and middle managers. They may have done a good job when the company was smaller. But they are very operations-focused, and now they also need more knowledge of management and strategy to be able to cope with the future challenges.

He perceives Strohm's communication and management style as counter-productive in relation to his integration project: "The managers in Strohm say that they are international, but they are still very German. It's incredible how much of the information we get that's in German. And they have this fundamental culture that can be hard for us Scandinavians to accept. When a manager issues an order, he expects to be obeyed and that people click their heels and say 'Yes, Sir'. But that's not Danish culture. Danes ask: 'Why? Couldn't we do it this way instead'?"

He characterises the German managerial style as more authoritarian, involving top-down communication with commands and intensive control of subordinates. He sees the Danish managerial style as characterised by compromise-seeking nego-tiation and thus as a helper to his integration project. The Danish way to carry out management, strategy, and team building is also viewed as far more advanced than the German way. Moreover, the German managers could learn from the Danish managers that they should be more aware that an integration process following an acquisition, is also 'people business'. The Danish general manager thus emphasises that it is crucial for the acquiring company to be aware of the uniqueness of a company such as Fonodan. This company is a knowledge-based organisation, where managers and employees are committed to innovative problem-solving.

The shop steward's second narrative – May 1998

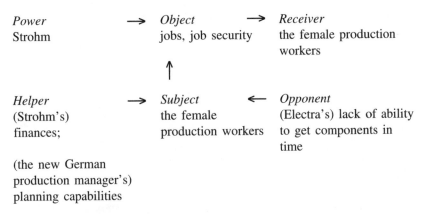

At a lower level in the company hierarchy, we hear, once again, the voice of shop steward, Jonna Jensen, speaking on behalf of the female production workers, the subject of her narrative.

In May 1998, as well as in her first narrative from the Electra era, she is primarily focused on getting jobs for the members of her union, and on obtaining as much job security as possible. Between 1995 and 1998, British Electra has moved from a position as the power who provided the desired object to a position as an opponent who hinders the subject(s) in obtaining what they want. In both narratives, the former acquiring company and the former management are seen as opponents. In 1998, Electra's management is pointed out as the culprit, because the company was not able to get the needed components for production in time. Moreover, the shop steward now admits that it was difficult when all meetings with the British CEO in the company's works council were held in English: "We also get more information than before. Now the meetings are in Danish again, and that's a relief. Though they were briefer before. . . ."

The helpers are indicated rather vaguely in the shop steward's narrative: "Gerhard Strohm is an old company, and they know about production. They know that you need good tools and machinery." Strohm's stronger financial situation is a positive factor in the creation of jobs and more job security in the production plant, too. It is also mentioned as something very positive that the German production manager has learnt Danish – in contrast to the former British CEO who did not make any such efforts during the 2½ years he stayed in Denmark.

The shop steward expects it will be a big change to the workers when they move to the new factory, which at that time was still under construction. She says: "A couple of us were sent to Germany to look at a factory down there. There were a lot of good things, but there were no colours or plants. We would like it to be more cosy here. But I believe that the good spirit we have in this firm will continue; no one feels controlled and we can talk freely. That's important. That's what we are known for. That's what attracts new girls to jobs in the production department."

The Danish CEO's second narrative – June 1999

A year later, a new series of interviews are made. In the meantime, the Danish company has moved to a new building with administration offices, a larger research and development department and a huge plant with mass production facilities. The number of employees has increased from 1014 to 1488, since May 1998. Strohm Telecom DK is now the biggest private company in the region of Northern Jutland.

In the global market of mobile phones, the competition among a still decreasing number of players has been intensified. In 1999, Strohm Telecom has 3.2% of the world market, whereas the three global giants Finnish Nokia, Swedish LM Ericsson and US-American Motorola have 27, 22 and 19% respectively. Rumours are circulating in the company and in the media that

Strohm is looking for a strategic partner. The alternative may well be to be 'swallowed up' by one of the bigger players or even to close down. In the following, we will discuss how different central actors in the Danish company interpret this situation. First, the Danish CEO, Erik Nielsen:

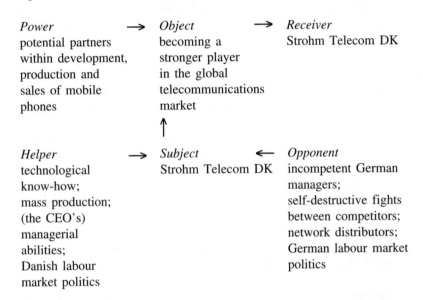

Power ➞ *Object* ➞ *Receiver*
potential partners becoming a Strohm Telecom DK
within development, stronger player
production and in the global
sales of mobile telecommunications
phones market

Helper ➞ *Subject* ⬅ *Opponent*
technological Strohm Telecom DK incompetent German
know-how; managers;
mass production; self-destructive fights
(the CEO's) between competitors;
managerial network distributors;
abilities; German labour market
Danish labour politics
market politics

Erik Nielsen still speaks on behalf of Strohm Telecom DK. He describes his project as making the company a stronger player in the global market for telecommunications. He characterises himself in this way: "I am a world champion to fall on my ass and get up again." He sees it as an important aspect of his managerial competence that he has survived many ups and downs in the Danish company's history. With an undertone of irony, he states: "I am cool as a cucumber." No difficulties can seriously affect him; he will strive to make the company survive any difficulties it faces.

In June 99, he sees quite a few opponents to his project, among them his counterparts and superiors in the German acquiring company. In general, he sees German labour market regulations as an obstacle to dismiss incompetent managers and employees, something which is easier according to Danish labour market regulations. Moreover, in Denmark there is a tradition of mobility between companies, due to the fact that most companies are small or medium sized. This makes the Danish work force more flexible. At a more concrete level, he experiences Strohm's personnel policy as an additional hindrance, because this big MNC, like many other major German companies, has developed a tradition of life-long careers. Thus, he experiences some of the managers in the Strohm Telecom division as opponents, because they have made their career in other divisions of the MNC, such as the automotive division (brake production, car radios). They make decisions with important implications for the Danish company, but according to the Danish CEO, they do not have the necessary insight in the unique conditions for research, development and marketing of mobile phones.

The global competition is very strong, and the Danish CEO views the competitors as engaged in a (self)destructive fight to get larger market shares. Another destructive force is the telecommunication network distributors who sell the phones to customers at extremely low prices that do not correspond to the costs of research, development and production: "The market is completely crazy. It grows with 50% a year, but it's a war – we use up all our strength trying to kill each other ... The only winner is likely to be you as a customer! If you look at the PC market 10–15 years ago, the exact same thing happened: huge growth and they all killed each other, only 3–4 survived." According to the Danish CEO, the best way out of this difficult situation is to be involved in strategic alliances with other financially strong companies: "As I see it, Strohm has three possibilities: Closing us down, investing billions in marketing, factories and development, or they can find someone to collaborate with. This is a game for the big boys, so: buy, join, merge."

The research and development manager's second narrative – June 1999.

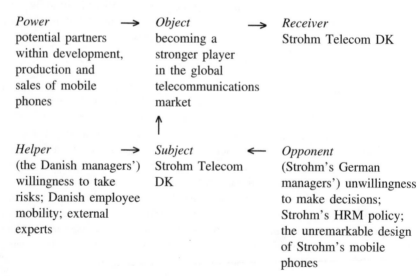

Power	→	Object	→	Receiver
potential partners within development, production and sales of mobile phones		becoming a stronger player in the global telecommunications market		Strohm Telecom DK

Helper	→	Subject	←	Opponent
(the Danish managers') willingness to take risks; Danish employee mobility; external experts		Strohm Telecom DK		(Strohm's German managers') unwillingness to make decisions; Strohm's HRM policy; the unremarkable design of Strohm's mobile phones

The Danish research and development manager also emphasises that the Danish employees' mobility is a helper in the project that he shares with the CEO, i.e. to strengthen the company's position in the global telecommunications market. The solution he recommends is external recruitment of experts who could add value by improving the design of the mobile phones, as well as develop the marketing to end users. However, Strohm's HRM policy is characterised by internal recruitment, no matter which competencies are needed, and this is seen as an obstacle and an opponent to the Danish R&D manager's project.

Frede Sonne still respects Strohm's competencies and highly needed experience of large-scale mass production. These are helpers, whereas the acquiring company's management style is perceived as a serious opponent. The R&D manager compares the present unstable and frustrating situation, where the German managers are not yet settled in their views upon the future strategy, with the situation Danish management experienced with Electra in 1996, when the British concern hesitated to invest more money. German managers fear to decide on investments that might fail and thus cost them their further career progression in Strohm. But in the meantime, several good managers and employees consider leaving Strohm Telecom DK because they are offered attractive positions by other electronics companies in the region.

The R&D manager also comments on the new production plant which is positively described by other narrators in the company. Many production workers are proud of Strohm Telecom DK's new big building that sticks out a mile in the environment. They also put emphasis on the fact that all managers and employees in the company are now working in the same building. It is easy to meet with other groups of employees, and you can even have your meals in the same canteen as the top managers. The managers in the Strohm Telecom division in Germany are also very satisfied with the new building, and have even considered erecting more buildings in Germany and abroad using the same design. The research and development manager describes the company's new premises from quite another point of view: "In the old building where the R&D department was located, my colleagues and I made all our decisions without interference from others. Nearly everything was possible. We gave the anarchist tendencies among the R&D people free scope. The new building is much more influenced by Strohm's thorough and painstaking character. You have to behave according to certain rules which apply to all groups of employees working in this building, from production workers to the CEO. You are asked to arrange everything in an ordered whole, in a system that you haven't had any influence on. You can no longer move any of the walls. You cannot invite your family and show them your workplace due to security systems. You are not allowed to move chairs to the open-air terrace when the weather is nice. There are no cosy places, no chat-rooms, no intimacy, and no room for spontaneous contacts. I cannot help referring to this big building as the one and only open prison in Northern Jutland."

In the contrasts between the old building and the new one, binary oppositions are constructed that may be interpreted as part of the narrator's underlying value system determining his identification with the Danes, against the German acquiring company. The Danish way of life and the Danish organisational culture in an entrepreneurial company is here associated with the old building, characterised by possibilities, anarchism, no interference from outsiders. It is possible to link workplace and family life, and the rooms are cosy, intimate, with spaces where you can chat and make spontaneous contacts. The new building is connotated with the German organisational culture and characterised by the narrator as dominated by control and restricted by a number of rules. The employees have no influence on their workplace, and the company is closed to the local environment. The atmosphere is cold, the social relations are formal. There is no space for chat, only for scheduled meetings.

The R&D manager never identified strongly with the company, whether under Danish, British or German ownership. Frede Sonne has always had a strong professional identity as an engineer and as an employee in the R&D department, though. But, as he emphasises in this last narrative: "I did not plan to work in Strohm Telecom DK. And I know that I can easily find a good job elsewhere. I am not born into the Strohm family, I do not share career perspectives with our German expatriate managers. I cannot imagine that I will stay here until I retire. As long as I have some fun with my job and find it challenging, it is OK, but if not, then . . ."

The research and development manager admits that the drastic enlargement of the Danish company, from 800 to 1500 employees in one year, has "drawn some teeth out of the Danish company. The organisation is right now suffering from severe stress symptoms; but nevertheless it has been a tremendous learning process. However, some of the people most intensively involved have to make up their minds if they want to continue at top gear with the risk of a burnout – or maybe even a too early death. Or if they prefer to leave the company in time." There seems to be some sort of identification with the people who are considering other life projects which in some aspects makes this narrative similar to the second narrative told by the human resource manager, in April 1994, in a situation close to burn-out.

Half a year after this interview, the R&D manager decided to leave the company to work as manager and co-owner of a smaller Danish R&D company that is a supplier to the giant competitors Nokia and L. M Ericsson. The German Strohm managers were shocked: "How can we make him change his decision?

Didn't we pay him enough?" but they did not succeed in convincing him that he should stay in Strohm Telecom DK.

DISCUSSION AND CONCLUDING REMARKS

The narratological perspective applied to the interviews analysed in this essay offers insight into interpretations based on different perspectives and at the same time displays that central actors within an acquired company may have very different goals and worldviews.

The narratological analyses have also made it clear how different organisational narrators and actors construct different plots and account for causalities from different points of view. The analyses have demonstrated that the plots and causalities in the narratives told must be seen as a result of both individual and collective processes of selection, hierarchisation and sequencing of organisational actions and events.

The narratological analyses have also focused on different modes of storytelling. We have analysed rationalistic, seemingly objective, accounts told on behalf of the company, or a department within it, enthusiastic stories about individuals' visions and future plans for the company, and tales of personal triumph and managerial success. But we have also analysed tales of trial and failure told by both top management and people lower in the workplace hierarchy, who blame others' actions or look for cultural differences, at a national or an organisational level, as explanations of failed plans and projects.

The many different voices and their differing narratives about acquisitions seem to indicate that the popular concept of 'shared narratives' in organisations may be a rather problematic managerial tool, and in some cases even counterproductive to implement through conscious effort. For instance, many employees shared the interpretation of Electra's positive role which the shop steward and the human resource manager expressed in their first narratives from the company's Electra-era. But a core group in the company, the ambitious R&D engineers who succeeded in developing one of the first GSM phones in the world, thereby making the company attractive for investors, certainly disagreed with this uncritical narrative about the Electra management. They did not support the British CEO's narrative about the need for cost consciousness and wage restraints.

Our longitudinal perspective on the organisational changes as they are experienced and interpreted by different central actors in an acquired company has enabled us to see some patterns in the way the narrators' stories change and develop over time: from the suspension of payments in 1993, through British and German acquisitions of the company, to the current development, where the company is searching for another strategic partner to survive in the global competition.

Notably, the acquiring company seems to move from a position as power and/or helper, to a position as opponent or a cause of problems, as soon as some time has passed and a new company is about to take over, or already has taken over. Both top and middle managers tend to see themselves as decisive agents when the company experiences success, but they tend to tone down the impact of their own decisions when problems arise. In times of trial, managers typically point to contextual factors outside their control as causes of problems – the market, the competitors, the technological development and consumers' changing preferences. Other organisational actors – in our case company for instance the shop steward, the production workers, and the secretaries – represent themselves as agents to a much lesser extent, regardless of whether things go well or not.

The managers, then, are more than ready to take responsibility when things go well, but they are quick to identify opponents in the environment, including the foreign acquiring company, when things go less well. In this way, managers' accounts may distort researchers' conclusions, if such tendencies in managers' story telling are not detected in studies of factors that lead to success or failure in mergers or acquisitions. Therefore, it is probably wise to interpret causal explanations with a grain of salt when relying on qualitative interviews. A narratological perspective on interviews can help us to see that the truth of managers' and employees' stories may not lie in the 'facts' that they recount, but rather in the way they construct their stories and, retrospectively, try to make sense of a course of actions and events.

When reading through stories told to us by managers and other employees in the acquired company, it becomes clear that the shifting CEOs have had demanding roles to fill. Not just in terms of work load and formal responsibility, but also at the psychological and interpersonal level. Although the CEO's personality has a bearing on the way he leads the company, his role and professional identity is, of course, not defined by him alone, but also by the employees. This makes it very difficult or risky for him to deviate too much from their expectations concerning the role he is to play. The CEO's role is generally expected to be that of central and, preferably, heroic character who assumes personal responsibility for the company's fate. This implies that it will not be acceptable for him to voice too much uncertainty and indecision, not even in the face of problems obviously outside his control.

According to Czarniawska (1997), one of the leader's most important functions is to provide the rest of the organisation and its environment with the illusion of controllability: The CEO is in charge, so the employees need not worry. But to uphold this illusion, even when the company meets challenges, the leader will also have to act as scapegoat. If he is not dismissed in case of failure, it is implicitly admitted that he is not responsible for what happens and so, everyone has to face the uncontrollability of organisational life. But if he is dismissed and a new CEO takes over, the old leader can safely be blamed, and everybody, except perhaps the new CEO, can feel secure again and tell each other that someone more competent is now responsible for the development. Their hopes and positive expectations are then projected on to the new CEO.

It is evident that former leaders, when we are told about them in retrospect, tend to act as scapegoats in the narratives told in the Danish acquired company, e.g. the pre-acquisition Fonodan management team and the British CEO Danny Allen. It also seems like the managers themselves are, to some degree, aware of the risks inherent in their role. Some of them tend to see their job in the context of a war or a game and they are very concerned with their personal position. They are more into concepts of power and success/failure than other employees, and they describe their work life as dramatic and exciting, but also dangerous.

All this means that it may be misleading to use managers' success narratives as the basis of practical guidelines in research aiming at normative conclusions or in consultants' reports. At least from our perspective, it is a pitfall if organisational research in general, and research on mergers and acquisitions in particular, is based on interviews with managers alone – but that is actually fairly often the case. We find that one of the advantages of the narratological approach which we have applied to our empirical data is it includes the voices of more organisational actors, and thereby offers a corrective to a purely managerial perspective on mergers and acquisitions.

NOTES

1. This name as well as all names of companies and persons in the following are fictitious in order to protect the anonymity of our respondents.

REFERENCES

Bakhtin, M. M. (1981). *The Dialogic Imagination.* Austin: University of Texas Press.

Bal, M. (1985). *Narratology. Introduction to the Theory of Narrative*, Toronto: University of Toronto Press.

Boje, D. (1991). The story-telling organisation: A study of story performance in an office-supply firm. *Administration Science Quarterly, 36*, 106–126.

Bruner, J. (1990). *Acts of Meaning*, Cambridge, Massachusetts, Harvard University Press.

Bruner, J. (1991). The Narrative Construction of Reality', *Critical Inquiry, 18*, 1–21.

Chatman, S. (1978). *Story and Discourse. Narrative Structure in Fiction and Film*, Ithaca and London: Cornell University Press.

Currie, M. (1998). *Postmodern Narrative Theory*, Houndmills and London: Macmillan Press.

Czarniawska, B. (1998). *A Narrative Approach to Organisation Studies*, Thousand Oaks, London and New Delhi: Sage Publications.

Czarniawska, B. (1997). *Narrating the Organisation. Dramas of Institutional Identity*, Chicago and London: The University of Chicago Press.

Genette, G. (1980). *Narrative Discourse. An Essay in Method*, Ithaca, New York: Cornell University Press.

Gertsen, M. C., & Søderberg, A. M. (1998a). Fonodan – en case om et virksomhedsopkøb. In: J. Strandgaard Pedersen, (Ed.),. *Fusioner på tværs – fra plan til praksis*, Copenhagen: Jurist- og økonomforbundets forlag, 1998, 144–164.

Gertsen, M. C., & Søderberg, A.-M. (1998b). Foreign Acquisitions in Denmark: Cultural and Communicative Dimensions. In: M. C. Gertsen, A-M. Søderberg, & J. E. Torp, (Eds.), *Cultural Dimensions of International Mergers and Acquisitions*, Berlin and New York: de Gruyter, 167–196.

Gertsen, M. C., & Søderberg, A.-M. (1999a). A business systems perspective on international acquisitions: The case of a Danish company with British and German owners – part 1, *Strategic Change, 7*(8), 413–419.

Gertsen, M. C., & Søderberg, A.-M. (1999b). A business systems perspective on international acquisitions: The case of a Danish company with British and German owners – part 2, *Strategic Change, 8*(8), 473–485.

Gertsen, M. C., Søderberg, A.-M., & Torp, J. E. (1998). Different Approaches to the Understanding of Culture in Mergers and Acquisitions. In: M. C. Gertsen, A-M. Søderberg, & J. E. Torp, (Eds.), *Cultural Dimensions of International Mergers and Acquisitions*, Berlin and New York: de Gruyter, 17–38.

Grant, D., Keenoy, T., & Oswick, C. (Eds.) (1998). *Discourse and Organisation*, Thousand Oaks, London and New Delhi: Sage Publications.

A. J. Greimas, (1966). *Sémantique Structurale*, Paris: Larousse.

Hobsbawm, E., & Ranger, T. (Eds.) 1983. *The Invention of Tradition*, Cambridge: Cambridge University Press.

Horsdal, M. (1999). *Livets fortællinger (Autobiographical Narratives)*, Copenhagen: Borgen.

Lieblich, A., Tuval-Mashiach, R., & Zilber, T. (1998). *Narrative Research. Reading, Analysis, and Interpretation*, Thousand Oaks, London and New Delhi: Sage Publications.

Martin, J. (1982). Stories and scripts in organisational settings. In: A. H. Hastrof, & A. M. Isen, (1982). *Cognitive social psychology*, New York: North Holland-Elsevier, 165–194.

Martin, J. (1992). *Cultures in Organisations. Three Perspectives*, Oxford: Oxford University Press.

Martin, W. (1986). *Recent Theories of Narrative*, Ithaca and London: Cornell University Press.

Olins, W. (1995). *The New Guide to Identity*, London: Cower.

Polkinghorne, D. E. (1988). *Narrative Knowing and the Human Sciences*, Albany: State University of New York Press.

Propp, V. (1968). *Morphology of the Folktale*, Austin: University of Texas Press.

Rimmon-Kenan, S. (1983). *Narrative Fiction*, Contemporary Poetics, London and New York: Routledge.

Weick, K. (1995). *Sensemaking in Organizations*, Thousand Oaks: Sage Publications.

White, H. (1987). *The Content of the Form*, Baltimore, Maryland: The John Hopkins Press.

White, H. (1973). *Metahistory. The Historical Imagination in Nineteenth Century Europe*, Baltimore, Maryland: The John Hopkins Press.